Multinational Corporations
and the Politics of Dependence

Written under the auspices of
the Center for International Affairs,
Harvard University

A list of other Center publications
of related interest appears at the back
of this book.

Multinational Corporations and the Politics of Dependence

COPPER IN CHILE

Theodore H. Moran

PRINCETON UNIVERSITY PRESS

PRINCETON, NEW JERSEY

To my family

Contents

List of Tables

Statistical Appendix

Preface and Acknowledgments

This book is the work of a skeptic trying to use training in the fields of political science and economics to carry out a study of the political economy of foreign investment. I have found that in fact there are tools in both of these disciplines to do a respectable job. If I had recognized this sooner, and got on with the job, as some of my friends ably suggested, I would have made faster and more effective progress. The fact that the overwhelming bulk of work in these fields is of such low quality is due to laziness, complacency, and lack of imagination on the part of the practitioners more than to the unavailability of useful tools.

A comment should be made about the methodology and tone of this study. Chilean political leaders, scholars, *técnicos* were required to make awesome decisions directly affecting the destiny of their country in a way only rarely equalled elsewhere—often under conditions of great stress, great uncertainty, and great popular pressure. The methodology of this study is based on the retrospective reconstruction of the accuracy, adequacy, and wisdom of those decisions. It benefits from the ease of academic reflection, from the exactitude of hindsight, and from the beginnings of a comparative perspective. The purpose of such second-guessing is not to pass judgment in a supercilious fashion on various episodes in the history of copper in Chile, but rather to extract lessons and suggest analytical tools for a political economy of foreign investment that can be used for other industries in other countries in the service of both scholarly analysis and policy formation.

I have benefited from the extensive and intimate help of persons in most of the Chilean political parties and interest groups studied here, in the North American copper companies, and in the United States government. Many of them still hold positions of responsibility and should not be mentioned by name. They will greet this work with varying degrees of enthusiasm.

Special mention should be made of the encouragement I received from Nancy and Martin Zimmerman, Clinton Bourdon, and Susan and Paul Drake. They will welcome this book if only because they will no longer have to hear me talk about it. To the extent that I followed editorial suggestions of my brother David, readers have grounds to rejoice.

I have had valuable commentaries and incisive critiques from Sam Huntington, Joe Nye, Hendrick Houthakker, Richard Caves, and Raymond Mikesell. And I have received help from the Foreign Area Fellowship Program, the Harvard Center for International Affairs, Vanderbilt University, and the Brookings Institution.

To Harlan Parker, Charles Ackerman, Nadav Safran, Barrington Moore, and Raymond Vernon I owe much of my intellectual inspiration. They might acknowledge it with some reluctance.

Finally, to my wife JoAnn I must give thanks for real sacrifices in her own professional calling. Why I and little Robbie should pursue our careers at the expense of her work in medieval history can only be ascribed to ill-concealed sexism.

The merits of this study come largely from the help of my friends and advisors. The faults, as they have frequently reminded me, are entirely my own.

T.H.M

Cambridge, Massachusetts
Nashville, Tennessee
Washington, D.C.
December 1973

Multinational Corporations
and the Politics of Dependence

CHAPTER 1

Introduction

In 1912, looking back over the history of nitrates and forward toward the future of copper, the celebrated Chilean writer and historian Francisco Encina regarded with despair the process which he called the "denationalization" of those industries that exploited the country's basic natural resources.[1] He was distressed by the spectacle of the nation's vital industries falling more and more completely into the hands of foreigners, whether British or North American —and he lamented a course of development in which Chileans were content to play essentially a secondary and supportive role to foreigners who were taking over the most important centers of economic growth.

Encina's term was *denacionalización*, and he longed for Chileans bold enough to recapture the sources of their own natural wealth and recover control over their own destiny. In the quarter of a century following the Second World War, the new term to describe Chile's plight became *dependencia*. And, at last, there were men bold enough to answer Encina's call and talented enough to be capable of taking over and running the industries.

Between 1945 and 1970 the Chileans closed in on the foreign-dominated copper industry in their country, successfully surrounded it, and proceeded to take it over. During that period they developed the skills necessary to mine copper, smelt it, refine it, and by the early 1970's they possessed the capacity to carry out all the operations of production on a large scale on their own.

The early formula for recovering control over the national destiny was, logically, the opposite of *denacionaliza-*

---

[1] Francisco A. Encina, *Nuestra inferioridad económica, sus causas y sus consequencias* (Santiago: Imprenta Universitaria, 1912).

ción—namely, *nacionalización*, or putting authority for basic decisions in Chilean hands—although the early Chilean writers would never have entertained the thought of state ownership as part of the notion.[2] The more recent formula for recovering control over the national destiny has been, with equal logic, the opposite of *dependencia*—that is, *independencia*, or *autonomía*. In the early 1970's Chile in fact nationalized the copper industry. The reassertion of sovereignty over the exploitation of natural resources is, in all likelihood, one of the few undertakings with support deep enough to survive, in one form or another, even the most intense domestic conflict.

I

This is an analytical history of the formation of copper policy in Chile from World War II through the end of the Allende regime in 1973. It is the history of the interaction of two systems—a system of multinational copper companies operating under unstable conditions of imperfect competition, and a system of domestic interest groups in Chile trying to respond to rising demands for national development and national welfare—both struggling to take advantage of each other and reduce each other to manageable proportions.

The Chileans characterized their side of this interaction as the struggle against *dependencia*.

What the idea of *dependencia* gained in popularity after the Second World War, however, it unfortunately lost in precision—in academic as well as political discussion. From the debates on copper policy, this study will abstract three definite objectives that were associated with the movement against *dependencia*: first, the objective of asserting Chilean sovereignty over its own economic and political life; second, the objective of forcing or enticing the foreign cor-

[2] *Ibid.*; Julio Kaulen, *Las empresas mineras extranjeras en Chile y la economía nacional* (Santiago: 1916); Machiavello Varas, *El problema de la industria del cobre* (Santiago: 1923).

4

porations to make more of a contribution to Chilean goals of growth and welfare; third, the objective of freeing Chile from having to contribute "captive production" to a vertically integrated corporate system that did not serve Chilean interests.

I shall argue that the first two meanings of *dependencia* embodied legitimate concerns toward which Chilean administrations, despite costly setbacks, made cumulative progress. The third meaning of *dependencia*, however, was based upon an inadequate analysis of international oligopoly behavior and did not acknowledge the limits within which any oligopolistic producer must pursue his individual interests. Pursuit of this objective may put Chile (as well as other nationalistic "independents") in a weak position outside the international copper oligopoly, rather than secure for the country a strong position of interdependence within the international industry.

The quarter-century struggle against *dependencia*, then, which has been necessary to mobilize national skills and gain national confidence in bringing the copper sector more and more under national control, could finish by substituting one kind of international dependence for another—perhaps worse.

II

The introduction of foreign corporations into the center of national life represents a complex challenge to the interests and to the sovereignty of the host country.

Natural resource companies, such as Anaconda and Kennecott, are large, oligopolistic, vertically integrated. They have substantial discretion in formulating investment policy, pricing policy, marketing policy. A tight hold on the combination of capital, technology, and experience that are necessary to find ore-bodies, bring them on-line, and process and market the output gives them the power to exclude competition. They make their policy decisions according to a global strategy based on their own internal needs—not purely in response to market forces (as an atomistic company in a situation of perfect competition would), nor purely in response to the environment created by the host country (as a domestic company would).

At the same time the potential contribution of such corporations to host countries is very great. The economic impact that Anaconda and Kennecott had on Chilean society was enormous. The total value of copper production by these two companies alone accounted for 7% to nearly 20% of Chilean Gross Domestic Product. Tax revenues from copper financed from 10% to 40% of government expenditures. Copper exports ranged from 30% to 80% of all hard currency earnings. No domestic decision about the rate of economic development, the strength of the balance of payments, the level of aggregate employment, the breadth of social welfare programs could be made without a careful calculation, from outside, of how the foreign copper companies might be going to exercise their discretionary power.

This produced an ambivalence about conflict and cooperation, an edge of hostility beneath the game of mutual accommodation. On the one hand, responsible Chilean statesmen wanted to please the foreign companies and obtain as many benefits for their country as possible by cooperative methods. On the other hand, responsible Chilean statesmen felt a mandate to bring the foreigners more and more under national control, force them to serve domestic goals, make them responsive to the society over which they exercised so much power.

The idea of *dependencia* grew out of this ambivalence. Its most fundamental meaning came from a sense that basic decisions about the pace and direction of national development were being dictated by North American corporate officials, unaccountable to any Chilean body politic, according to the internal logistical needs of the vertically integrated companies that those officials served—or, occasionally, according to the foreign policy preferences of their government. No matter how appreciative of the contributions of the foreign copper companies, Chileans of diverse political and economic views nursed a simple mistrust of concentrations of power, mistrust of alien self-appointed and self-perpetuating economic organizations whose private, secret, and often mystifying decisions affected the welfare and prosperity of the entire national community. The struggle against *dependencia* sprang from the desire to "restore" sovereignty and independence over the course of national development.

The result was a fight for control over a society's destiny beside which the populistic movements in the United States to regulate the banks, the railroads, and the "trusts" dwindle in magnitude and in difficulty.

All of *Fortune's* 500 largest US corporations combined do not play nearly the role in the economy of the United States or pay more than a fraction of the percentage of US taxes that Anaconda and Kennecott alone supplied in Chile. All the ranches in Texas, the banks in New York, the aerospace industry in the Northwest are not as responsible, economically, for the fate of their respective states as the copper industry is for Chile. The Rockefellers and the Morgans with all their affiliates at their height were minor operators in comparison to the position that Anaconda and Kennecott occupied for half a century in Chile. Yet if any of these groups were controlled and operated by foreigners according to obscure strategies linking them to headquarters and affiliates outside the United States, it is unlikely that the fear of international dependence and the sense of political frustration would be as comparatively muted and cautious as the Chilean reaction.

The tension about "foreign control" had a strong hold on many Chilean groups even when the foreign presence was considered clearly indispensable for the copper industry. Once the foreign presence was not considered absolutely necessary, the movement toward national control was very rapid—despite warnings that such a policy would have substantial real costs. As Chilean competence in carrying out operations at the production stage increased, the political appeal of national take-over became irresistible. Chilean leaders could not refuse the opportunity to "recover" control over the country's basic natural wealth and "restore" sovereignty over the course of national development.

III

Alongside the challenge to Chilean sovereignty, *dependencia* incorporated a feeling that the powerful foreign companies were not performing dynamically enough to satisfy the needs of national development. This interpretation of *dependencia* stimulated cycles of pulling, pushing, and shoving to encourage or oblige the foreign corporations to commit more of their resources to Chile and share the rewards more generously. With varying degrees of success, these cycles produced a movement to overcome the fundamental disparities of power between the copper companies and successive domestic administrations, and to use ever greater bargaining strength in the service of Chilean goals. In this sense, the struggle against *dependencia* took a course that reflected a fundamental evolution in the balance of power between the international investors and the host country.

In natural resource oligopolies where the largest barriers to entry exist at the production stage—petroleum, copper, and natural gas are the most important—the balance of power between foreign investors and domestic governments begins very much tilted in favor of the foreign producers and tips inevitably away from them toward the host governments. Foreign investors in the typical copper project, for example, must make a large lump-sum investment under conditions of great risk and uncertainty with little possibility of testing or adjusting incrementally. They will not invest unless they have the promise of substantial returns.

When the initial concession is negotiated, the host country is able to evaluate the location and value of prospective mineral deposits even less adequately than the foreign in-

8

vestors. Since the foreign companies enjoy near-monopoly control over the techniques and resources needed to bring a major mine on-line, the host country has little choice but to accept terms weighted heavily in favor of the foreign investors. But once one or more foreign enterprises commit themselves and invest, and once the mines are successful, the bargaining strengths change abruptly. Uncertainty is reduced, and the old doubts are forgotten. The host government gazes out at a profitable operation, carrying off resources the country was sure it had all along, in which a large part of the revenue is flowing away to foreigners. The price paid to the foreign investor seems, in retrospect, too high, and the government in power (or its opponents) point out that the country is being cheated. The foreign company, on the other hand, has sunk its capital and won its bet, and has an attractive mine that it will now continue to operate up to some point even though its share of the revenues may be reduced. Empirically, few large natural resource concessions in underdeveloped countries remain long unchanged. The terms of the original agreement are tightened in favor of the host country.

During the process of loosening conditions to attract new investments and tightening conditions after they have proved successful, the host country gradually moves up a learning curve of negotiating skills and of direct operating skills for the industry. Historically, most Third World countries began to watch the growth of new resource industries with very little domestic capability to monitor industry behavior, very little knowledge of terms of concessions in other countries, and very few skills in negotiating sophisticated agreements. Once the industry was established, the government had an incentive to build a skilled bureaucracy, bring in foreign consultants, demand hiring of nationals in supervisory positions, and require participation of its representatives in the arrangement of international marketing and finance. As the host country invaded those areas that were once the exclusive province of the foreigner, it could play the game of mutual accommodation in a tighter and tighter fashion. As the country gained direct operating skills, the cost of replacing the foreigner was lowered. With agonizing slowness, Chile accumulated both negotiating and operating expertise as part of the drive against a dependent relationship with the North American copper companies in the post-World War II era. Despite clear instances in which particular domestic groups moved against the trend to serve their own private interests, the broad movement to push the copper sector by various means (some successful and some counterproductive) to provide the resources for sustained national development gained momentum. Despite widely advanced hypotheses to the contrary, as the foreign copper companies expanded operations in Chile over time they did not gain power, or influence, or allies on the domestic scene. Rather, their power became attenuated, their position became more precarious, their alliances proved most fragile.

Nowadays the direction of the shift in bargaining strength in natural resource industries is clear. At the end of the Second World War and through the 1950's, it was not. Rather, sanctity of contract (together with the paraphernalia of 99-year concessions and 20-year government guarantees of "inviolability") served the function of attempting to cement the relationship between foreign investor and host government on the initial favorable terms to the foreigner. But in a situation where rapidly diminishing uncertainty meant that *ceteris* did not long remain *paribus*, sanctity of contract could not have much operational meaning. Sanctity was steadily "violated" by "undependable Latins" no less than by "untrustworthy Arabs" and other "firebrand nationalists" in a process that reflected frustration about the original terms and shifts in relative bargaining power.

In retrospect this process can be observed to have taken place in various natural resource industries whose output was vital to the functioning of industrial societies and whose largest barriers to entry were located at the production stage—such as in copper or oil. In the petroleum industry the shift in the balance of power toward the host governments began to become clear, after some painful experiences, by the early 1960's. In the copper industry, the consciousness of this shift came more slowly. Chile, no less than Venezuela or Iran, had to suffer the emotional, political, and ideological turmoil required to push history in the direction that now seems both logical and inevitable.

IV

The use of the word "dependence" to characterize some of the key problems of Chilean development grew out of the domestic desire to reassert sovereign control over the economic and political life of the nation. It was also a reaction against the disparities of power that had historically conditioned relations between the foreign copper companies and the host country. The result was a determination to bring the foreign investors under tighter scrutiny as the country's bargaining position improved and to use the country's power to get more from the copper sector for Chile.

But there was a third dimension to *dependencia*. The rationale for moving in on the copper industry and finally taking it over did not originate entirely in concerns about the division of returns or the loss of sovereignty. Rather, Chileans elaborated the idea of *dependencia* even as their country gained experience in tough bargaining with the foreigners and got higher relative as well as absolute returns from the copper industry. This third aspect of the attack on *dependencia* grew out of the Chilean experience of frustration about corporate pricing and marketing behavior, and became a fundamental critique of corporate strategy and corporate integration.

Dependencia, in this dimension, was a sense that the country contributed "captive production" to an integrated system that by nature rendered the struggle for national development extraordinarily difficult while accentuating by

11

a large factor the share of costs and risks in the international system that had to be borne by Chile. From this premise the conclusion emerged that if *dependencia* meant being a "captive" part of the integrated corporate system, *independencia* required being free of that system or even destroying it. A war on the system of private corporate integration became war on the idea of integration *per se*. The mind slipped easily from identification of the problem to prescription of the solution—from dependence to independence, from *dependencia* to *independencia*.

The result would be not only *autonomía*, or more sovereign control over decisions affecting national growth and welfare, but also a chance to achieve at last the full returns as an independent producer from the rich natural resources in Chile. National control of the copper industry would mean that the country would at last break the chains of "captive production" in a larger integrated system, that the country would at last be free to use the full force of its market power to serve its own national interests.

V

This is an analysis of the domestic politics of economic nationalism that have produced the idea of *dependencia* and mobilized the broad reaction against it in Chile since the end of the Second World War. It is also an analysis of the alternative futures for economic nationalism in Chile as the country now faces the semi-integrated world industry as a major independent producer.

This study will not only ask how the idea of *dependencia* gained support and test whether that idea has provided an adequate interpretation of Chile's past. It will also analyze to what extent the reaction against *dependencia* can provide an adequate guide to Chilean strategy in the future as the international industry reacts to protect itself against the threats of economic nationalism.

This study will argue that the idea of *dependencia*, often left vague or purposefully endowed with a variety of mean-

12

ings as it grew out of the Chilean experience, served better to inspire Chileans to close in on the copper companies when the country was in a position of strength, served better to build up domestic competence for exercising the rights of sovereignty in bringing the foreign corporations under national control, than it did to enlighten them about oligopoly strategy in the international industry.

There are dangers as well as opportunities as Chile now fashions its own policy as a large national producer. The country can come to occupy a strong position within the international oligopoly or a very weak position outside it. Unfortunately, there are indications that the heritage of economic nationalism in Chile has not well prepared the country to recognize the opportunities and separate them from the dangers.

There can be no doubt of the poignancy of the feelings about *dependencia* or of the strength of the desire for *independencia* or *autonomía* on the part of many Chileans as long as control of the copper remained in foreign hands. It is less clear, however, whether important Chilean groups of various political and economic ideologies have yet analyzed these concepts with sufficient care to understand the limits within which they can exercise their hard-won liberty or autonomy.

The successful end to their struggle against "dependence" can only come through recognizing the boundaries of their "independence." Whether or not this will be possible within the continuing dynamics of Chilean politics is difficult to predict. If the pressures and ideas used to mobilize opposition against the foreign companies continue to dictate national strategy vis-à-vis the semi-integrated global industry, the outlook cannot be favorable.

VI

The importance of the Chilean struggle goes beyond the fortunes of any particular ideology or particular regime in one country. It demands study by any producing country that wants to use an endowment of natural resources to serve the national welfare in a world where resource industries are integrated from mine or well to consumer by multinational coporations. It requires study by any consuming country that wants access to raw materials in a world where more and more of those materials must come from the hands of sovereign economic nationalists.

The Chilean experience occupies a position of global significance in a world of nations growing increasingly interdependent and increasingly autonomous at the same time.

This work tries to combine the case study of the Chilean copper industry with broader issues of theory and policy in three areas.

First, there is an analysis of the question of what constitutes international "dependence" in a global natural resource oligopoly. Chapters 2, 7, and 8 examine the evolution of structure and strategy in the international copper industry to show what Chile's position has been within the larger corporate-controlled industry in the past, and to identify what are the strengths and weaknesses of the country's position as an independent producer facing the future. They contrast these findings with evolving Chilean perceptions about the dynamics of the global oligopoly. Thus, they provide the setting for the case study of policy formation in Chile. More generally, however, they aim to elucidate the relationship between "dependence" and "interdependence" for any natural resource-producing country trying to shape an effective strategy in the international economy.

Second, there is an analysis of the reaction of domestic groups in the host country to the challenge posed by international "dependence". Chapters 3, 4, 5, and 6 penetrate beneath the abstraction called the "host country" to examine the behavior of Chilean political parties and interest groups at each of the major renegotiations of relations with the foreign copper companies in the post-World War II period. These chapters test and reject hypotheses about "reactionary alliances", "neo-imperialism", and the "consolidation of underdevelopment"—as well as hypotheses about "good investment climate" and "good corporate citizenship" —before placing the Chilean experience within the context of an alternative model of the evolution of the balance of power in natural resource concession agreements in developing countries.[3] Building on top of this dynamic model, Chapter 6 offers the beginnings of a general theory of foreign investor–host country relations and shows how such a theory would explain the course of economic nationalism among natural resource producers in the Third World.

Third, there is an attempt at broad policy proposals, for both producing and consuming countries. From an analysis of Chilean strategy to pursue its goals as an "independent" national copper producer, Chapter 7 delineates the margins within which any economic nationalist must fashion its policy as an oligopolist to serve its own national interest. Then, Chapter 8 tries to suggest ways in which the major consuming countries can encourage the restructuring of multinational corporate relations to preserve many of the benefits and reduce some of the costs inherent in international resource development.

[3] In the course of fitting this alternative model of the evolution of the balance of power between foreign investors and host countries together with the Chilean experience, Chapter 6 offers its own definition of "exploitation" and "complicity in exploitation" that can be clearly identified, and its effects measured, at various crucial points in Chilean history.

Chapter 2

Structure and Strategy in the International Copper Industry

The success of any oligopolistic industry—whether generating private corporate profits, or generating funds for public welfare and national development—comes from exacting an economic rent from final consumers. Such rent is a higher-than-"normal" return that results from the restriction of competition.[1] And the restriction of competition, in turn, is a function of three factors: barriers to the entry of newcomers into the industry; availability of substitutes that can be used in place of what the industry produces; and ability of the members of the oligopoly to coordinate pricing and investment policy (formally or informally) among themselves.

To generate a flow of high earnings, a raw materials producer—whether private company or state agency—must ensure that he can profit from the restriction of competition at some stage that he controls and can pass the commodity at "high" prices continuously on downstream.

In fashioning a strategy to achieve this, the producer must make important but necessarily uncertain judgments about the potential entry of new producers to share his high profit rate, about the potential substitution of alternative products for his, and about what fellow members of the oligopoly will do in response to his choice of moves. In addition, he must try to calculate how best to protect himself from meeting concerted monopoly or oligopoly power at some stage that he does not control downstream from his operations, and how to avoid making his own behavior

[1] The higher-than-"normal" return also of course includes a "Ricardian" or scarcity rent, resulting from the particular characteristics of the Chilean mines that render them superior to the properties of the other members of the oligopoly.

seem like unacceptable monopoly power to his customers downstream—if they have any possibility of integrating backwards to his sphere of operations.

The threat of dilution of the original oligopoly through the entry of new competitors and the threat of substitution of alternative products put limits on the market power that industry members can successfully exercise. These threats define the margins within which the producer must formulate his price and investment strategy and try to coordinate that strategy with the other members of the oligopoly. No oligopoly that faces any possibility of dilution or substitution can exercise all the market power it possesses all the time. It must maintain some delicate balance between the strength that it has to demand "high prices" in the short run and the restraint it must show to keep that strength in the long run.

These considerations have dominated corporate strategy in the past. They must dominate Chilean strategy for the future.

But a sympathetic appreciation of the need to nurture and protect oligopoly power is probably not, to put it mildly, the way a host country first perceives its relationship with a foreign-controlled natural resource industry.

Rather, the initial task that confronts an underdeveloped country trying to use its primary export sector to spur domestic growth is to mount an assault on the power imbalance that characterizes its relations with the foreign investors. The same oligopoly power that gives the corporations leverage vis-à-vis final consumers also gives them leverage vis-à-vis the host country. They use their strength not only to exact high returns from consumers but also to demand from the host country the right to retain a large share of those returns for themselves.

To reduce its own helplessness in this situation, the host country must mobilize a domestic attack on the "power of the foreign corporations". The objectives of such an attack are to invade the foreigners' monopoly of skill and experi-

17

ence, to dispel the country's ignorance of industry practices, to strengthen the country's bargaining position, and to enable the country to have to concede less for what the foreigners offer in return.

For a host country beginning uncertainly to fashion a strategy to deal with large natural resource investors, this turns the problem into a predicament: the host country benefits from the strength and invulnerability of an oligopoly exporting from a base with high barriers to entry within the host's jurisdiction, and gains by acting so as to preserve the strength of the oligopoly. But at the same time the country wants to chisel away at that foreign strength and invulnerability in a way that improves its own ability to claim greater returns from the industry.[2]

The formulation of a sustained policy to deal with this predicament may in fact be too subtle for popular campaigns or simple slogans about "monopoly power" and "foreign control". In Chile, it was not easy to decipher what power should be preserved and what power attacked, what power should be restrained and what power unleashed in the drive to use the natural resource industry to finance domestic development. It was still less easy to sort out the answers in the course of fiercely contested electoral debates. Important domestic groups in Chile felt that national interests were threatened by the size and seeming invulnerability of the large multinational copper companies, and they attacked them as "foreign monopolies". The same or different groups also felt that national interests were threatened by the corporate propensity to exercise moderation in the market place, and they attacked the "exploitative sys-

---

[2] In addition, the country wants to assure itself that in response to its growing challenge the foreign corporations do not begin to shift their profits away from the host's jurisdiction and recapture the bulk of the returns from the industry farther downstream. The hypothesis that the foreign copper companies might have been transferring their profits to integrated subsidiaries outside of Chile is tested (and rejected) later in the chapter, pp. 40–45.

tem" of "foreign control". Finally, they were afraid that their own increasing assertiveness might be forcing the companies to siphon off their oligopoly profits outside of Chile. These fears about foreign strength and foreign restraint and foreign control came together in the idea of *dependencia*—came together in the idea that the system of private corporate integration from mine to consumer was retarding and hindering the course of national development.

It is clear, after the fact, what purpose the debate about monopoly power and foreign control consciously and unconsciously served. It led the country to demand that the companies make a growing commitment to Chilean welfare —sometimes in the form of expanded total revenues, other times in the form of a larger share of existing revenues. It inspired the cycles of pulling, pushing, and shoving to get the foreign-dominated primary export sector to serve the national interest. It moved Chile to invest time and energy and resources to develop confidence that the country could monitor and finally duplicate production operations with less and less reliance on the foreigners.

But at the same time the debate gave false clues about strategy in regard to the international oligopoly—both as to what the companies were doing during their tenure in Chile and as to what the country should do to serve its interests best as an "independent" producer after nationalization.

Now that Chile has taken over the domestic copper industry, it will have to fashion its own strategy from a combination of power and restraint. The movement to nationalize the foreign copper companies was founded on a critique of Anaconda's and Kennecott's actions as large members of the international copper oligopoly. In the future, Chilean domestic growth and welfare will depend on the country's capacity to reproduce many aspects of the same strategy. The momentum of the reaction against *dependencia* and the attack on private (formal and informal) corporate integration will no longer serve the interests of the country as an independent national producer.

This chapter will trace the evolution of oligopoly strategy in the international copper industry as Chile began to feel closed in a system of exploitation. It will test alternative hypotheses to explain that strategy and to evaluate charges that the strategy did or did not harm Chilean interests. It will analyze the rationale for the persistence of some forms of vertical integration in the industry, and examine the way in which the country can be helped or hurt by such integration.

This chapter provides a background for understanding the Chileans' perception that their country was a captive in a system that did not serve its interests well. It also delineates the limits of that perception and the boundaries within which the country must now reconstruct its own national strategy.

I

In the second half of the nineteenth century, copper was mined only from veins of rich ore averaging 10%–15% in copper content. The metal was used for kitchen utensils and some construction work, but demand began growing exponentially only as the electrical industry developed. By the early twentieth century, revolutionary methods of extracting and processing lower grades of porphyry ore (nonvein deposits of 1%–2% copper content) were gradually brought into practice in the western United States. By the end of the First World War, large-scale open-pit mines and block-caving underground mines began to serve the soaring needs of the electrical and construction industries.[3]

[3] For background on the history of the copper industry, the best sources include: Orris C. Herfindahl, *Copper Costs and Prices: 1870–1957* (Baltimore: Resources for Freedom, Johns Hopkins Press, 1960); William Y. Elliott *et al.*, *International Control in the Non-Ferrous Metals* (New York: Macmillan, 1937); A. D. McMahon, *Copper: A Materials Survey* (Washington, D.C.: U.S. Department of the Interior, Bureau of Mines, 1964); Isaac F. Marcosson, *Anaconda* (New York:

The International Copper Industry

The technology that was required to extract metal from low-grade ore was only one of the reasons for early foreign predominance as the copper industry began to grow in Chile. The amounts of capital and the scale of operations involved in constructing huge mines with concentrators, smelters, and railroad facilities in the midst of the Atacama desert or the Andes mountains—the high risk and relatively low profits—were other disincentives to domestic competition. Chilean capital gravitated toward the more speculatively profitable nitrate industry, the rich copper-vein mining, urban commerce, or toward conservative cattle raising in the fertile Central Valley.[4]

In 1904, as the possibilities of vein mining were running

Dodd, Mead, 1957); and John McDonald, "The World of Kennecott", *Fortune*, November 1951.

[4] The best histories of copper in Chile include: Francisco A. Encina, *Nuestra inferioridad económica, sus causas y sus consequencias* (Santiago: Imprenta Universitaria, 1912); Julio Kaulen, *Las empresas mineras extranjeras en Chile y la economía nacional* (Santiago: 1916); Machiavello Varas, *El problema de la industria del cobre* (Santiago: 1923); and Markos Mamalakis and Clark Reynolds, *Essays on the Chilean Economy* (Homewood, Ill.: Richard D. Irwin, Inc., 1965).

The "denationalization" of the Chilean copper industry, or why it came to be controlled by foreigners, was a sensitive issue in Chile after the First World War. Julio Kaulen asked: "Are Chileans capable of running mines? Yes! If there is so little initiative in Chilean entrepreneurs, why does Chilean capital work such large [nitrate or silver] mines in Bolivia as Llallagua, Optoca, Oruro, Corocoro? The fact is that El Teniente does not have the character of being an adventure that attracts the Chilean entrepreneur. . . . [Low-grade copper mining] is a work of perseverance, which is not a predominant quality in the Chilean."

On the same subject, Macchiavelo Varas quoted a writer in *El Mercurio* (December 1918) who said: "Mr. Braden was right in saying he was convinced that the [copper] mining industry was not the type of business that interested Chileans. At the beginning, at El Teniente and Potrerillos, he had wanted to associate himself with Chileans, but as the latter did not soon get their dreamed-of dividends, they got rid of all or almost all of their stock, allowing one more step toward the denationalization of the copper industry."

21

out, the Chilean owners of El Teniente, a mountain of ore located in the Andes about 100 miles southeast of Santiago, sought financial support from fellow-Chileans and from potential investors in England, France, Germany, and Yugoslavia to no avail. They finally sold out to William Braden, an American mining engineer, who was himself forced to sell to the Guggenheims in 1908, who in turn transferred control of El Teniente to Kennecott in 1915. Under Kennecott ownership, El Teniente was built into the largest underground copper mine in the world. The output of the Kennecott subsidiary, Braden, reached 115,000 metric tons in 1934, climbed to 145,000 metric tons in 1937, and stayed close to that level as an upper capacity of production until 1969.

In 1913, work was begun on the Chuquicamata property in the Atacama desert of northern Chile, a property sold to Anaconda in 1923, which became and has remained the world's largest open-pit copper mine. In 1926, Anaconda began production at a second mine at Potrerillos several hundred miles southeast of Chuquicamata.[5]

There can be no doubt of the skill, imagination, and risk involved in the early development of the Kennecott and Anaconda mines. And the North American entrepreneurs were given ample opportunity to enjoy the fruits of their initiative through the copper boom of the 1920's. Complete data are not available, but Clark Reynolds estimates that the total taxes paid by Kennecott in the period 1913–1924 amounted to only 0.8% of gross sales.[6] An income tax was not initiated until 1922 and amounted to only 12% until 1932. In the late 1920's Kennecott was making 20%–40% per year on its investment in El Teniente, and Anaconda recovered over 14% per year on its two properties.[7]

---

[5] On Anaconda's early operations in Chile, see Marcosson, *Anaconda*; and Mamalakis and Reynolds, *Essays on the Chilean Economy*.

[6] Mamalakis and Reynolds, *op.cit.*, p. 226.

[7] Throughout this study I have used the official historical statistics of the Corporación del Cobre de Chile as they were compiled through the beginning of 1970. To my knowledge, they have not been changed

Foreign control of the technology, capital, and managerial skills necessary for large-scale low-grade mining placed the companies in a strong position to expect, or demand, generous initial concessions from the Chilean government. In 1916 the newspaper *El Mercurio* called the employment that Kennecott provided for Chilean labor (plus

---

during the Allende or the military regimes. Where they differ significantly from company figures, I try to give an explanation. For yearly entries, see the Statistical Appendix.

According to the Corporación del Cobre, the book value of Kennecott's subsidiary Braden was approximately $36 million during this period, while the book value of Anaconda's subsidiary at Chuquicamata was approximately $113 million and at Potrerillos $80 million.

These figures involve some controversy. Kennecott claims (*Expropriation of the El Teniente Copper Mine by the Chilean Government*, Kennecott Copper Corporation, 1971) that the total investment value of Braden in the late 1920's was about $72 million. This figure, however, would appear to be gross investment, before deducting accumulated depreciation charges. The Chilean figure of $36 million roughly fits what one would compute if he started with the agreed book value of Braden in the 1960's and subtracted net investments (gross investments minus depreciation charges) made since the late 1920's. Therefore, I have stuck with the Chilean figure for the book value of Braden at the end of the 1920's.

For Anaconda, Chilean historical statistics actually only record a book value of about $19 million for Chuquicamata because $94 million from the purchase of the Chuquicamata property was never transferred onto the books of the branch operating in Chile (Chile Exploration Company) but rather was retained for tax purposes on the books of a holding company subsidiary (Chile Copper Company) in the US. I have sided with the Anaconda position in stating that book value for Chuquicamata in the late 1920's was about $113 million.

This method of estimating initial net worth to calculate return on investment means that Kennecott's subsidiary appears by far the more profitable venture, since the Guggenheims sold Chuquicamata to Anaconda in 1923 as a highly successful on-going operation at a commercial price. If one were to calculate the rate of return on the value of the initial investment at Chuquicamata, one would produce a high figure much more closely approximating Kennecott's.

The average profits for the years 1928 and 1929 for Braden are $14.5 million, yielding a return of 40% per year. The average profits for the two Anaconda subsidiaries for the same two years are $27.5 million, yielding over 14%

a small amount of import duties and fares on the national railroad) a blessing![8] These "blessings" multiplied as the state cautiously imposed 6%, then 12%, then 18% income taxes on Anaconda and Kennecott.

From the Second World War onward, however, the Chilean perception of what constituted a "fair" distribution of the earnings from the copper industry, and the Chilean willingness to remain helpless and passive vis-à-vis the foreign monopoly on expertise and experience in running the copper industry, changed dramatically. This changing perception coincided with a shift in bargaining power away from the foreign investor toward the host government.[9] During the Depression, the copper companies had been in such precarious financial condition that Chilean governments did not push taxes much above 20%.[10] But with the boom conditions of the Second World War, the country declared an excess profits tax that raised the total tax burden to about 50%. By 1952, the total tax burden had been pushed above 70%. Anaconda and Kennecott, with their investments sunk and their operations a success, did not begin to think seriously of abandoning or even cutting back on their Chilean operations. In the 1947–1949 period, for example, with taxes approaching 60% of earnings, Kennecott was still receiving above 40% per year on its investment and Anaconda 12%.[11]

[8] *El Mercurio*, June 28, 1916, quoted with disapproval by Julio Kaulen.

[9] A dynamic model of the evolution of bargaining strength between foreign investors and the host country is developed in Chapter 6.

[10] The actual income-tax rate was only 18%, but after 1931 the Chilean government required Anaconda and Kennecott to buy pesos for local expenses at an artificial exchange rate which, as inflation raised the price of domestic goods and services, became an increasingly heavy indirect tax. This tax is described in more detail in Chapter 3.

[11] For the two years 1947 and 1948, Kennecott's subsidiary Braden earned $30 million on an investment of $32 million. Anaconda earned $54 million on an investment of $223 million.

The judgment about what constituted a "fair" distribution of the earnings from the copper industry between foreign investors and host country was based implicitly on a
yardstick that was changing as time went along. The companies measured their contribution to the country against
what the country would have had if they had never come
to invest. Until the day they were nationalized, Anaconda
and Kennecott were recounting feats of risk and endurance
in the lonely deserts and treacherous mountains that had
occurred fifty years earlier.

The Chilean government looked out on the successful
operations and the reduced uncertainty and the fixed investment and began to measure the foreign contribution
against what the situation would be like if the companies no
longer had a monopoly control over technology, experience,
and entrepreneurship.

Unfortunately for the clarity of the debate, however, the
shift in the perception about what constituted fair shares
of the copper earnings came about within a muddled attack
on the "monopolistic" nature of the international copper
industry in general. More and more arguments after the
Second World War took the form that the country was suffering because company profits were "too high", and that
they were too high because the foreigners were "monopolistic". Summarizing the history of the copper companies in
Chile, Senator Contreras Labarca typified the feeling by
arguing that the magnitude of the profits Anaconda and
Kennecott had been able to earn on operations in Chile
were "the cause of the country's underdevelopment".[12]

This was the kind of argument that had a certain rhetorical importance in the shift from laissez faire to national control over copper policy, but as a hypothesis linking international oligopoly power with domestic underdevelopment
it was more confusing than enlightening. It confused the
size of the returns generated by the foreign companies'

[12] *Historia de la ley 16.425* (Chilean Congressional hearings on
"Chileanization"), Vol. 1, September 6, 1965, p. 204.

operations with the relative distribution of those returns between foreign investor and host country. It confused one kind of "monopoly" power, the power of the companies vis-à-vis final consumers (allowing the former to charge the latter a price that was substantially above marginal cost), with another kind of "monopoly" power, the power of the companies vis-à-vis the host country (allowing the former to keep a large share of the revenues at the expense of the latter).

But for all this kind of argument lacked in clarity, it made up for in domestic appeal. Shortly after the Second World War, Chileans began to cite a study of the copper industry, carried out by the US Federal Trade Commission in 1947, that declared: "Practically all the copper entering into world competition is controlled by less than a dozen companies or financial groups. They have one common interest, profits, and probably can be counted on to take whatever steps, organized or unorganized, as may seem most expedient, to attain their ends of high profits."[13] The report then boldly went on to identify *six men* who, the study claimed, "directly or indirectly, are in a position to dictate the production and price policies of about 60% of the world output of primary copper"! Chilean production was included.

Hostility to monopolies, especially foreign monopolies, is not surprisingly a frequent theme in Chilean nationalistic or populistic thought. But Chilean writers and politicians took the argument against the international copper industry, constructed for the benefit of consumers, and transposed it to Chile, a producing country, as part of their struggle against the profitability, invulnerability, and foreignness of Anaconda and Kennecott.

The economist Aníbal Pinto was one of the first of a long line of Chilean writers to point to the Federal Trade Commission study of the copper industry. He began in the early 1950's to warn of the "semi-monopolistic international nexus"

[13] *Report of the Federal Trade Commission on the Copper Industry* (Washington, D.C.: GPO, 1947), pp. 176 *et seq.*

that it revealed.[14] Senator Izquierdo of the Agrarian Labor Party prefaced his remarks on the revision of the Chilean mining legislation in 1955 by saying that "the country cannot afford to be at the mercy of private foreign economic groups with links to strong consortia and monopolies in the United States".[15] In debates on copper policy in the mid-1960's, Sr. Contreras Labarca, the Senator from the Communist Party, who had described the size of copper profits as the "cause of the country's underdevelopment", attacked Anaconda and Kennecott because they were "grand consortia that dominate almost without counterweight the world trade in copper".[16] At the same time Senator Carlos Altamirano, later to become president of the Socialist Party under Allende, asserted that "nobody who knows the problem could say that the interest of Chile is associated with a foreign commercial monopoly".[17] A writer for the national copperworkers' union in 1964 cited the old FTC study in attacking the companies because their "cartel prevents free trade".[18]

The Chilean argument against monopolies, based on their own experience with small domestic markets, was indisputable: monopoly power is "by nature" exploitative. It is used to dictate high prices and exact high profits. But this is an argument designed to protect the interest of final consumers, not producers.

When the greatest barriers to entry of competition (and therefore the source of monopoly or oligopoly power) exist at the production stage, those who control the mines have

[14] Aníbal Pinto Santa Cruz, *Hacia nuestra independencia económica* (Santiago: Editorial del Pacífico, 1953), p. 182.

The groups that these spokesmen represented and the domestic interests that these arguments served will be traced in Chapters 3, 4, 5, and 6.

[15] *Historia de la ley 11.828* (Chilean Congressional hearings on the *Nuevo Trato*), Vol. 1, January 20, 1955, p. 1361.

[16] *Historia de la ley 16.425*, Vol. 1, September 6, 1965, p. 204.

[17] *Ibid.*, October 7, 1965, p. 591.

[18] Juan Agarte Solas in *Cobre*, February 3, 1964.

the potential to exact an economic rent from users and consumers downstream. Foreign producing companies and the domestic taxing authorities join together in exploiting the final consumer, and split the resulting revenues in some proportion between themselves. What that proportion is may be vitally important to the host country, and the government may want to do all that it can to increase its own bargaining power in dealing with the foreign companies. But this does not alter the fact that the stronger the international monopoly power of an industry that produces within a country and sells outside it, the more advantageous for the host country.

II

Unfortunately for producers and their host governments, however, the efforts of the international copper oligopoly to control price at a "high" level have had continually decreasing success. At the same time that Chile was pushing the foreign mining companies for more and more revenues, the major international copper producers, including Anaconda and Kennecott, were finding it harder and harder to maintain oligopolistic control over the industry.

Since the beginning of the twentieth century there have been at least seven major attempts to form and hold an international cartel in the copper industry.[19] Anaconda and Kennecott were both regularly involved in producers' agreements and exporters' associations outside of the United States. But all of the cartel activities were short-lived and unsuccessful. Orris Herfindahl finds that none of the attempts to create a producers' monopoly were long

---

[19] For a history of these attempts at cartelization in the international copper industry, see Herfindahl, *Copper Costs and Prices: 1870–1957*, chs. 4–6, and Elliott *et al.*, *International Control in the Non-Ferrous Metals*. On the history of copper mining in Africa, see L. H. Gann, "The Northern Rhodesian Copper Industry and the World of Copper: 1923–1952", Human Problems in British Central Africa xviii, *Rhodes-Livingstone Journal*, No. 18, 1955.

effective either in maintaining price or in controlling production.[20] Cornelius Kelley, the head of Anaconda, complained in the mid-1920's that outside competition, price
chiseling, and defections all worked to make cartel arrangements impossible.[21]

The lure of profits similar to the 40% per year realized by
Kennecott in Chile was attracting new entrepreneurs into
the industry. The availability of untouched copper sources
in Africa and South America, Canada and the United States
gave some of them great success. Even the established
members of the producers' oligopoly could not coordinate
their own actions. They cheated on each other to bring additional production from new sources to the market at discount prices.

During the Depression the most successful of all the cartel attempts lasted from 1935 through 1939. Still, Rhodesian
producers, with low labor costs and extensive ore-bodies,
pushed for and got quotas during that period giving them
a larger share of the market at the expense of the rest of the
cartel. Similarly, in Canada there were also increases in capacity. From 1935 to 1939 Canadian mine production increased by 45% while the increase for cartel members was
28%.[22]

Since the end of the Second World War there have been
no formal attempts by the major private producers to control production or raise prices. Yet the discovery of new
sources of copper and the dilution of the strength of the
producers' oligopoly have proceeded even more rapidly.

In the United States, the "Big Three" copper producers
(Kennecott, Anaconda, and Phelps Dodge) held their
share of domestic mine production above 80% from 1947
through the Korean War. This was the level of concentration that gave rise to the Federal Trade Commission report
on monopoly in the copper industry. But by 1960 the share

[20] Herfindahl, *op.cit.*   [21] Cited in *ibid.*, p. 95.
[22] *Ibid.*, p. 111.

of the Big Three had dropped to 69%. And by 1970 their share had declined to 61%.[23]

The dilution of producer concentration is even more striking on the international level. From the end of the Second World War to the end of the Korean War, seven companies, including the Anglo-American and Roan-American Metal groups in Northern Rhodesia (Zambia), the Union Minière group in the Congo (Zaire), and International Nickel of Canada, as well as Anaconda, Kennecott, and Phelps Dodge, produced an average of from 65% to 70% of "Free World" copper. By 1960 their percentage of world production had declined to 60%. By 1969, their production was 54% (see Table 1).

TABLE 1
Copper Production of Leading Companies[24]
(thousand short tons)

	1948	1960	1969
1. Kennecott	514	571	699
2. Anaconda	362	476	597
3. Phelps Dodge	247	234	284
4. Roan-AMC group	134	241	368
5. Anglo-American Group	118	392	426
6. Union Minière	171	331	399
7. International Nickel	118	155	110
Total "The Seven"	1664	2400	2883
Percentage of World Production	70%	60%	54%

[23] These figures have been computed on the basis of standard industry statistics from appropriate issues of the *Yearbook* of the American Bureau of Metal Statistics (New York).

[24] The Roan-American Metal Climax group includes Mufulira and Roan Antelope as well as Matahambre (Cuba) for 1948. For 1960, Chibuluma Mines was added and Matahambre dropped. For 1969, Chambishi was added.

The American Metal Climax Corporation has historically owned

If, in 1969, one added American Smelting and Refining, the Newmont Mining majority holdings (Magma in the United States and O'okiep in South Africa), plus all the Japanese domestic producers as a group, the result would still account for only about 65% of world output.

To get a figure above 70% of "Free World" production, the list would have to include a sizable number of those large mining companies producing between 50,000 and 100,000 tons per year—some of which are almost large enough to have been included among "The Seven" after World War II. There are more than fourteen in this range: Southern Peru Copper Company, Rio Tinto Zinc (including Palabora in South Africa and Cia. Española de Rio Tinto in Spain), Mt. Isa in Australia, Copper Range in the US, Inspiration Copper in the US, Pima Mining in the US, Duval Copper in the US, Bolidens in Sweden, Cerro de Pasco in Peru, Noranda Mines in Canada, Hudson Bay in Canada, Atlas Consolidated in the Philippines, Freeport Sulphur in Indonesia, Ecstall-Texas Gulf Sulphur in Canada, plus a number of potentially large properties under development in British Columbia and in Southeast Asia–Oceania.

These companies are not all strictly independent since American Smelting and Refining, Phelps Dodge, Cerro, and Copper Range have interests in Southern Peru Copper Company; Newmont Mining has interests in Palabora (29%) and in Atlas (4%); Anaconda has a 25% interest in

---

about 42% of the Roan Selection Trust Ltd., 18% of O'okiep Copper Company Ltd., and 17% of Copper Range Company.

The Anglo-American group includes Nchanga and Rhokana for 1948; by 1960 Bancroft had been added. Hudson Bay Mining Company was not included with the Anglo-American group despite the latter's 28% interest. The Anglo-American Corporation of South Africa also had equity interests in some of the mines operated by Roan Selection Trust—30% of Baluba Mines; 31% of Chisangwa Mines; 34.4% of Mufulira; and 14% of Mwinilunga Mines.

The last year before the full impact of economic nationalism made itself felt in Chile, Peru, and Zambia was 1969.

Inspiration; Anglo-American has a 28% interest in Hudson Bay; and American Metal Climax has an 18% interest in O'okiep and 17% in Copper Range.

But the trend toward dilution of the international copper oligopoly is unmistakable. Since the end of the Second World War, the oligopoly on a world level has grown from seven major producers to at least twenty, even before allowing for the force of economic nationalism further breaking up the producing units.

This trend toward a more diluted concentration in the copper mining industry is related to five major factors. Their impact has been to weaken the strength of the international producers' oligopoly throughout the period when Chile and other host governments have been pushing the companies for higher revenues.

(1) First, there has been the continuing discovery of large new sources of copper. This began as a process of geographical discovery in the 1920's as large new ore-bodies in Canada and Africa were added to those in the United States. After the Second World War new finds were made in the United States, Canada, Peru, and Zambia. More recent areas of major discovery include the South Pacific (Indonesia, Bougainville, Australia), the province of British Columbia in Canada, Siberia, Iran, and parts of Africa.

The possibility of geographical discovery has been aided by the process of technical discovery, with the development of the ability to work very low-grade ore-bodies successfully on a large scale. The bulk of the world's copper reserves are located in large low-grade porphyry ore-bodies, accessible only to open-pit methods. The initial shift from vein to bulk mining opened the possibility of working ore with 0.7%–2.0% copper content. Now, with operations of huge scale and capital intensity, the range of recoverable copper has been significantly expanded. In the middle 1960's the Japanese were thinking of signing a contract to "re-mine" the huge waste dumps and slag heaps left by Anaconda in the northern desert near Chuquicamata. They never signed, owing to fears of economic nationalism. But the Japanese (and others) are now successfully working new ores in Canada with a lower copper content than the Anaconda waste!

In Arizona, Anaconda and Duval are working ore with as little as 0.3% copper content (less than seven pounds of copper per ton of rock). Reserves of such copper in the United States are immense. These ore-bodies are only from one-third to one-fourth as rich as the major mines in Chile or Peru or Zambia.

The amount of capital and scale of operations necessary to begin such low-grade mines may constitute a major absolute barrier to entry, especially for the governments of less developed countries acting on their own. But they will not be a high barrier to entry to companies with access to finance and with experience in large operations.

There are other technological discoveries in view that could further increase the potential supply of copper. The most promising include chemical processes of treating ore, and mining from the seabed.

(2) Second, the dilution of concentration in the producers' oligopoly has been stimulated by government subsidies, especially wartime subsidies in the United States. The Premium Price Plan during the Second World War and the Defense Production Act of 1950 provided grants or loans for new facilities that were to be paid back in new output.[25] These programs offered financing to new companies, or helped small companies to expand their operations. The Silver Bell Mine, which substantially increased American Smelting and Refining's position as a primary producer, was developed under DPA subsidies. The White Pine Mine, another DPA property, moved Copper Range from obscurity to the status of major producer. Magma's output tripled in 1956 when its San Manuel Mine, subsidized under the Defense Production Act, came on-line. As

[25] Cf. James L. McCarthy, "The American Copper Industry, 1947–1955," *Yale Economic Essays*, Vol. IV (Spring 1964).

recently as 1970 the Duval Corporation became a major producer by bringing its Sierrita property into production with a loan from the General Services Administration under the Defense Production Act of 1950.[26]

In the 1960's and 1970's the governments of Japan and Germany have increasingly been willing to provide easy credit to stimulate the development of secure sources of copper. Chapter 7 will discuss the probability that these programs of government subsidy will continue or even be expanded in reaction to the "threat" of economic national-ism in some producing countries.

(3) Third, the pressure toward creating new sources of copper has come from the desire of smelting, refining, and fabricating companies to integrate backwards to their own supplies. American Smelting and Refining, American Metal Climax, and major Japanese refining and fabricating groups have been moving upstream to develop sources at the min-ing stage. German, Belgian, and British firms appear to be heading in the same direction.

Such smelting, refining, and fabricating groups already possess many of the skills and expertise necessary to man-age an integrated copper business. Entry into the mining stage, alone or in conjunction with other miners, does not involve overcoming such high barriers as those faced by a newcomer to the industry.

(4) Fourth, and related to the third point above, the growth of new entrants in the field of copper mining has been a function of the willingness of fabricators and con-sumers of copper to finance the growth of new small cop-per miners and be paid back in output. Thus, fabricators and consumers have by-passed having to buy from the tra-ditional giant mining companies and have provided capital to smaller mining companies or to new mining companies to expand production.

[26] For Duval's experience, cf. George P. Lutgen, "Open-pit Guide: Sierrita Makes It with Big Equipment", *Engineering and Mining Journal* (August 1970), pp. 70–73.

Japanese companies have been the leaders in financing the development of new sources. Mitsubishi, Nippon, Sumitomo, and Furukawa have loaned substantial amounts to small companies or new companies in Africa, Canada, South America, and the South Pacific in return for long-term contracts for metal and concentrates. German refiners and fabricators, led by the Norddeutsch Affinerie–Metallgesellschaft Aktiengesellschaft group, have been following the same practice in Africa and the South Pacific.

(5) The fifth factor that has caused the dilution of concentration in the international copper mining oligopoly has been a drive on the part of natural resource companies that have not traditionally been associated with copper to diversify by forming or buying a mining subsidiary. Petroleum and sulphur companies have been particularly successful in diversifying into copper mining. Duval, which has grown to be the fourth largest domestic copper producer in the United States and eighth largest in the corporate world, is a wholly owned subsidiary of Pennzoil United. Cities Service has two growing copper mining affiliates. Freeport Sulphur has developed one of the world's largest new copper deposits at Ertsberg in West Irian, Indonesia. Texas Gulf Sulphur is a major copper producer, with its Ecstall Mining Division in Canada.

Also, copper is often found in conjunction with nickel deposits, which has resulted in International Nickel of Canada becoming one of the largest copper producers in the world. The same process is occurring in Australia's nickel boom, with the Pechiney–Tréfimétaux group of France, and others, anticipating relatively large increases in copper output as a result of their expanded nickel operations.

These large multinational natural resource firms are already familiar with the problems of production and global distribution, and have access to the large amounts of capital necessary for mining. Thus, they do not face barriers to entry into the copper industry as high as do the smaller or newer companies. The lure of copper profits and the corporate preference to diversify, then, have combined to contribute heavily to the erosion of concentration at the mining stage of the copper industry.

Consequently, the trend that started with the failures of the international copper cartels in the 1920's and 1930's has continued. Copper deposits have not been scarce enough nor the technology of extraction esoteric enough to permit effective control of prices and production. There has been a steady dilution in the international oligopoly at the production stage and a long-term downward trend in prices.

Orris Herfindahl has charted the course of copper prices from 1870 to 1957, deflated it by the wholesale price index in the United States, and found the overall trend line to be distinctly downward.[27] This trend continued through the beginning of the Vietnam War.

The profit rates for the major copper-producing companies have also been declining[28] (see Table 2).

TABLE 2
Average Rate of Return on Stockholders' Equity
for Major Copper Companies

	1946–1956	*1957–1966*
Anaconda	7.2%	5.8%
Kennecott	15.9%	9.5%
Phelps Dodge	17.1%	11.2%
American Smelting and Refining	13.6%	8.9%

[27] Herfindahl, *op.cit.*, chart entitled "Price of Copper Deflated by Wholesale Price Index", Trend Line (3). This trend line includes what Dr. Herfindahl calls both "normal" and "abnormal" periods of pricing. He suggests that since the end of World War I there has been a long-term stability in the deflated price of copper.

Another study that emphasizes the competitive nature of copper pricing in the postwar years is B. R. Stewardson, "The Nature of Competition in the World Market for Refined Copper", *Economic Record*, June 1970.

[28] Computed from figures given in the *Annual Reports* of the companies by the Charles River Associates, Inc., *Economic Analysis of the*

In comparison to other oligopolistic industries, Professors Joe Bain and H. Michael Mann have found that, from 1936 to 1960, the copper industry could be classified as having "substantial barriers to entry" at the production stage, but not those "very high entry barriers" where the profit rate, at least from 1950 to 1960, was a full five percentage points higher.[29]

In short, the monopoly or oligopoly power of those "grand consortia that dominate almost without counterweight the world trade in copper", in the words of Senator Contreras Labarca, has in fact been on a steady decline, and with it the ability to generate high earnings has been diminished. Who has won and who has lost from this process? Over the long term, final consumers have been winning. And primary producers and their host governments have lost.

To a large extent, however, the waning power of producers to exact economic rents from consumers has not been apparent to Chile (or Zambia, or Peru, or the Congo) because the ability of the host governments to demand more of a contribution from the foreign companies has been simultaneously increasing.

III

In the face of gradually increasing competition at the production stage of the copper industry, one corporate response has been a strategy of trying to regain tight oligopoly control farther downstream at the fabrication stage.

Copper Industry (Cambridge, Mass.: March 1970), p. 191. All of these companies—especially Phelps Dodge and Kennecott—have substantial US mining operations. Thus, the decline in profit rate is not primarily attributable to higher foreign taxes.

[29] Joe S. Bain, *Barriers to New Competition* (Cambridge, Mass.: Harvard University Press, 1956), pp. 192–195; and H. Michael Mann, "Seller Concentration, Barriers to Entry, and Rates of Return in Thirty Industries, 1950–1960", *Review of Economics and Statistics*, Vol. 48 (August 1966).

Anaconda was the first and most vigorous North American company to move forward into the fabricating business.[30] The company had begun as a mining enterprise in Montana at the end of the nineteenth century, spread its mining operations into Arizona, Nevada, and eventually Chile, building or acquiring large smelters and refineries as it went. In 1922, Anaconda acquired the American Brass Company, which was then the largest and most technologically advanced fabricator of non-ferrous metals in the world. With this move Anaconda became the leader in an industry undergoing relatively rapid technological change to serve the needs of construction—developing strong, flexible, non-corrosive alloys in the form of sheets, strips, and rods, flexible metal hoses, and large- and small-diameter seamless tubing.

In 1929 Anaconda moved into the wire and cable business by bringing together a group of smaller enterprises under the name of the Anaconda Wire & Cable Company. Here, too, the development of the new science of metallurgy was important in fashioning magnetic and non-magnetic wires, cables, and coils of both large size and miniature dimensions for the rapidly growing electrical and electronics industries.

Shortly after Anaconda's moves toward forward integration, Kennecott imitated the strategy by acquiring the Chase Brass and Copper Company.[31] By early 1929 Kennecott was also a major fabricator of brass products. In 1935, Kennecott bought out the American Electrical Works to add a wire and cable subsidiary.

In the United States, the same broad pattern was repeated by Phelps Dodge, American Smelting and Refining, and Cerro; in Canada, by Noranda; in Europe, by the

[30] On Anaconda's history, see the *Annual Reports* and Marcosson, *Anaconda*.

[31] For Kennecott's history, see the *Annual Reports*; McDonald, "The World of Kennecott"; and Rush Loving, Jr., "How Kennecott Got Hooked with Catch–22", *Fortune*, September 1971.

Union Minière-Société General du Belgique group; and in Japan, most prominently by Sumitomo, Mitsubishi, and Nippon.

It is not possible to judge on the basis of the available data the relative weight given to various motivations for integrating vertically into the fabricating stage. On the one hand, copper fabrication seemed to offer the possibility of excluding competition. Metallurgical technology and expertise in skilled production might create barriers to entry sufficiently high to limit competition. In addition, integrated operations would give the mining companies the option of using variable pricing to squeeze independent fabricators out of business. This would discourage newcomers. From this point of view, the strategy could be seen as an aggressive attempt to regain at the fabrication stage some of the oligopolistic control that was being threatened at the production stage.

On the other hand, the strategy was also a defensive reaction taken to protect profits obtained upstream in mining. Copper producers need a secure outlet for their metal, and the fabricating stage appeared as a potential bottleneck. As Anaconda's biographer states: "Ryan and Kelley [Anaconda's president and executive vice-president in the 1920's] realized that it was imperative to seek outlets for the output of Anaconda then inert. These outlets would permit a constant flow of metals from the plants at all times even when there might be a temporary surplus of metal in the market. Their studies led them to the inevitable conclusion that Anaconda must enter the field of fabrication."[32]

In other words, there was a threat that fabricators could act, in periods of slack demand, as monopsonists (oligopsonists) and force producers to sell below average cost. In an industry such as copper mining where there are high fixed costs and low variable costs, any monopoly power downstream can force the producer to sell well below the

[32] Marcosson, *Anaconda*, p. 167.

high average cost needed to depreciate all the capital invested in mining, smelting, and refining. To insure himself of an outlet and avoid the necessity of pricing right down to the low variable cost, the producer will make a defensive investment in the stage that offers the potential threat.

For offensive and defensive reasons, then, corporate strategy in the copper industry between the two World Wars, and to a certain extent after them, was directed toward vertical integration into the fabricating stage. Once Anaconda had made the major move into brass works and wire and cable fabrication, other major producers felt compelled to follow. Anaconda's slogan, "From Mine to Consumer", seemed to indicate the trend for the future.

If the technology and expertise in copper fabrication had in fact been esoteric enough to exclude competition, or if variable pricing to fabricating subsidiaries could in fact have been used to destroy competition, forward integration could have helped the copper industry to bolster its slipping oligopoly control. Although this would have helped to preserve the total oligopoly rents generated in the chain from mine to consumer, it would at the same time have posed a threat to those countries that were host to the production stage alone. Vertical integration would then have given the copper companies the option of collecting those rents outside the tax jurisdiction of the governments where the mines were located. Such an option would be exercised by charging "low" transfer prices between producing and fabricating subsidiaries that had the same parent. As a producing country like Chile pressed for a greater share of the industry earnings, the subsidiaries in Chile could have been made to show low accounting profits for tax purposes, and the total economic rent collected in the international oligopoly would have been little shared with the Chileans.[33]

[33] If an industry is totally integrated, there is no way a taxing authority can reallocate income on the basis of what prices would be if intersubsidiary sales were conducted as arm's-length transactions. The only solution in such a situation would be an artificial set of

This was a hypothesis that provoked legitimate Chilean fears. Luís Corvalán, the leader of the Communist Party, made the charge: "The producers are also fabricators, and thus they keep prices low so that they can collect the difference from their fabricating outlet."[34] Raúl Ampuero, an influential Chilean Senator from the Socialist Party, asserted: "We know that these trusts can displace their profits from one step to another down the line—for them, a transfer of mere accounting; for us, a crisis of brutal magnitude."[35]

Such a hypothesis could have been subjected to direct and indirect tests, even with the evidence then available—but such tests were not attempted.[36] To transfer "profits" out of Chile and recapture them farther downstream, the foreign copper companies would have had to sell only to their own fabricators with absolute discretion over the transfer price, or else would have had to sell to their own fabricating subsidiaries at a low transfer price and to independent fabricators at a higher real price.

Such was not the case.

In the first place, competition could not be excluded at

"posted prices" used for tax purposes similar to the practice in the petroleum industry.

For the purposes of this study, primary production of copper will include mining, smelting, and refining. Although smelting and refining create value-added (so that it was in the Chilean interest to push for such operations to be done in Chile), they do not constitute stages to which oligopoly rents can be shifted.

[34] *Historia de la ley 11.828*, Vol. 1, September 16, 1954, p. 3930.

[35] *Ibid.*, Vol. 2, January 19, 1955, p. 1293.

[36] Unfortunately, able and sophisticated Chilean economists concerned with copper policy did not bother to examine the structure of the industry or the level of profits at various stages within the industry. Rather, a vague suspicion that the companies could "transfer profits from one stage to another at will" was allowed to persist. Cf. the defense of Anaconda's pricing behavior by Rudolfo Mitchels in *Panorama Económico*, No. 31, 1951.

To make up for the scarcity of published information, Chilean authorities could have obliged Anaconda and Kennecott to submit a financial breakdown of mining and fabricating operations.

the fabricating stage. As metallurgy became a more mature science after the end of the Second World War and as the technology of most copper fabrication became more standardized, the barriers to entry were lowered and independent fabricators proliferated. Concentration in the US copper fabricating industry declined in almost all Standard Industrial Classifications of copper mills and foundries between 1954 (where data are available), 1958, and 1963.[37] The level of concentration varied greatly, depending upon the importance of technology, from a classification for electrical wire manufacturing plants (SIC 33572) where the top four firms still controlled 67% of the market in 1963, to a classification for copper-based castings (SIC 33620) where the top four firms only controlled 17% of the market in 1963. Rather than using the fabricating subsidiaries as a new point to collect oligopoly rents, the reports of the major copper companies constantly complain of excess capacity, "excessive" competition, and "unacceptable" profit levels at that stage.

In the second place, after the Alcoa case in 1945, differ-

---

[37] These data come from *Concentration Ratios in Manufacturing Industry, 1958* and *Concentration Ratios in Manufacturing Industry, 1963*, Reports prepared by the Bureau of the Census for the Subcommittee on Antitrust and Monopoly of the Committee on the Judiciary, U.S. Senate, 87th Congress, 2nd Session (Washington, D.C.: GPO, 1962) and 89th Congress, 2nd Session, 1963 (Washington, D.C.: GPO, 1966). A convenient summary of these results has been reprinted by the Charles River Associates, *Economic Analysis of the Copper Industry*, p. 59.

Data on vertical and horizontal integration are more difficult to find for Europe and Japan. Incomplete evidence from *Beerman's Financial Yearbook of Europe* (New York: International Publishers Service, 1970) and *Non-Ferrous Metal Works of the World* (London: Metal Bulletin Books, Ltd., 1967) suggests that although there are some large fabricator groups (General Electric–Associated Electrical Industries or British Insulated Callender's Cables in England, the Metallgesellschaft Aktiengesellschaft–Norddeutsche–Vereinigte Deutsche Metallwerke group in Germany, and Sumitomo or Furukawa in Japan), in general concentration at the fabricating stage is relatively dispersed.

ential pricing and predatory treatment of independent fabricators became, in the United States, the object of close anti-trust scrutiny.[38] To avoid the threat of prosecution, the major producers began to allocate their copper between their own subsidiaries and independent fabricators according to historical buying patterns (i.e., without discrimination and at a uniform price even in periods of scarcity) in a conscious attempt, according to James McCarthy, to avoid squeezing the independents out of business.[39] As part of this system, the international mining companies sold Chilean output at the same price (the US "producers' price") to their own subsidiaries and to independents alike. Variable pricing was not used as a means to siphon profits out of 'Chile.

Finally, the major companies began to cut back on their own drive into fabrication and started to sell more and more of their output to unrelated buyers. Kennecott did not pursue its preliminary ventures into copper fabrication with any vigor and continued after the Second World War to sell about 80% of its output to independent fabricators and consumers. Even Anaconda, which had been the strongest mover in the direction of complete integration, allowed fabricator divisions to stagnate in comparison to mining and sold about 40% of its mine output to independents.[40]

In short, the North American companies could not have shifted profits out of Chile through this mechanism of vertical integration without losing those profits themselves.

[38] For a discussion of the "power to exclude" as one acceptable test for monopoly in the thinking of Judge Learned Hand, and later as accepted by the Supreme Court in the Alcoa case of 1945, see Merton J. Peck, *Competition in the Aluminum Industry, 1945–1958* (Cambridge, Mass.: Harvard University Press, 1961), pp. 8–14.

[39] McCarthy, "The American Copper Industry, 1947–1955", p. 92.

[40] In McDonald, "The World of Kennecott", p. 90; and *Prospectus*, The Anaconda Company (6⅝% Debentures due 1993), November 19, 1968, p. 16.

The evidence confirms that the bulk of the profits produced in the international copper industry continued to be
taken by necessity at the production stage. Disaggregated
figures for the mining and fabricating subsidiaries of semi-
integrated companies are not publicly available, but aggregate data support this proposition. From 1945 to 1955, out
of every dollar of Anaconda's sales from the mines in Chile,
37¢ were pre-tax earnings and subject to taxation by Chilean authorities; the corresponding figure for Kennecott was
38¢. For the global operations of Anaconda and Kennecott
—which would include profits realized by the large fabricating subsidiaries of Anaconda and the small fabricators
of Kennecott—the figures during the same period were 19¢
and 36¢ respectively. (The higher global figure for Kennecott is explained by the fact that its fabricating divisions
were smaller and its largest mine, the Bingham pit in Utah,
was generally acknowledged to be the most efficient mine
in the United States.) Mining, not fabricating, was the point
where most of the profits were generated and declared.

From 1955 to 1965, Anaconda's pre-tax income per dollar
of sales from Chile was 47¢; for Kennecott, 59¢. The corresponding figure for Anaconda's global operations (including fabricating earnings) was 23¢; for Kennecott, 34¢.

From 1958 through 1962 the non-consolidated figures are
available for the Anaconda Wire and Cable Company.[41]
They also support the proposition that the bulk of the profits in the copper industry were realized at the production
stage. During that period the pre-tax earnings of the wire
and cable subsidiary (the high-technology end of Anaconda's fabricating operations) were only slightly over 1¢
per dollar of sales, compared with a figure above 20¢ per
dollar of total Anaconda sales. Similar evidence is available
from Kennecott. From 1958 to 1965 the company owned the
Okonite Corporation, one of the larger and more technologically sophisticated specialty fabricators, and non-con-

[41] Disaggregated figures for the Anaconda Wire and Cable Company
are found in a Proxy Statement dated November 15, 1963.

solidated figures are not available for that period. But in the preceding period, from 1952 to 1958, the pre-tax earnings of Okonite were about 7¢ per dollar of sales, compared with pre-tax earnings of about 36¢ per dollar of sales for Kennecott.[42]

Thus, the large copper companies could not recapture oligopoly control at the fabricating stage, nor were they able to shift oligopoly profits downstream without losing them. Those companies and host countries that shared control of the production stage were the fortunate ones in the industry. But their fortunes were waning.

IV

High profits at the mining stage of the copper industry attracted the entry of new competition to share in (and drive down) the profit rate. High profits at the fabricating stage attracted an even greater number of new competitors. From the 1920's through the Korean War the behavior of the international copper industry shifted from (unsuccessful) attempts to force prices up through cartel arrangements to a more cautious and conservative use of market power.

There was a new factor beginning with the Second World War, however, that hastened the shift to a defensive strategy: the threat of substitution by aluminum.[43]

[42] Cf. The Okonite Corporation, *Prospectus*, June 1, 1967. The Justice Department forced Kennecott to sell Okonite in 1965.

[43] The aluminum industry began its dynamic growth curve with the construction of light airframes in the First World War. But the threat of substitution for copper does not appear to have been a major concern in the strategy of the large copper producers until World War II. On the aluminum industry, see Peck, *Competition in the Aluminum Industry, 1945–1958*; Sterling Brubaker, *Trends in the World Aluminum Industry* (Baltimore: Resources for the Future, Johns Hopkins Press, 1967); and Martin S. Brown and John Butler, *The Production, Marketing, and Consumption of Copper and Aluminum* (New York: Praeger, 1967). The figures on aluminum growth are taken from these sources and from *Metal Statistics* (Frankfurt am Main: Metallgesellschaft, A.G., annual).

Aluminum is lighter and cheaper than copper. Supply and price are subject to fewer fluctuations. But aluminum is bulkier and much less efficient in conducting electricity (and heat) than copper. The substitution of aluminum for copper involves a trade-off among price, bulk, and efficiency in which both metals have certain distinct advantages. Because of the large contrasts in bulk and efficiency, substitution at the margin has not been considered easy— to replace copper with aluminum requires a major decision about engineering redesign that is costly and, once undertaken, not easily reversed. The rule for the copper industry seemed clear: demand lost to aluminum was lost for good.

From the Second World War onward there was no doubt that aluminum was cutting severely into copper's traditional areas of use. From 1939 to 1943 "Free World" production of aluminum more than tripled, while copper production increased only about 25%. The experience during the Korean War was similar. Between 1949 and 1953, "Free World" production of aluminum again more than doubled, while copper production gained slightly less than 20%. Over the long term, from 1945 to 1965 world aluminum production increased at a rate of nearly 11% per year, while copper only managed a rate of growth close to 5% per year.

During both the Second World War and the Korean War the major copper producers complained about what Cornelius Kelley, Anaconda's chairman, called a "systematic campaign [on the part of US government officials] that practically amounted to propaganda urging the substitution of aluminum for copper."[44]

The *Engineering and Mining Journal*, an independent publication representing the aluminum as well as copper industries, provided subtle examples of more than mere "propaganda": in the midst of the Korean War (1952), the

[44] Statement of Cornelius F. Kelley, chairman of the board of Anaconda, in the *Engineering and Mining Journal*, February 1952.

National Production Authority was allocating to auto manufacturers enough steel and other materials to produce 12%
more vehicles than would the corresponding copper allocation.[45] The copper companies naturally represented this as
a "campaign" to promote the substitution of aluminum for
copper.

The threat of substitution by aluminum, like the threat
of new competition in copper production itself, recommended an oligopoly strategy of moderation in pricing.[46]
When representatives of the major international producing
companies negotiated price ceilings in Washington to extend throughout the Second World War for all Allied countries, the price agreed upon was actually lower (11.775¢
per lb.) than the average market price had been in 1937
(13.167¢ per lb. with a high of 16.775¢) at the end of the
Depression. Similarly, the price ceilings negotiated for the
International Materials Conference during the Korean War
were only slightly higher (24.200¢ per lb.) than had prevailed in the market place in 1948 (22.038¢ per lb. with a
high of 23.200¢).

This was in marked contrast to price behavior during the
First World War and, later, the Vietnam War, when there
were no ceilings and open-market prices soared 200%–
300%.

The "low" price ceilings of the Second World War and
the Korean War, freely negotiated by the private companies
at a level much lower than the market would bear in wartime shortage, became a source of scandal in Chile, as

[45] *Ibid.*

[46] The strength of this threat was later confirmed by econometric
studies of the cross-elasticity of demand for copper and aluminum.
Cf. Charles River Associates, *Economic Analysis of the Copper Industry*; and Franklin M. Fisher and Paul H. Cootner, in association
with Martin Neal Baily, "An Econometric Model of the World Copper Industry, I+II",' *Bell Journal*, Vol. II, No. 1 (Autumn 1972).
These findings are discussed in Chapter 3, pages 81-83.

The copper prices (range and average) cited above are taken from
Metal Statistics.

Chapter 2 will point out. Such corporate behavior "proved" that producers and consumers in the industrial heartland were allied in an unquestionable (and hence unexamined) conspiracy of interests to deny Chile and other members of the underdeveloped periphery their rightful earnings.

Moderation in pricing policy was not the only response of the international copper industry to the threat of substitution. Many of the major copper producers, including both Anaconda and Kennecott, diversified into the aluminum business themselves. Kennecott began a program of portfolio investments in aluminum and other metals in 1949 and by 1959 had acquired a position in Kaiser Aluminum valued at almost $100 million.[47] Anaconda began to diversify directly into the aluminum industry in the mid-1950's with its Anaconda Aluminum Company smelter at Columbia Falls, Montana.[48] The company extended the process of diversification into aluminum in the 1960's with major investments in bauxite sources in Jamacia.

The timing of these diversification moves, partly as a matter of chance, had a substantial adverse effect on Chile. It put strong pressure on corporate funds just at a time when, as we shall see in Chapter 4, Chileans were being persuaded that a "good investment climate" would induce the companies to invest in copper expansion in Chile. A "good investment climate" was defined as a high cash flow with no strings attached. The lure of additional profits, so the argument went, would provide an "automatic stimulus" for additional investment to expand copper production.

But the result in the late 1950's was a legislative program in Chile that opened the way for a large increase in funds

[47] Cf. *Annual Reports* of Kennecott; McDonald, "The World of Kennecott"; and Loving, Jr., "How Kennecott Got Hooked with Catch–22".

[48] Cf. *Annual Reports* of Anaconda; Marcosson, *Anaconda*; Thomas O'Hanlon, "The Perilous Prosperity of Anaconda", *Fortune*, May 1966; and "Anaconda: The Domestic Problems of an International Giant", *Forbes*, December 15, 1968.

flowing *out of* Chile to finance the diversification of the parent corporations elsewhere.

Warnings about the threat from the substitution of aluminum were almost never expressed by either North Americans or Chileans in Santiago. Rather, corporate behavior remained a mystery. And, to the fear of the companies for being large, and foreign, and "invulnerable" were added suspicion about the diabolic nature of corporate strategy and hostility to the corporate use of moderation in the market place.

V

Chilean suspicion about corporate strategy and Chilean hostility to corporate moderation had a common target during the postwar period—namely, the system of "producers' prices" used by Anaconda and Kennecott. For many of the large mining companies in the international copper industry, the attempts of the 1920's and 1930's to form a producers' cartel with the aim of keeping prices "high" gave way after the Second World War to a producers' price system of informal integration designed in large part to keep prices "low".

It has already been argued that the trend toward vertical integration into the fabricating stage through formal ties of ownership makes sense not just as an aggressive attempt at control farther downstream. It also can be justified as a defensive attempt to protect profits generated upstream. In an industry such as copper production, where there are high fixed costs and low variable costs, any monopoly power downstream can force the producer to sell well below the high average cost needed to recover sunk capital expenditures. Surges in production and/or slumps in demand can give fabricators and final consumers a sudden monopoly position vis-à-vis the producer. To hedge against this threat, the producer has an incentive to seek a "secure outlet".

Similarly, just as producers want to be assured of a secure outlet when there is a glut, so fabricators and consumers want to be assured of steady, dependable sources of copper when there is shortage—sources at least providing them with the same relative supply at the same price as their competitors. Fabricators and consumers, like producers, do not want to find themselves at the mercy of sudden monopoly power at some stage they do not control.

Between buyers and sellers in the copper industry, then, as in other settings of bilateral oligopoly, both sides have an incentive to establish a pattern of risk-avoiding behavior. In the copper industry, inelasticities of supply and demand in the short run tend to shift market power abruptly from producer to consumer and back again. The possibility of a copper workers' strike in the United States or a mudslide in Zambia creates the risk of large blocks of copper unpredictably being removed from the market, creating shortage. Political pressures or the burden of large fixed costs make cutbacks in production difficult at the margin during recessions, creating gluts. To hedge against the risk of facing these uncertainties at a serious disadvantage in relation to one's competitors means that there will exist a strong preference among both producers and consumers for some kind of vertical integration.

It soon became apparent that formal ties of vertical ownership were not the only way to avoid risk and meet the needs of "security". The same end could be achieved through a producers' price system that reflects what Simon Strauss of American Smelting and Refining has called "the lasting relationship", "the community of interest between the man who produces copper and the man who fabricates it".[49]

Producers' prices are infrequently changed quotations for transactions between the major producers and their regular customers, with both agreeing to trade in established

[49] Simon D. Strauss, executive vice-president, American Smelting and Refining, in "The Experts' Corner: Copper's Future" *Barron's,* March 9, 1970.

and dependable patterns.[50] The price level can reflect a mutually acceptable judgment about basic trends in supply and demand, and avoid the chaotic short-run price gyrations that are prevalent in open-market copper training. The participants agree, implicitly or explicitly, to trade in regular patterns with each other over long periods of time, and pay a premium or accept a discount from the open market price at various stages of the business cycle in order to maintain an informal system of vertical integration. Thus, in periods of heavy demand, major copper producers become in effect allocators or rationers of scarce low-priced copper, which they sell to their regular customers on the basis of historical buying patterns. The cost of this loyalty is later exacted from the fabricators or consumers in periods of slack demand when the fabricators or consumers must forgo the temptations offered by low prices in the open market and pay the producers' price instead.

Informal integration through the producers' price system has served the interests of copper producers in ways other than giving them a secure outlet. Moderation in the use of

[50] On copper prices and marketing, see Hendrik Houthakker, *Report of the Subcommittee on Copper to the Cabinet Committee on Economic Policy* (Washington, D.C.: The White House, May 13, 1970, mimeo); "Copper: The Anatomy of a Malfunctioning Market", remarks delivered by Dr. Houthakker at Duke University, Durham, N.C., March 11, 1970; "The Copper Industry in a Changing World", remarks made by Dr. Houthakker before the American Metal Market Copper Forum, New York City, June 12, 1970; and Press Conference of Dr. Houthakker, Washington, D.C., May 22, 1970.

See also John E. Tilton, "The Choice of Trading Partners: An Analysis of International Trade in Aluminum, Bauxite, Copper, Lead, Manganese, Tin, and Zinc", Ph.D. thesis, Department of Economics, Yale, 1966, with a shortened version published in *Yale Economic Essays*, Vol. vi (Fall 1966).

Martin S. Brown and John Butler, *The Production, Marketing, and Consumption of Copper and Aluminum*; Charles River Associates, Inc., *Economic Analysis of the Copper Industry*; Fisher and Cootner, "An Econometric Model of the World Copper Industry, I+II".

market power during periods of scarcity has retarded the dilution of the producers' oligopoly by backward-integration of processors and consumers. This chapter has already pointed out that a major source of new competitors at the production stage has been those smelters or refiners or fabricators or consumers that have by-passed the traditional producers to finance or develop their own sources of supply. A "low" producers' price when there was heavy demand and a soaring open market has served the traditional producers as a strategy to minimize the feeling among customers that the latter were facing a situation of intolerable monopoly power.

Since the end of the Second World War there have been several sets of producers' price quotations. The United States producers' price has been the most important, followed by the Canadian and Japanese. South American copper has generally moved through the sales organizations of the major North American producers at the US producers' price. Companies in Africa and Western Europe have had less success in establishing a pricing system far removed from the level of the open market in London, but they have followed the practice of trading in long-term established patterns with regular customers that is prevalent in the United States, Canada, and Japan.

Thus, the great bulk of trade in copper has been carried out between producers and fabricators or consumers who have built what John Tilton has called "organic ties" among themselves.[51] He finds that trading partners maintain regu-

---

[51] Tilton, "The Choice of Trading Partners". Tilton uses a linear programming transportation model to calculate what would have been the trade pattern if relative prices and transportation costs had determined the international flows of copper (and aluminum, bauxite, lead, manganese, tin, and zinc) according to classical, Heckscher-Olin, or location trade theories. He finds that the choice of trading partners has been strongly influenced by non-price factors, such as international ownership ties, political blocs, governmental regulation and participation, and "established buyer–seller ties". Tilton then uses a single equation multi-variate regression analysis to show that international

lar patterns over time—patterns that deviate significantly from what the structure of trade would be if only price (and transportation costs) were taken into consideration. In many cases formal ties of ownership determine this structure of trade. In other cases long-term contracts, joint financing arrangements, or minority equity positions have produced a regular historical pattern. Finally, annual contracts with provisions for perpetual renewal ("evergreen provisions") between arm's-length buyers and sellers have in many instances defined the structure of informal vertical integration.

The true open markets for copper—the London Metals Exchange and the New York Commodity Exchange—have traditionally handled only a very thin volume of the trading in copper. They function as spill-over markets for the marginal needs of buyers and sellers that are not covered by direct contract. And they serve as hedge-markets for speculation against future fluctuations in price. The daily quotations do reflect the play of supply and demand—but only on a very small volume of copper. They are therefore subject to rapid fluctuation, to manipulation, and they are not necessarily representative of an equilibrium position for the industry as a whole.

In theory, one might predict that the aim of a producers' price system would be to balance out premiums and discounts from the frequently fluctuating open market quotations over the long run. Since 1945 there have been periods when the London or New York open market quotations were above or below the producers' price quotations. But, because of the threat of new competition in copper mining and of substitution by aluminum, the producers' price has been kept more frequently below the quotations of the major open markets than above them.

This moderation in using market power, like the accept-

---

ownership ties exert the greatest force in shaping trade, followed by established buyer–seller ties, political blocs, and so on.

ance of "low" price ceilings during the Second World War and the Korean War, was particularly infuriating to the Chileans as they were forming their first ideas of *dependencia*.

The pattern of informal integration in international marketing revealed to them a strong private corporate system that conspired not to raise prices but to keep prices low, to benefit the industrial metropolis at the expense of the underdeveloped periphery, and to deny Chile its just returns from the country's rich natural resources.

VI

Thus, the international copper industry was an oligopoly that found itself unable to hold prices "high" through a cartel of producers, or to recapture tight control farther downstream from primary mining, smelting, and refining. It was an oligopoly suffering gradual dilution at the production stage and rapid dilution at the fabrication stage. The international copper industry was an oligopoly slowly shifting from an unsuccessful offense to a moderately successful defense—a process of reorientation that accelerated rapidly after the Second World War with the fear of substitution by aluminum. It was an industry increasingly conscious of its relations with customers and trying to maintain a semi-integrated structure of regular, long-term ties to the large (capitalist) industrial consumers.[52]

---

[52] This does not mean that the aims or behavior of all major oligopoly members were identical: Kennecott, Phelps Dodge, the Roan-American Metal group, the Union Minière group, and the Anglo-American group were generally acknowledged to be the lowest cost producers with ample reserves of rich ore-bodies. They were broadly in favor of "low" prices for copper, a strategy that would both eliminate higher cost competitors and minimize the risk of substitution or of new entry at the production stage. International Nickel of Canada had no production strategy, since its large copper output was mined as an adjunct to its main business—nickel mining. It is likely that International Nickel favored "higher" prices for copper. Anaconda was generally considered to be the price leader in the copper industry

Both Anaconda and Kennecott, like other members of the international copper oligopoly, felt threatened by new entrants at the production stage and by the possibility of substitution of aluminum for copper. They were cautious in their use of market power and careful to maintain close marketing ties to regular customers. They were open to certain kinds of pressures to force them to bring more of their corporate resources to the service of Chilean development; against other kinds of pressures they were particularly intransigent.

Their pricing and marketing strategies did not prevent either themselves or the Chilean governments from collecting substantial revenues from operations in Chile. From 1945 to 1955, Anaconda and Kennecott received $275 million in profits from Chile, and Chilean governments collected $328 million in direct income taxes. From 1955 to 1965, the companies realized $465 million in profits from Chile, and Chilean governments collected $909 million in direct income taxes.

But the interaction of the two systems—a corporate system operating under uncertain conditions of imperfect competition, and a political system operating under great pressures for domestic change and development—produced conflict and confusion. Many of the conflicts were inevitable; fewer of the confusions were.

Chile tried to push, pull, and shove the foreign copper companies into contributing more and more to the nation's welfare. In learning to play the game of conflict and co-

---

before the Second World War, a role it shared with various smaller independent companies much of the time in the postwar period. Anaconda wanted to keep operations profitable at its high-cost US mines, improve its financial position (which was much weaker than Kennecott or Phelps Dodge), and respond to demands for higher revenues in Chile where the bulk of its production was located.

On the different strategies of various companies within the producers' oligopoly, see McCarthy, "The American Copper Industry, 1947–1955".

operation, Chile attempted at various times to maximize its receipts from each ton of copper mined, to maximize the total output from Chile, to press the companies to generate more earnings through higher prices and more "aggressive" marketing. It sought to attack the cautious, dependable structure of corporate integration. In the process, the country built up momentum against any strategy of restraint or any system of integration.

From both the successes and the failures of Chilean copper policy came the country's frustrations in the postwar period and the consequent sense of *dependencia*.

For the future, as an "independent" national producer, the country's strategy for copper will have to move beyond the reaction against *dependencia*.

CHAPTER 3

The Multinational Copper Companies in Chile and the Growth of Economic Nationalism, 1945–1954: Declining Terms of Trade and the Early Elaboration of a Framework for *Dependencia*

A satisfactory analysis of the development of economic nationalism in Chile, of the growth of the idea of *dependencia*, would require an essay in intellectual history. As the usage of the term *dependencia* grew in popularity after the Second World War, as diverse Chilean groups found the concept useful or accurate or convenient in describing their country's relations with the foreign copper companies, feelings were generated that moved men to make crucial decisions about the future of their nation. Yet the meaning of *dependencia* was often left vague, clouded with rhetoric, or allowed to suggest overlapping and contradictory hypotheses, only some of which are amenable to testing and verification or rejection by the methods of the social sciences.

In its broadest sense, *dependencia* was more a mood than a set of precise propositions. It drew upon many sources, discoveries, talents, and ideologies while remaining greater than its parts and different from any of them. This mood emanated from the desire for industrialization and for an elusive "fundamental structural change" in economy and society; it sprang from a kind of disillusionment with classical economics and the conventional doctrines of export-led growth. It was a reaction to the pains of the Depression and the Second World War, and to the surprising inward growth (*crecimiento hacia adentro*) that these "adverse conditions" stimulated. The mood was formed in antagonism to "inequitable" treatment by Chile's international allies during World War II and the Korean War; in an-

57

tagonism to "unfavorable" treatment by the United States government as a pawn in the Cold War.

This mood included suspicion of foreign ideology, foreign practices, the foreign presence in the midst of Chilean affairs. The reaction to *dependencia* sprang from the desire to establish sovereignty and restore control over the pace and direction of national development.

For a country responding to growing domestic pressures for development, the behavior of the copper industry had an overwhelming impact through its effect on government revenues and foreign exchange earnings. In the first years after the end of the Second World War, copper prices ranged from 13¢ to 22¢ per pound. Each penny variation in the price of copper meant a difference of $10 million in exports (2% of all Chilean exports) and a difference of more than $5 million in government revenues (3% of all revenues). A one-cent variation in price could raise or lower the absolute amount of foreign exchange received by the country from the industry by 5%–10%. A dip in the business cycle in the United States, such as the recession of 1949—during which prices fell 7¢ per pound (or 40%) and the output of the Chilean subsidiaries of Anaconda and Kennecott was cut back by 30%—could have a disastrous effect on the Chilean economy. Conversely, a boom in the industrial business cycle could have an extraordinarily buoyant effect, but—as we shall see in this chapter—seldom did.

In every stage of the business cycle, then, responsible Chileans from all political and economic groups were obliged for their own welfare to focus attention on the behavior of the international copper oligopoly, on each actual or potential change in strategy open to Anaconda and Kennecott. Yet to their dismay, as Chileans became increasingly sophisticated in economic analysis and in perception (and misperception) of the dynamics of multinational corporate behavior, a good deal of evidence after the Second World War seemed to suggest that the decisions taken by foreign corporate officials to meet the internal needs of the companies they served were proving more and more detrimental to the Chilean struggle for development.

This chapter will analyze the first attempt in Chile to relate the behavior of the foreign copper companies to the problems of domestic growth. The Prebisch model of declining terms of trade for primary products provided the first coherent framework for the idea of *dependencia,* the first coherent framework for judging the behavior of the companies. The Prebisch model brought together Chilean antagonisms to both the strength of Anaconda and Kennecott and the moderation of oligopoly strategy in the international industry. It provided what was regarded as a clear indication of how Chile ought to fashion its own copper policy to defend its interests. It provided a justification for the Chilean state sales monopoly of 1952 as a way of moving away from the condition of *dependencia.*

I

The Depression of 1930, followed by the Second World War, had had the effect in Chile, as elsewhere in Latin America, of stimulating the process of industrialization through import substitution. The sharp drop in foreign exchange earnings together with protectionist measures taken to defend the balance of payments had resulted in the development of manufacturing industries that produced goods for domestic consumption. From 1925 to 1929 consumer goods had averaged 44% of all imports; from 1946 to 1951 the composition of imports included only 30% consumer goods; and from 1952 to 1954 they had dropped to 25%. The total industrial sector had grown in the meantime (1925–1950) by a factor of four.[1]

[1] The figures on the composition of imports are taken from a study by Bitran-Viveros, "El papel del comercio exterior en el desarrollo económico chileno", based on data from the United Nations Economic Commission for Latin America, and cited in Aníbal Pinto Santa Cruz, *Chile: Un caso de desarrollo frustrado* (Santiago: Editorial Universitaria, 1959), p. 116. The data on aggregate industrial production come

The central concern in the early postwar period for many Chilean groups—left and right, labor, business, and academic—was the protection and expansion of the light industrial base that had been built with such effort and expense. Their attention was centered on the "capacity to import" those capital goods and raw materials necessary for further economic growth. Consequently, the terms of trade between the price of copper received by Chile and the price for imports paid by Chile assumed a crucial position in the struggle for development.

But the prospects for a vigorous export-led growth were becoming more and more frustrating. Now that Chile had strong groups who for the first time were actively interested in promoting domestic industrialization, Aníbal Pinto complained, the export sector had stopped playing the dynamic role it had played in earlier periods.[2] The United Nations Economic Commission for Latin America recorded figures showing that the Chilean capacity to import during conditions of Korean wartime demand from 1950 to 1953 was 40% lower than the capacity to import had been in 1925–1930.[3] Since Chile did not produce the capital goods needed to preserve and expand the national manufacturing sector, the ability to import would have to be defended if growth were to continue. The behavior of copper prices in relation to the prices of Chilean imports was identified as the major brake on the process of national development.

This idea did not become widely accepted in Chile until the US recession of 1949, followed rapidly by the Korean War the following year. But the cycle of frustration with the foreign corporate system that stimulated the Chileans'

---

from Oscar Muñoz G., *Crecimiento industrial de Chile, 1914–1965* (Santiago: Universidad de Chile, 1968), p. 158. See also P. T. Ellsworth, *Chile: An Economy in Transition* (New York: Macmillan, 1945).

[2] Pinto, *Chile: Un caso de desarrollo frustrado*, pp. 107–113.

[3] *Ibid.*, p. 116.

sense of *dependencia* was traced back to the beginning of the Second World War.

That cycle of frustration went as follows: the export price for Chilean copper had been fixed by the Allied governments during the Second World War at a figure about equal to or slightly lower than late-Depression levels. Electrolytic wirebars were assigned a ceiling of 11.775¢ per pound for the period of the war; average prices from 1937 to 1940 had ranged from 10.000¢ to 13.167¢.[4] Chilean estimates of the losses they suffered owing to the arbitrary price ceiling ran from $107 million to $500 million.[5] At first Chileans were proud to claim, rightly or wrongly, that they had contributed more per capita to the Allied war effort, in terms of earnings forgone, than any other power. But as their problems with development mounted they went on to add, with increasing bitterness, that they had contributed more per capita during the Second World War (while remaining an underdeveloped country) than the Marshall Plan would later give per capita to build up the industrial countries of Europe.

[4] These and other prices are taken from the averages reported in appropriate editions of *Metal Statistics* (Frankfurt am Main: Metallgesellschaft A.G.). The quotations are for electrolytically refined wirebars. Since most Chilean copper was refined at Anaconda and Kennecott plants in the United States, the price realized by the Chilean subsidiary was lower. Markos Mamalakis and Clark Reynolds, *Essays on the Chilean Economy* (Homewood, Ill.: Richard D. Irwin, 1965), p. 372, calculated that the average price realized during the Second World War in Chile was about 11¢.

[5] Eugenio Vidal, president of the Association of Importers, arrived at a figure of $107 million in additional revenues if Chile had received the price of 17.35¢ that was allowed for subsidized mines in the United States ("La situación del cobre", *Panorama Económico*, no. 31, 1951). Senator Salum claimed that Chilean losses should be calculated on the basis of a 24.5¢ level in the open market, producing a result of $500 million (*Historia de la ley 11.828*, Vol. 1, September 16, 1954, p. 3907). Mamalakis and Reynolds, *op. cit.*, p. 240, cite a study of the Chilean Copper Department by Wacholtz that also arrived at the $500 million figure.

Chilean reserves of $70 million or $80 million did accumulate from sales of copper at the fixed price, but were (generally) frozen in the United States for the duration of the war. When the war ended, all US prices were released and the Chilean reserves were free to be spent on goods unavailable earlier. But, by the time the accumulated dollars could be used, their purchasing power had substantially declined in the inflationary US economy. In addition, prices for copper exported from Chile to the United States did not rise as rapidly in the postwar period as the cost of manufactured goods imported from the United States. This process of deterioration in the Chilean position lasted throughout the US economic expansion of 1946–1948.

Then, with the business recession in the United States in 1949, copper prices dropped precipitously (by nearly half), and the North American companies cut back their production in Chile further than at many of the mines in the United States.[6] To protect the US industry, Congress was

[6] Exact evidence on the extent of the cutback in production at individual mines in Chile or the United States, or on what had been planned if the Korean War had not erupted, is not available. Senator Larraín Vial, of the Conservative Party, claimed that the US companies planned to reduce production by 30% in Chile but were prevailed upon to limit the cutback to 20% (*Historia de la ley 11.828*, Vol. 1, September 16, 1954, pp. 3909–3910).

There was widespread feeling in Chile that disproportionate reductions at the Chilean works were regularly used by the North American companies to regulate price in the world market. For a history of this practice, see the speech by Senator Silva Ulloa of the Socialist Party, *Historia de la ley 11.828*, Vol. 1, September 15, 1954, pp. 3734–3770.

James L. McCarthy, "The American Copper Industry, 1947–1955", *Yale Economic Essays*, Vol. IV (Spring 1964), p. 111, confirms that the reduction of production in Chile by Anaconda and Kennecott in 1949 was greater than their reductions in the United States. But, according to McCarthy, the suspension of the US copper tariff was achieved through intense lobbying on the part of Anaconda and Kennecott in 1949 was greater than their reductions in the United States. But, according to McCarthy, the suspension of the US copper tariff was achieved through intense lobbying on the part of Anaconda and Kennecott against great pressure from domestic producers.

considering a reimposition of the 4¢ tariff on copper that had been passed during the Depression with disastrous results for Chile. Thus, Chile faced rapidly falling prices, disproportionate cutbacks in production, and the prospect of a stiff duty on copper imported into the United States through the integrated system of Anaconda and Kennecott. "The policy of the Good Neighbor," Senator Wallace F. Bennett of Utah told the United States Congress in a speech that provoked outrage when it was quoted in the Chilean Senate, "should not be extended to the point of letting our own people go hungry!" This was the thanks, Chileans exclaimed, that their country received for giving the US cheap copper during the war and receiving depreciated payment afterwards![7]

But the 1949 recession ended abruptly with the beginning of the Korean War in the spring of 1950. And, without even consulting the Chilean government, United States officials in conjunction with representatives of the US copper companies again unilaterally set a new ceiling on the price of Chilean copper.

In short, Chile was being denied full enjoyment of the boom side of the business cycle in the developed countries while having the recession side of the cycle exported with exaggeration into the Chilean economy. The system of relations between Chile as an exporter of raw materials and the industrial countries as exporters of manufactured products seemed to work, coherently and perhaps even intentionally, to frustrate Chilean efforts to build its own industrial base, provide for its own national welfare, and promote the broad process of development.

II

A sense that center (US)–periphery (Chilean) relations, linked through the private corporate integration of Anaconda and Kennecott, constituted some kind of "obstacle"

---

[7] For Bennett's quotation and the reaction in the Chilean Senate, see *Boletín Minero*, June 1949.

to Chilean development did not arise immediately after the Second World War.

The initial effect of the war had been to restore a measure of prosperity to both Chile and the foreign companies. With Anaconda's two mines at Chuquicamata and Potrerillos and Kennecott's single mine at El Teniente working at close to full capacity, Chilean foreign currency reserves began to improve markedly. Domestic employment was high, and the process of import substitution, begun during the Depression, was pursued with more vigor.

Undoubtedly it was this progress and prosperity, combined, as Senator Julio Durán of the Radical Party pointed out, with the enthusiasm of cooperating in the common cause against Fascism, that led to a general acquiescence in the wartime price structure.[8]

There was indeed widespread concern when the war ended about the country's ability to buy the machinery and materials from the United States that would be needed to consolidate and develop the new industrial base in Chile. This was the theme of meetings with Nelson Rockefeller (US Coordinator for Post-War Affairs in Latin America) in New York in 1945 and 1946, and it was the basis for discussions between Chilean business groups and various commercial missions from the United States in 1947.[9] The Chilean left shared the preoccupation of the right with the future of industrialization. *El Siglo*, the Communist Party newspaper, supported the search for foreign capital to finance the machinery needed to expand basic industry, such as refineries for copper (Paipote), steel (Huachipato), and petroleum, although it feared that conservatives in the government of President González Videla might sell out the country in the process.[10]

[8] Cf. Senator Julio Durán in *Historia de la ley 11.828*, Vol. 1, September 16, 1954, p. 3907.

[9] On the meetings with Nelson Rockefeller, see the accounts in the magazine of the National Society of Manufacturers (Sociedad de Fomento Fabril), *Industria*, January 1945 and January 1946.

[10] *El Siglo*, May 7, 1947.

But, for the moment, the problem of foreign exchange was seen as a matter of unfreezing the accumulated wartime reserves in Washington and gaining access to foreign credits. Chilean economic missions to the United States in the period 1945–1948, composed primarily of prominent and talented Chilean conservatives, were not complainers. Guillermo del Pedregal, Victor Santa Cruz, and Flavian Levine promised good treatment for US investors and for holders of Chilean bonds in return for small amounts of American generosity in offering lines of credit.[11] The Chilean Chamber of Commerce and other business groups gave a warm reception to Winthrop Aldrich, president of the Chase National Bank, who headed the most important of several US commercial expeditions to Santiago. They asked for credit to buy needed imports, and Mr. Aldrich promised help with the Export-Import Bank, the IMF, and private banking groups in securing the necessary finance.[12]

Through the end of 1948 the hunger for hard currency to finance Chilean domestic growth had not yet been translated into a concerted attack on the foreign copper companies. What would quickly become, in 1949–1950, the central elements in the idea of *dependencia*—constantly unfavorable terms of trade, a growing foreign exchange gap, the straitjacket of being "captive production"—were not yet widely perceived together as a whole.

---

[11] The first important postwar Chilean mission to seek foreign credit was headed by ex-Finance Minister Guillermo del Pedregal in April–May 1947. For official reports of that mission, see *La Nación*, April 26 and May 17, 1947. For an insider's account of the negotiations, see the Congressional testimony of Senator Hernán Videla Lira, reprinted in the *Boletín Minero*, January–June 1955.

The relationship between the search for credits in the United States and the expulsion of the Communist Party from the government of González Videla is discussed in Chapter 6.

[12] Accounts of the meetings with Aldrich are contained in *El Mercurio*, April 19–20, 1947, and *El Diario Ilustrado*, April 20, 1947. There were also important commercial visits by representatives from Standard Oil, Esso, City Bank of New York, and Coca-Cola.

For the time being, the way to Chilean development seemed to be to go hat-in-hand to the country that had come out of the economic experience of the war so well.

III

But the arbitrary decision taken in Washington at the beginning of the Korean War to set price-ceilings for Chilean copper without even consulting the Chilean government was what provoked the first direct outcry against the foreign companies and their government.[13] The dictated price-ceiling was a challenge to Chilean sovereignty as well as to Chilean development. The system of free trade and free enterprise was evidently being allowed to work only when it benefited the interests of the developed countries—not when it could do the greatest service to Chile.

If it was the challenge to Chilean sovereignty that first provoked the emotional reaction to the sense of *dependencia*, it was the Prebisch model of declining terms of trade for primary products that provided the first theoretical framework and prescription for policy.

Raúl Prebisch and other economists associated with the United Nations Economic Commission for Latin America (ECLA) built a model in the 1950's asserting that the gains from technological change and increased productivity were unequally spread through the international trade mechanism, with most of the benefits accruing to the developed "center" while few of the benefits remained in or were transmitted to the underdeveloped "periphery".[14] The un-

[13] Curiously, although the United States government neglected to invite or inform the Chilean government about the Washington meetings to set prices for the Korean War, it was the United States that wanted Latin American and other Third World representation on the International Control Board, while the British wanted only the US, Great Britain, and France as members. The US position prevailed. *Engineering and Mining Journal* (January 1951), pp. 90 *et seq.*

[14] The main statements of the Prebisch model are: Raúl Prebisch, *The Economic Development of Latin America and Its Principal Problems*, Economic Commission for Latin America (Lake Success, N.Y.:

even spread of gains is reflected, according to this conceptualization, in a long-run decline in terms of trade between primary products exported from the underdeveloped countries and manufactured goods imported from the developed countries. In contrast to classical trade theory, Prebisch argued that industrialization through government-sponsored import substitution was the only path for authentic national development. This amounted to a fundamental attack on the doctrine of comparative advantage and export-led growth.

The foundations for this model were laid in Santiago in the late 1940's. Prebisch's work on Chilean data provided him and other members of the Economic Commission for Latin America with much of the evidence that first inspired their view of international trade. And the beginnings of the Prebisch model first provided Chileans with a framework for analyzing their relations with the foreign copper companies.

Shortly after the end of the Second World War, the International Monetary Fund released terms-of-trade figures for Latin America showing the relationship between the prices of exports and the prices of imports as they had

---

United Nations, Department of Economic Affairs, 1950); and Raúl Prebisch, "Commercial Policy in the Underdeveloped Countries", *American Economic Review*, Vol. 49, No. 2 (May 1959).

Similar arguments were developed by H. W. Singer, "The Distribution of Gains between Investing and Borrowing Countries", *American Economic Review, Papers and Proceedings*, Vol. xl, No. 2 (May 1950).

For analyses and criticisms of the Prebisch model, see Paul T. Ellsworth, "The Terms of Trade between Primary Producing and Industrial Countries", *Inter-American Economic Affairs*, Vol. 9 (Summer 1956); Gottfried Haberler, "Terms of Trade and Economic Development", in *Economic Development for Latin America*, Howard S. Ellis, ed. (London: Macmillan, 1961); Werner Baer, "The Economics of Prebisch and ECLA", *Economic Development and Cultural Change*, Vol. 10, No. 2, Part ii (January 1962); and M. June Flanders, "Prebisch on Protectionism: An Evaluation", *Economic Journal*, Vol. lxxiv, No. 294 (June 1964).

evolved since the end of the Depression. These statistics were reproduced by Prebisch in the ECLA *Economic Survey of Latin America* for 1948[15] (see Table 3).

TABLE 3

Terms of Trade of Thirteen Latin American Countries in 1946
(price indexes, base: 1938 "equals" 100)

	Exports	*Imports*	*Terms of Trade*
Brazil	277	200	138
Argentina	258	215	120
Ecuador	268	227	118
Mexico	192	169	114
Costa Rica	195	175	111
Guatemala	195	175	111
Colombia	200	190	105
Cuba	233	234	100
Venezuela	160	168	95
Nicaragua	178	190	93
Peru	195	217	90
Chile	163	198	82
Bolivia	193	237	81

Of these thirteen countries, Chile's terms of trade had declined the furthest, except for Bolivia. The export price index itself for Chile was lowest of all the countries except Venezuela—and 1946 had been a year of rapidly rising copper prices![16]

Between 1948 and 1950, Raúl Prebisch completed his pioneering study that attempted to demonstrate a long-run downward trend in the terms of trade between manufactured products exported from Great Britain to Latin America and primary products imported into Great Britain from Latin America since the late nineteenth century.[17] On the

---

[15] United Nations, *Economic Survey of Latin America* (New York: 1948), p. 220; reprinted in *Panorama Económico*, No. 32, 1951.

[16] Copper prices had risen about 75%, from 11.775¢ per pound at the beginning of the year to an average of 19.275¢ at the end.

[17] United Nations, *Economic Survey of Latin America* (1948); United Nations, *Relative Prices of Exports and Imports of Underdeveloped Countries* (New York: 1949); and United Nations, *The*

basis of these data, the "Prebisch thesis"—charging that a systematic deterioration in terms of trade between the center and the periphery was responsible for the economic difficulties of the latter—started to take shape.

In Chile, all of this seemed self-evident. With the transfer of exaggerated effects of the US recession of 1949 into the Chilean economy, leaders of the political left, right, and center had already joined the increasingly prestigious economic *técnicos* associated with ECLA and the Instituto de Economía of the University of Chile in calling for measures to protect the economy from the effects of the international trade cycle, and to preserve and expand the industrial base built up during the war. Eduardo Frei, the young Falangista (later Christian Democratic) Senator, and Alberto Baltra, the Radical Minister of Economy and Commerce in the González Videla government, argued that industrialization and the defense of domestic employment were necessary responses to the vulnerability created by the system of international trade.[18] Professors of political economy, such as Luís Escobar and Carlos Oyarzún, called for Keynesian measures to protect Chilean development from the recessions transmitted to Chile through the copper industry.[19]

Economic Development of Latin America and Its Principal Problems (1950).

Paul Ellsworth has claimed that a large proportion of the decline in British prices paid for primary products from 1876 to 1905 can be accounted for by a substantial decline in inward freight rates.

Gottfried Haberler argues that the annual index of the United Kingdom's commodity terms of trade is too narrow a statistical base for the allegations that Prebisch makes.

As a further criticism of the Prebisch position, evidence of a systematic upward bias in export indexes of the industrial countries is discussed in footnote 37.

[18] See the round-table discussion on the economic cycle published in *Panorama Económico*, June 1949. Baltra's position was stated on the tenth anniversary of the Corporación de Fomento, reprinted in *Panorama Económico*, April–May 1949.

[19] Round-table discussion on the economic cycle, *Panorama Económico*, June 1949.

Octavio Larraín, the conservative president of the Association of Exporters, and Clodomiro Almeyda, a member of the central committee of the Socialist Party (and later to be Foreign Minister in the Allende government), explained the country's fundamental structural weakness in terms of international dependence vis-à-vis the industrial countries of the northern hemisphere.[20]

Then, with the sudden advent of the Korean wartime boom, the argument shifted from the cyclical aspects of international trade to the long-term deterioration in the Chilean position. Beyond outrage at the challenge to Chilean sovereignty represented by the decisions made without consultation in Washington, the fixed price for copper during a period of intense demand focused attention in Santiago on the downward trend in the terms of trade. *Panorama Económico*, Chile's leading journal of economics and business, republished in 1951 the ECLA figures from 1948. In the same year, the Central Bank of Chile demonstrated that, even in the midst of a wartime shortage of copper, the export-import price index for the country was lower than it had been in the midst of the Depression[21] (see Table 4).

The prices that Chile received for its exports has been consistently lower during the Second World War and the late 1940's than the prices the country had had to pay for imports, in comparison to the situation in the late 1930's. Despite the demand generated by the Korean War, the terms of trade for Chile were still significantly lower than they had been in 1936–1937!

This had profound implications for the process of national development. Chile's "capacity to import" the goods and materials needed for industrial growth was diminishing. Aníbal Pinto, one of the foremost spokesmen for the ECLA position in Santiago, showed that the physical volume of exports had risen after the Second World War a full 12% above the prosperous levels of the period 1925–1929. But

[20] *Ibid.*

[21] *Balanza de pagos 1951* (Santiago: Banco Central, 1952).

the nation's "capacity to import", or the total of what could be bought with that increased volume of exports, had declined by 27.2%. "This means," concluded Pinto sadly,[22] "that although we sell more, we must buy less."

Chile's predicament, he argued, reminded him of *Alice in Wonderland*. " 'Here, you see,' the Red Queen told Alice, 'you have to run as fast as you can simply to stay in the

TABLE 4

Net Terms-of-Trade Relation: Price Index for Chile
(1938 = 100)

	Exports	*Imports*	*Terms of Trade*
1936	100.5	88.5	113.6
1937	129.7	96.9	133.8
1938	100.0	100.0	100.0
1939	107.5	94.7	113.5
1940	105.4	104.2	101.2
1941	109.2	113.1	96.6
1942	118.4	150.1	78.9
1943	120.9	168.7	71.7
1944	125.6	179.6	69.9
1945	129.7	183.2	70.8
1946	151.1	200.6	75.3
1947	201.1	245.4	81.9
1948	221.1	250.8	88.2
1949	220.3	246.1	89.5
1950	222.1	237.0	93.7
1951	279.4	276.9	100.9

same place. If you want to get somewhere else, you must run at least twice as fast as that.' "

The behavior of copper prices and the declining terms of trade seemed to bind all the problems of Chilean economic growth together into a coherent (although frustrating) system. The prescription for policy appeared obvious. The structure of "captive" relations had to be broken, the terms of trade had to be "defended". *Industria*, the official publi-

[22] Pinto Santa Cruz, *Chile: Un caso de desarrollo frustrado*, ch. vi.

cation of the National Society of Manufacturers, editorialized that the need to maintain the relative terms of trade was crucial to industrialization.[23] They phrased their argument cautiously: the country needed the expertise of foreign investors. Physical output of copper had to be expanded. Steps should be taken to diversify exports. But, fundamentally, Chile had to get off the treadmill and find a way to achieve *precios justos* for the commodity in which the country had the greatest comparative advantage. The president of the Manufacturers Society, Dr. Walter Müller, went to Washington to underline the extent of the problem to US government officials, businessmen, and financial representatives.

Spokesmen for the Santiago Chamber of Commerce, the National Agriculture Society, and the National Association of Importers all acknowledged their abhorrence of state intervention in a free economy—but then proceeded to argue that the declining terms of trade for copper justified drastic action by the Chilean government.[24] "I am against nationalization, and in general against state intervention," declared Eugenio Vidal, president of the National Association of Importers and a former Minister of the Economy, "but this is an exceptional case. We need a government sales monopoly."[25]

Frei and Tomic of the Falangistas (later Christian Democrats), Baltra and Duran of the Radicals, and Almeyda and Allende of the Socialists all joined in identifying copper prices, marketing patterns, and the deterioration in terms

[23] *Industria*, March 1951. See also Dr. Müller's summer lectures at the University of Chile, 1951, on the process of industrialization in Chile (*Industria*, February 1951); and correspondence between Dr. Müller and C. Heriberto Horst, president of the Chamber of Commerce (reprinted in *ibid.*, April 1951).

[24] *Memoria*, Cámara de Comercio de Santiago, 1951, pp. 31 *et seq.*; *Industria*, April 1951, pp. 203 *et seq.*; *Panorama Económico*, No. 31, 1951.

[25] *Panorama Económico*, No. 31, 1951.

of trade as constituting a system of dependence that retarded or prevented the process of broad national development.[26]

IV

This should not suggest that Chilean copper policy after
the Second World War was formulated consciously and
consistently according to precepts drawn from the Prebisch
model. Until the beginning of the Korean War, copper policy was not devised according to any coherent strategy.
Rather, it was the product of malign neglect on the part of
the host country.

Chile had emerged from the Second World War with a
number of tensions in the copper industry. Two of the more
important of these tensions were bound up with the country's devouring need for foreign exchange; a third sprang
from the structure of international marketing. Rather than
confronting the issues involved directly and trying to resolve the tensions, both Chile and the foreign copper companies repressed their frustrations until the explosions of
1951–1952.

The foreign exchange issues were focused on the system
of *retornos parciales* or "partial returns" and the system of
costos legales or "legal costs" of production. "Partial returns" meant that receipts from the sales of the Chilean subsidiaries of Anaconda and Kennecott were allowed to be
kept with the accounts of the parent corporations in New
York. Only those amounts of hard currency necessary to be
exchanged for local expenses were ever passed through the
financial institutions of Chile. This "disgraceful privilege",
as Mariano Puga Vega called it, which was permitted to no

[26] Cf. Frei in *Panorama Económico*, June 6, 1952; Tomic in *Panorama Económico*, November 11, 1955, and May 27, 1955; and further
references to Tomic in *Historia de la ley 11.828*, Vol. 1, p. 3898;
Allende in *El Siglo*, January 20, 1953; Almeyda in *Panorama Económico*, June 1949.

domestic companies, was widely believed to hurt the Chilean balance of payments.[27]

The system of "legal costs" meant that the subsidiaries of Anaconda and Kennecott in Chile were required to buy local currency for local expenses at the fixed rate of 19.37 pesos per dollar. As the official dollar price for pesos rose, this meant a rising implicit tax had to be borne by the foreign companies.

The complaints made by Chileans about the damage to their balance of payments were largely without basis. The complaints made by the companies about the increasing level of implicit taxation had very great basis indeed.

If there had been a system of "total returns" wherein all the receipts from copper sales were deposited in Santiago, with a quarterly dividend remitted to the parents in New York, the side of the Chilean balance of payments showing claims on dollars would have been higher. But the figures showing the foreign claims on Chilean claims on dollars would also have been higher by an equal amount, reflecting the demands of foreign suppliers or the parent on the dollar balances. Thus, if a system of *retornos totales* had replaced the system of *retornos parciales*, the figures in the Chilean ledger of credits and liabilities would have still balanced each other.[28]

---

[27] Mariano Puga Vega, a Liberal congressman, later became ambassador to the Organization of American States in Washington, 1957–1958, and president of the Liberal Party in 1962. He was a particularly outspoken critic of the system of *retornos parciales*. His speeches and writings on copper policy have been collected in *El cobre chileno* (Santiago: Editorial Andes Bello, 1965).

Other Chilean conservatives were highly critical of the system of partial returns. See the remarks by Senators Correa Larraín and Larraín Vial of the Conservative Party in *Historia de la ley 11.828*, Vol. 2, November 5, 1954, p. 940.

[28] There were diverse Chilean schemes to oblige the foreign copper companies to invest a certain percentage of their profits in Chile, or to buy Chilean government bonds (presumably at an interest rate lower than such bonds could be floated in New York or Europe). These measures would have improved the Chilean balance of pay-

As would become clear during the Allende administration, the real disadvantage to Chile with the system of *retornos parciales* was not economic but diplomatic. If the foreign companies were suddenly expropriated, the receipts from recent sales and from shipments in transit would be deposited in the accounts of the Kennecott Sales Corporation or the Anaconda Sales Corporation in New York. And, if the Chilean government then wanted to go through the international legal system to claim those receipts, the parent companies would have a stronger bargaining position in negotiating compensation for their operations in Chile.

With regard to the companies' complaint about the fixed exchange rate for local expenditures, however, it is clear that the implicit tax burden was increasing rapidly. During the Second World War the official dollar price for pesos rose to 30, signifying that at the 19.37 rate the companies had to pay an indirect tax to the Chilean government almost equal to their local expenditures. By 1948 Rudolfo Mitchels, Chilean vice-president of Anaconda, declared that the effective tax rate had risen from 50% to 64%, owing primarily to implicit taxes.[29]

Clark Reynolds has suggested that the overvalued exchange rate may have discouraged expenditures in the local economy, and this is quite plausible.[30] Aníbal Pinto, on the other hand, has argued that, given the large sunk investments, the implicit taxes on Anaconda and Kennecott served to stimulate substantial increases in productivity in the mines.[31] Between 1928 and 1948 output per man-year

---

ments. But merely to shift from a system of "partial returns" to a system of "total returns" (in which the parent corporations still had claims on the dollar accounts) would not have helped the balance of payments for Chile.

[29] *Panorama Económico*, No. 31, 1951.

[30] Mamalakis and Reynolds, *Essays on the Chilean Economy*, p. 248 *et passim*.

[31] Aníbal Pinto Santa Cruz, *Hacia nuestra independencia económica* (Santiago: Editorial Universitaria, 1958), ch. 13.

increased from 15.7 tons of copper to 27.3 tons (compared with 20 tons per man-year in the United States). The system of indirect taxes pressured the companies to keep real production costs among the lowest in the world, and passed on the gains in productivity to Chile.

From 1945 through 1949 there were intermittent promises from the companies and the Chilean authorities to "rectify" both the system of *retornos parciales* and the system of *costos legales*. But no real movement was ever made, and the Chilean share of the revenues generated by the copper companies rose steadily.

The third area of conflict in the early postwar period did not involve foreign exchange and the balance of payments directly. Rather it had to do with the process of marketing Chilean copper and with whether or not the companies were aggressive enough in pressing for the highest possible prices. The issues here bore on the question of the declining terms of trade, but again were not dealt with directly. Rather, as in the case of "partial returns" and "legal costs" of production, the tensions generated were allowed to build up and contribute to the general "sense" of *dependencia*.

All of the copper mined by Anaconda and Kennecott in Chile was sold through the sales subsidiaries of the parent corporations in New York. Some went to the refining or fabricating subsidiaries of the corporations themselves, and the rest went to regular customers in the United States or (predominantly) in Western Europe. The copper was sold at the producers' price of the major copper companies in the United States (the Connecticut Valley producers' price). And it was forbidden by the United States government to be sold to any customers in the Soviet bloc, or to any "undependable" intermediaries who might dispose of it within the Soviet bloc.

The ban on sales to socialist countries was an ideological abomination to the Chilean left, and a slap at national sovereignty even to many members of the Chilean right. Some of those who defended the US position in Santiago did fear that sales to the Soviet bloc would throw Chile into the "communist camp". But most of those who wanted to diversify Chilean markets aimed at selling a portion behind the Iron Curtain only when higher prices could be had there.[32]

Radomiro Tomic and Aníbal Pinto argued that if the US system of corporate integration and government control did not satisfy Chilean interests through improving the terms of trade, the country was "justified in taking whatever steps are necessary to defend its capacity to import".[33] As prices deteriorated in the capitalist markets, they claimed, their country should not be bound by the doctrine of the "forbidden zone" in Eastern Europe. The result need not be a break with the United States but merely a gradual expansion of markets. And if the foreign companies were forbidden by US law to trade with the Soviet bloc, they concluded, then a Chilean state agency would be the logical instrument to take charge of international marketing.

There was also strong advocacy for selling through a Chilean government agency to customers in the major capitalist markets as well. The corporate policy followed by Anaconda and Kennecott of marketing in established patterns to regular customers at little-changing producers' prices seemed particularly dull and unaggressive to many Chileans. Except for the recession of 1949, producer copper seemed to be in chronic shortage, and the *Engineering and Mining Journal* brought continual reports to the Ministry

[32] Even the position of the Communist Party, before the Korean War, involved only marginal expansion into non-capitalist markets. Cf. *El Siglo*, "Política Commercial Independiente", leading editorial, May 21, 1947.

For the post-Korean War debate on commercial policy in the copper industry, see *Panorama Económico*, May 9, 1952; September 26, 1952; August 28, 1953; August 13, 1954 (Sunkel); April 3, 1958 (Lagarrigue); August 1958 (Allende); October 31, 1958 (Letelier). A long debate in *Ultima Hora* in 1953 was reprinted in Aníbal Pinto, ed., *El cobre: Comercio y política* (Santiago: Editorial Universitaria, 1954).

[33] *Panorama Económico*, April 10 and June 10, 1953.

of Mining of brisk demand for real deliveries (not just hedge operations) in the major commodity markets to supply the postwar boom in consumer durables.[34] Even in peacetime, the open markets of Great Britain, Europe, and the United States frequently recorded prices as much as 10%–15% above the corporate quotations.

The London Metals Exchange and the New York Commodity Exchange in fact represented thin markets, clearing marginal amounts of copper that were bought by new or small or sporadic users who had not yet built up a "historical buying position" on the sales books of the major corporations.[35] But this was not clearly understood in Chile or carefully explored. Nor was the rationale examined for a "low", slowly changing producers' price in the face of strong substitution by aluminum. More exciting was the exercise of finding an open-market quotation higher than the producers' price, multiplying it by Chilean output, and calculating the additional foreign exchange that could be generated by a more aggressive marketing strategy. Thus, when E. T. Stannard, president of Kennecott, announced in the midst of the 1948 boom, for example, that Kennecott was against any increase in the US producers' price, many Chileans reacted by demanding the creation of a state agency that would defend "Chilean" rather than "corporate" interests.[36] The sense that Chile contributed "captive production" to a semi-integrated private corporate system was added—unexamined—to the general concern about foreign exchange, capacity to import, and declining terms of trade.

[34] Cf. *Engineering and Mining Journal*, December 1945 and February 1947. This journal, one of the major industry publications, was received in Chile, and the National Mining Society frequently reprinted selections from it in Spanish.

[35] For a good description of the history and operations of the London Metals Exchange, see Martin S. Brown and John Butler, *The Production, Marketing, and Consumption of Copper and Aluminum* (New York: Praeger, 1967).

[36] Cf. *El Siglo*, May 6, 1948, editorial.

The possibility of forming a Chilean government agency that, with little effort or experience, could dictate price and marketing policy more imaginatively than the stodgy corporate officials in New York (who sold only to their old friends or own subordinates) became more and more appealing.

V

The declining terms of trade, the weak capacity to import, and the desire for industrial growth were concerns that occupied the attention of most Chilean political and economic interest groups in the early postwar period. Unfortunately, however, a thorough analysis of the Prebisch model of international trade and development was never attempted for the case of Chile as a copper exporter, nor was there careful reflection about whether the Prebisch model was giving the proper signals for copper policy.

Rather, a Prebisch "cast of thought" was permitted to flourish—ECLA phrases became a part of the jargon of politics and business—without any insistence that the able and sophisticated Chilean economists think through the technical aspects of their model and the implications for policy in the copper industry.

The Prebisch explanation of declining terms of trade depended upon comparing the price- and income-elasticities of demand for primary products exported from the underdeveloped periphery with the price- and income-elasticities of demand for manufactured products exported from the developed countries. It hypothesized that demand for primary products in the industrial countries would not rise as rapidly when those countries grew as demand for manufactured products in the periphery would rise when countries in the periphery grew. Furthermore, owing to market imperfections in manufacturing that were assumed not to be as prevalent in natural resource production, the Prebisch model hypothesized that gains in productivity in primary products would be passed on to consumers in the form of lower prices, whereas gains in productivity in manufactured goods would not.

The slow growth in demand for primary products, upon which Prebisch's analysis depended, could be explained in the case of agricultural products by Engel's law, and by protective measures adopted by the developed countries. Engel's law asserts that as incomes rise, consumers will spend a smaller and smaller proportion on food, and more on manufactured products. For other primary products the slow growth of demand might be explained by advances in technology that save on inputs, or by the development of synthetics. These hypotheses about price- and income-elasticities of demand and about market imperfections led Prebisch to conclude that governments in the periphery cannot accept the classical view about trade and development— namely, that benefits of technical progress and increases in productivity will be distributed equally over all regions. In the real world of comparative advantage, Prebish argued, some advantages are more equal than others—namely, the advantages that accrue to industrialized countries. As a result, states in the periphery should take extraordinary (protectionist) measures to industrialize.

This model of the terms of trade was never specifically tested—if, indeed, it could have been tested—for the case of Chile. More important, no close analysis was made of what relation the model had to the formulation of strategy for the copper industry.

Clearly, evidence from the Chilean experience would have supported some aspects of the Prebisch model: (1) It was true that Chilean demand for imports from the industrial countries of the "center" was rising rapidly as Chile developed; that even as imports of consumer goods declined, demand for capital equipment and raw materials rose; and that, consequently, the process of broadening the Chilean industrial base demanded a high, and growing, level of foreign exchange earnings. (2) It was true that the terms of trade for Chile between exports (primarily copper) and imports (including a large proportion of manufactured goods) probably[37] were declining. (3) It was true that, regardless of how the terms of trade would have behaved in a free trade system, the interference of the foreign corporations and their governments in copper pricing worsened those terms of trade for Chile. (4) It was true that, to, the extent that protected industrialization could be justified with infant-industry or second-best arguments, the "capacity to import" did have to be defended.

But it was *not* true that the demand for copper in the industrial countries of the "center" was price- and income-inelastic, as the Prebisch model assumed, or that the best Chilean strategy to "defend" its capacity to import was state intervention to force prices up to their short-term maximum.

Subsequent econometric studies have shown conclusively that demand for copper is highly elastic in relation to increases in industrial activity in the developed countries; that demand for copper (which is relatively price-inelastic in the short run, owing to the difficulty of substitution by

[37] There are a number of important problems in constructing terms-of-trade indexes. One of the most important of these is the difficulty of comparing the "value" of import packages of the same price where the composition changes rapidly over time owing to technological change and the appearance of new goods. A second major difficulty is caused by the fact that export price indexes for manufactured goods have been discovered to show a systematic upward bias. By the time manufactured goods are registered on export indexes, they are at a "mature" point in their life cycle, after their prices have already dropped significantly. The result is a systematic upward bias in reporting export prices for manufactured goods—or, stated another way, prices for exported manufactures do not appear to decline in export indexes when in fact they already have fallen significantly. Cf. Robert Stobaugh, "Systematic Bias and the Terms of Trade", *Review of Economics and Statistics*, Vol. XLIX (November 1967). For further discussion of the "product cycle model", see L. T. Wells, "Test of a Product Cycle Model of International Trade", *Quarterly Journal of Economics*, Vol. LXXXIII (February 1969); and Raymond Vernon, *Sovereignty at Bay: The Multinational Spread of U.S. Enterprises* (New York: Basic Books, 1971), ch. 3.

aluminum at short notice or with easy reversibility) becomes much more price-elastic over the longer term; that cross-elasticity of demand in relation to the price of aluminum is very high.[38]

Such studies obviously were not available in the period 1945–1950. But it should have been clear, if careful thought had been given to the problem, that copper did not fit well into the Prebisch model and that, in any case, the proper policy conclusions to serve Chilean national development were not being drawn.[39]

Every set of statistics that was available indicated that the use of copper was rising very rapidly as the United States, Western Europe, and Japan recovered from the war. As incomes rose in the industrial countries, as the "center" enjoyed construction and automotive booms and bought

[38] Charles River Associates, Inc., *Economic Analysis of the Copper Industry* (Cambridge, Mass.: March 1970); and Franklin M. Fisher and Paul H. Cootner, in association with Martin Neal Baily, "An Econometric Model of the World Copper Industry, I+II", *Bell Journal*, Vol. II, No. 2 (Autumn 1972).

These econometric analyses did not develop equations with respect to income elasticity of demand for copper, but only with regard to indexes of economic activity, industrial production, and use of construction materials in the US, Western Europe, Japan, and "rest of world".

Both studies found demand for copper to be very price inelastic in the short run, becoming much more elastic in the longer run. The Fisher-Cootner study obtained figures that were still inelastic at the point of means (−1.0 defining elasticity), ranging from −0.9 in the United States to −0.1 in Japan. Nevertheless, the cross-elasticity of demand for copper with respect to price of aluminum in Japan was even higher than in the United States.

[39] Two other criticisms of the Prebisch model could be made for the case of the Chilean copper industry: first, the system of implicit taxes pased on productivity gains to the Chilean state rather than to final consumers through lower prices (see pp. 75–76); second, the political and economic strength of Chilean mining unions constituted at least as powerful an "imperfection" in factor markets as the trade unions in industrial countries. These two factors rendered the Prebisch analysis less applicable to the Chilean copper case, but did not bear directly on the determination of copper policy.

more consumer durables and used more electricity, demand for copper shot up. As Prebisch predicted, the consumer in a developed industrial country might have devoted a smaller and smaller proportion of his income to bananas when his income rose, but he did not devote a smaller and smaller proportion to copper, which was included in the manufactured products he bought. Thus, the demand for copper was very responsive (elastic, not inelastic) to economic growth in the industrial heartland.

There should also have been a strong presumption of increasing price elasticity of demand for copper in moving from the short run to the long. The rapid entry of lower-priced aluminum, as well as of plastics, specialized steels, and other substitutes, into uses traditionally reserved for copper suggested that higher prices for copper, possible in the short run, would seriously weaken demand in the longer run.

As Chapter 2 pointed out, price behavior in the international copper industry was determined in reality by the fact that the metal was not scarce enough to restrict the entry of new competition at the production stage, and by the fact that the metal was not unique enough to prevent substitution if the relative price were kept "too" high. These factors led the private producer companies to acquiesce in "low" price ceilings during wartime, and to use their market power generally to keep producer prices "low" rather than "high" in peacetime.

What would have been the best Chilean strategy to "defend" the national interest, to maximize the capacity to import?

Chile was one of the lowest cost producers of copper in the world, with large reserves of high-grade ore. The national interests of Chile would have been best served by a policy of low prices, greatly expanded production, and as close a relationship between producers and consumers as possible. This would have enlarged aggregate demand for copper, increased the Chilean share in supplying that de-

83

mand, retarded the dilution of oligopoly power as well as the process of substitution, and made optimal use of the foreign-dominated industry to increase the Chilean capacity to import.[40] In this direction the Chileans could have most easily pushed the US companies. In other directions, they encountered much heavier resistance.

In summary, the Chilean capacity to import was not best defended by trying to reverse the trend in the terms of trade through pressing for the highest commodity prices market power would allow in the short run.

In contrast to what an optimal strategy would have been, however, Chile did press for higher prices. The country attacked the system of integrated relations between producers and consumers. It pushed the foreign companies sufficiently, without trying to attract any new companies into Chile, to find the country's share of world-wide copper production steadily declining.

VI

The rationale that could justify the "low" prices and the semi-integrated marketing system as being in the Chilean national interest was very poorly explained, if even understood, by Anaconda and Kennecott executives in Santiago. There was almost no mention of the threat of substitution by aluminum. Perhaps because the terms-of-trade issue was so sensitive, most corporate energy was spent in convincing the Chilean public that the companies were pushing for prices as high as the market could possibly bear. Rudolfo Mitchels, Chilean vice-president of Anaconda (and former ambassador to the United States), laid his prestige on the line by insisting that the US copper companies, like all companies in a free enterprise system, wanted as high a price

---

[40] Even if the demand for copper were not price elastic in absolute terms in the long run, Chile's best strategy as a low-cost producer with abundant reserves would have been to expand production at a lower price and have the aggregate loss to the industry borne by the higher cost producers while Chile increased its own market share.

as possible.[41] He asserted that there were no agreements to hold copper prices down, and that price level was determined by open-market supply and demand conditions.

These assertions were simply not true.

Kennecott was no better in explaining price and marketing strategy in the copper industry. The management contented itself with recounting (in a threatening way) how delightful alternative conditions were for mining companies in Africa, where docile governments and subsistence labor brought a corporate fantasy to life.[42] Such public statements did little to clarify the debate on marketing strategy. Rather, they invariably elicited responses from Chileans to the effect that the foreigners had to be stood up to rather than sold out to, that national interests had to be defended against corporate interests.

Much more persuasive were the domestic politicians, economists, and businessmen who pointed to the declining terms of trade and talked about the need to protect the capacity to import by pressing for higher copper prices. *Panorama Económico*, the academic journal of business and economics, and *Industria*, the journal of the National Society of Manufacturers, argued that "free trade" was a system that was allowed to work in the international copper industry only when it benefited the foreign companies and the developed countries—not when it worked to the benefit

[41] Rudolfo Mitchels, in *Panorama Económico*, No. 31, 1951. Mitchels probably believed what he was saying. He was not the first businessman to confuse free enterprise with perfect competition.

[42] Cf. *Panorama Económico*, March 27, 1953, and December 4, 1953; *Historia de la ley 11.828*, Vol. 1, September 16, 1954, p. 3944.

Mario Illanes, Assistant Manager of Commercial Operations for Kennecott's Braden in Santiago did bring a discussion of substitution by aluminum into his discussions over Chilean radio and in *El Mercurio*. Cf. *Boletín Minero*, January, 1957, p. 777.

Jorge Fontaine was a notable exception to the rule in introducing into his analyses the threat of substitution and the strategy of increasing output and selling at a lower price. *Panorama Económico*, May 27, 1955, and August 5, 1955.

of Chile. Chilean state control of marketing was necessary, they concluded, to defend the national interest against the US government-foreign corporation system of control that kept prices low and the terms of trade declining.

VII

Between 1945 and 1951, the dichotomy between "center" and "periphery", the systematically declining terms of trade, and the sense of *dependencia* caught and held the Chilean imagination. The country's experience as "captive production" in a system of foreign corporate integration seemed to provide ample evidence.

Aníbal Pinto and Luís Escobar lectured at the University of Chile on the detrimental effects which the free trade system had for Chile, and concluded that the government should intervene to fix higher Chilean prices.[43] The Radical Baltra, the Liberal Videla, and the business leader Müller explained to businessmen and bankers in Santiago and Washington about the permanent inequities that relations with Anaconda and Kennecott meant for Chile.[44] The moderate Falangistas, Frei and Tomic, argued that copper export prices should be directly pegged to the prices Chileans had to pay for imports to ensure against the declining terms of trade.[45] The Socialists Almeyda and Allende suggested that copper prices should be set through state intervention, and should be maintained by developing new commercial ties with socialist countries.[46]

[43] Cf. Luís Escobar in *Panorama Económico*, No. 31, 1951. In addition to Aníbal Pinto's constant writings in that magazine, see his books, *Hacia nuestra independencia económica, Chile: Un caso de desarrollo frustrado*, and *El cobre: Comercio y política*.

[44] Cf. Videla in *Boletín Minero*, June 1949, January 1951, and May 1952; Müller in *Industria*, February, March, and April 1951, and May and August 1952; Baltra in *Panorama Económico*, September 2, 1955.

[45] Cf. Frei in *Panorama Económico*, June 6, 1952; Tomic in *Panorama Económico*, October 8, 1954, November 11, 1955, and May 27, 1955.

[46] Cf. Almeyda in *Panorama Económico*, June 1949; Allende in *El Siglo*, January 29, 1953.

When, in June 1950, the United States Office of Economic Mobilization unilaterally set the price of copper at 24.5¢ per pound for the duration of the Korean conflict—while neglecting even to invite a Chilean representative to the discussions, much less allowing Chile to participate in deciding what the price ceiling should be—Santiago cried out in indignation. A Chilean delegation headed by the outraged president of the Senate Mining Commission, Hernán Videla Lira, and including the outspoken Senator Radomiro Tomic, went to Washington armed with reason and righteousness.

In the Washington Conference of May 1951 they managed to achieve certain substantial concessions, among which were an increase of 3¢ per pound for copper and the right of the Chilean government to sell up to 20% of its output independently at whatever "free" price it could command.[47]

But the success of the negotiations—and the extra revenues from prices as high as 55¢ per pound (or 100% above the price ceiling) on "free" sales in Europe—did not make the major economic and political groups in Chile think that their condition of *dependencia* was any more tolerable. In fact, the two-price system only confirmed their worst suspicions. The two-price system whetted Chilean appetites for greater returns and for greater justice.

Dependencia meant serving as captive production of large North American corporations and receiving the price decided upon by those corporations. If having the price on 100% of Chilean production dictated by foreign corporations was a challenge to national sovereignty and national

[47] The increase of 3¢ per pound was initially granted only to Chile and was paid directly to the Chilean government. The *Engineering and Mining Journal* reported that with this effort by the US State Department to "support another nation's inflated economy . . . the average American's sense of fair play was aroused". Soon the ceiling price for US producers was raised 3¢, too. *Engineering and Mining Journal*, July 1952, lead editorial.

growth, having the price dictated on 80% of Chilean production was not much improvement.

Cautions were brushed aside in the name of justice. In May 1952 President González Videla informed President Truman that his government was annulling the Washington agreements and establishing a state monopoly over all copper sales. Chile would find a just (higher) price, at last, not on 20% of its sales but on 100%.

With two local functionaries, two secretaries, and a man who worked half-days, a single small office in the Banco Central began trying to price and sell 13% of the world's copper output to customers on four continents.[48]

The Chilean sales monopoly of 1952 became the first major attempt to end the condition of *dependencia*.

[48] *Historia de la ley 11.828*, Vol. 2, November 5, 1954, p. 953.

CHAPTER 4

"Good Investment Climate" and the *Nuevo Trato* Mining Legislation of 1955: Death and Rebirth of the Idea of *Dependencia*

The first round in the postwar growth of economic nationalism in Chile began with tensions aroused by the desire for industrialization after the Second World War and ended with the Chilean sales monopoly of 1952. During this period the course of the relations between the country and the multinational copper companies gave rise to a feeling of *dependencia*, a sense that something was fundamentally wrong with the character of that relationship wherein foreigners controlled the Chilean copper industry and integrated it from mine to consumer.

Round two in the growth of economic nationalism in Chile began with the failure of the Chilean sales monopoly and ended in the late 1950's or early 1960's with the repudiation of Chile's basic postwar mining legislation—the *Nuevo Trato* or "New Deal" for the North American copper companies, which had been passed in 1955. During this period, the dominant Chilean thinking about relations with the US companies went through a complete cycle. The Chilean sales monopoly had been established to gain control over pricing and marketing policy. After the failure of the sales monopoly, a mood of laissez faire replaced the preoccupation with control. This reversal was sponsored most strongly by Chilean business interests and the political parties that represented them. The establishment of a "good investment climate" for the foreign corporations was part of their own domestic campaign to restrain government intervention in their activities. Although still preoccupied with the capacity to import, they became persuaded—after the disaster of the Chilean sales monopoly—that the strong drive of private enterprise (domestic and foreign) to increase profits would, if properly unleashed, serve both their own and the national interest. They claimed that the mining legislation would be a model for how they should be treated.

Consequently, the *Nuevo Trato* was constructed according to the philosophy that the foreign corporations would contribute the maximum to Chilean development if they were left unimpaired to pursue their own strategies, that they would greatly increase both their output and the returns to Chile "automatically" if given the opportunity to pursue higher profits with the stimulus of low taxes and a large cash-flow to the parents in New York.

But when the foreign corporations failed to respond with dynamism to the "automatic" stimulus of higher profits, to legal guarantees and tax provisions more generous than those enjoyed by many Chilean businesses, the sense of frustration returned. The failure of the *Nuevo Trato* to stimulate the multinational copper companies according to Chilean expectations renewed and reinforced the feeling of *dependencia.*

I

The rationale for establishing a Chilean sales monopoly in 1952 was to obtain a "just" price for Chilean copper, to end the condition of being "captive production" to the large foreign corporations, and to restore national sovereignty over commercial policy by opening up new channels of trade.

The "Washington Treaty" of 1951 had granted a 3¢ per pound price rise above the 24.5¢ ceiling payable directly to the Chilean government, and had allowed the Chileans to sell 20% of their output at whatever price the open market would bear (to non-Soviet bloc countries). Most of that 20% was sold on the European "free" market at about 54¢

per pound. These sales resulted in a substantial increase of revenues to the Chilean government in 1951–1952.[1]

Even then, however, in the midst of the Korean War, weaknesses in the Chilean marketing position were becoming evident. Chile wanted to sell to some imagined "new customers", but the evidence indicates that the country inadequately understood how thin and precarious the "free" market for copper actually was.[2] There was no Chilean institution that had experience in international marketing. The country did not have reliable data on the size or determinants of demand in the United States and Europe, let alone in the forbidden Soviet zones. Neither ECLA nor marxist economists gave any indication of being able to go much beyong coining wishful slogans about establishing "new commercial relations".

The fact was that those who had hard currency, wanted copper, and could afford the higher prices sought by Chile were mostly the subsidiaries and traditional customers of the large US or European-African companies. These were customers who valued their carefully built-up "organic ties" and "established relations" with the major producers, and who were willing to supply only their spill-over needs from independent producers in a high-priced open market in periods of scarcity. When Chile took control of all marketing operations in the first half of 1952, the regular customers had no short-run alternative but to pay a higher price.[3]

[1] Dr. Walter Müller estimated that the Chilean sales monopoly resulted in $23 million extra revenues in 1951 and $39 million in 1952 (*Industria*, May 1952, pp. 267 *et seq.*). Aníbal Pinto calculated the figure for extra revenues in 1952 at $70 million, in *Hacia nuestra independencia económica* (Santiago: Editorial del Pacífico, 1953), p. 178.

[2] On the Chilean sales efforts with the copper output 1951–1954, see *Historia de la ley 11.828*, Vols. 1–2; *Panorama Económico, Boletín Minero*, and *Industria* during that period; and Pinto, *op. cit.*, ch. 13.

[3] The Chilean marketing effort was undermined, according to Chil-

Nuevo Trato *Legislation of 1955*

Once wartime demand dropped and price controls were discontinued in February 1953, the Chilean government could not successfully maintain a quotation above the US producers' price on its traditional volume of output. The Chilean position as an independent supplier anxious to use the full extent of its market power was very weak in relation to the more moderate strategy of the corporate oligopoly. The preference of large consumers to buy in regular patterns from the traditional producers with whom they had historical ties was affirmed and reaffirmed.

Chilean copper policy was failing. The country's share in world production had been steadily declining since the end of the Second World War and had not recuperated much even during the Korean War. In 1945, the Chilean share of Free World production had reached a high of 22%; in 1951 that share was 15%; and by 1954 it had dropped to 14%.[4] Actual sales for 1953 and 1954 would have been even lower, since large inventories were accumulating.

This deterioration was complicated by the fact that the smallest of the three great mines in Chile, Anaconda's Potrerillos, was rapidly becoming depleted and would have

ean sources, by the decision of the International Materials Conference to deduct purchases from Chile from the quotas granted to the United Nations allies at the lower ceiling price. Thus, if France, for example, contracted to buy an "extra" 10,000 tons of copper from Chile at 54¢ per pound, the French allotment of 27.5¢ copper could be reduced by 10,000 tons by the International Materials Conference. (*Panorama Económico*, June 6, 1952; Pinto, *op.cit.*, ch. 13.)

The *Engineering and Mining Journal* (April 1952), p. 68, provides corroboration to the extent that some "restrictions on the sale and purchase of copper" were arranged by the International Materials Conference, and that these unspecified "restrictions" have narrowed the market for premium priced copper.

After the end of the Korean War, Anaconda and Kennecott appeared to ration their non-Chilean output among their regular large customers so as to keep their original marketing system intact and not "lose" customers to the Chilean sales agency.

[4] Official Codelco (Corporación del Cobre) statistics.

to be shut down before long. Chilean efforts alone, public and/or private, could not replace it.[5]

The implicit tax levied through the artificial exchange rate at which "legal costs" of production were covered served to buoy Chilean revenues somewhat. But this could be achieved only at great penalty to the companies. In the period 1951–1954 the level of effective taxation on Anaconda and Kennecott ranged from 65% to 92%.[6]

Chilean strategy was becoming counterproductive. Copper production was heading lower over time, and the absolute returns to Chile from the copper sector were falling. The government had huge stocks accumulating on its hands, weak prices, and a major mine about to give out.

In 1954 the president of the Senate Mining Commission, Hernán Videla Lira, told his colleagues that he had heard that Texas oil producers raised a statue to Mossadeq of Iran when the latter took over his nation's oil industry, because it meant an increase in the market for Texas. Peru and several states in Africa, said Videla, might be in the process of raising a statue to the Chilean Senate![7]

There was little disagreement that the time had come for a new set of fundamental negotiations with the foreign companies to set the direction of Chilean mining policy for the future. The balance of power between the Chilean government and the foreign companies, which had been tilted toward Chile since the 1920's, had shifted back in favor of the companies. Anaconda and Kennecott had something the host country needed—namely, the capital and technology necessary to expand production. Chile would have once again to strike a bargain to bring these resources to the service of the country.

[5] Editorial, *Boletín Minero*, June 1952.

[6] See the tables on direct and indirect taxation and explanation of calculations in the Statistical Appendix to this volume, pp. 265-266.

[7] Speech of Senator Hernán Videla Lira to the Chilean Senate, reprinted in *Boletín Minero*, March–April 1954, p. 1965.

II

The process of deciding to strike a fundamental new bargain with the foreign companies—in fact, to rewrite the country's basic mining legislation—was filled with rhetoric. But, beneath the rhetoric, the Chilean approach to how it could best serve its own interests was implicitly and explicitly based on a model of corporate behavior. The model came from domestic Chilean business groups and from the US companies themselves. The model was ideologically conservative and pro-business. More importantly, however, it was also erroneous.

What were the terms of the bargain to be struck?

Chile wanted a flood of new investment—to increase production substantially, to regain and maintain its former share of the world market. The country needed to entice the foreign companies into developing a new mine, or new mines, to replace the almost exhausted Potrerillos. Chile wanted refining capacity, especially electrolytic refining capacity, to serve the growing needs of the European market. To achieve these goals, the government was willing to dissolve the state sales monopoly, and Congress was prepared to rewrite the country's basic mining code to make it more attractive.

The companies, for their part, wanted a lower tax rate. In 1952, for example, the effective rate of direct income tax was 32.7%, while the rate of implicit taxation through exchange controls was 40.4%—for a total effective tax rate of 73.1% on the Anaconda and Kennecott operations in Chile. This provided plenty of room for strong bargaining. The companies wanted an elimination of the artificial exchange rate and the consolidation of all taxes into one income tax —in order to gain the full benefit of the United States Foreign Tax Credit. In addition, they wanted a special accelerated depreciation rate for new investments, plus liberal expensing allowances for mine development—this concession was particularly crucial for Anaconda, which was planning to replace the depleted Potrerillos mine. And the companies wanted to be given back control of sales and pricing policy from the Chilean state monopoly.

But the atmosphere that surrounded the writing of the *Nuevo Trato* hardly gave the impression of hard bargaining.

The key to the legislation was the idea of the "automatic stimulus" of the "good investment climate": private enterprises seek profits, and if profit rates could be made higher than alternatives elsewhere—so the argument ran—the companies would invest to expand operations and increase production; if tax rates could be made attractive enough, depreciation rapid enough, importation and expensing regulations generous enough, the companies would surely respond to these stimuli like rational economic creatures with higher output, new mines, new refineries.

"These US enterprises that have come to Chile," argued Senator Aldunate of the Liberal Party,[8] "are not religious congregations, nor cultural or scientific institutions, nor welfare foundations. They are the largest, most powerful and best-managed commercial and industrial enterprises in the world of private capital, which have come in search of attractive and secure investments. I think, in consequence, that it is an inexplicable error to deny that, when they are given adequate incentives, safeguards, and legitimate guarantees, they are going to feel compelled to work and to earn money. These companies are directed by the most able and talented men in matters of commerce and trade. They are not directed by mystics or philosophers who come to Chile for sentimental reasons. They come to fulfil their destiny, to realize what is inherent in their nature, to exploit to the maximum their capacity of production."

This model of rational economic behavior, reinforced as well as obscured by rhetoric, was propounded by copper

[8] *Historia de la ley 11.828*, Vol. 1, September 15, 1954, p. 3951.

company executives in public and in private. Mining legislation constructed to rely on the automatic incentives provided by a good investment climate was then and has since
been hailed as a "model" in the United States.[9] Both the
model and the rhetoric were received as revealed truth by
conservative political and business groups in Santiago in an
about-face from their earlier critical stance toward the foreign corporate system.[10]

"We would not be in the position we are today," commented the conservative Senator Bücher,[11] "if we had
adopted a policy of profit stimulus ten years ago."

Beneath the ringing phrases about the behavior of "free
men in free enterprise in a free society" there was a prediction that would have been rational from the perspective of
a simple firm producing a single product in a single country under conditions of perfect competition. Such a firm
would have responded to the incentive of increased profit
by investing to add production up to the point where marginal cost equaled marginal price.

But Anaconda and Kennecott were not simple firms
operating under conditions of perfect competition. And the
legislation did not have the desired result. This would be

[9] See, e.g., the lead editorial, *Engineering and Mining Journal*, June
1955, p. 67; and L. C. Raymond, "Chilean Mining's History and Fu-
ture", *Engineering and Mining Journal*, July 1969.
This is the position of Clark Reynolds in Mamalakis and Reynolds,
Essays in the Chilean Economy, and of E. N. Baklanoff, "Taxation of
United States-Owned Copper Companies in Chile: Economic Myopia
vs. Long-Run Self Interest", *National Tax Journal*, Vol. 14, No. 1
(March 1961).

[10] Some businessmen and conservative politicians were critical of
the rhetoric of *estímulos automáticos*. Dr. Walter Müller felt that the
obligations of the US copper companies should be spelled out more
clearly (cf. *Industria*, August 1952, pp. 260 *et seq.*). Jorge Fontaine
argued that in return for modifications in the tax system the foreign
copper companies should have to sign well-defined *compromisos* with
respect to the new investments they would undertake (*Panorama
Económico*, May 27 and August 5, 1955).

[11] *Historia de la ley 11.828*, Vol. 1, September 16, 1954, p. 3902.

the last major instance when these conservative groups identified their own interests with the strategy that motivated the large US copper companies.

The *Nuevo Trato*, then, was designed to remove the "artificial" restrictions and impediments that were restraining corporate behavior. It was primarily a codification of the stimuli, rights, exemptions, and advantages that Chile was offering to the companies. Anaconda and Kennecott got literally all the concessions on their shopping list—a lower initial effective tax rate; generously low base production figures which, if doubled, would reduce the companies' tax to about 50%; the immediate elimination of artificial exchange controls; special accelerated depreciation on new investments; liberal expensing allowances; free import rights on equipment; and the return to the companies of control over pricing and marketing.[12]

The sliding tax structure was particularly significant since it was occasionally lauded as the *Nuevo Trato*'s single non-automatic stimulus. The tax assessment after 1955 was constructed so that, to a rate of 50%, a 25% surtax would be added that was reduced to zero when a given production base was doubled. But the production base was set quite low—95% of the average production of each firm from 1949 to 1953, a period which, as has been shown, contained constant difficulty and decline. Bickering over sales and pricing policy during the Korean War had prevented any large expansion to meet wartime demand. And 1949 and 1953 represented prewar and postwar slumps. Thus, a 100% increase over the "production base"—which would have eliminated the surtax entirely—represented an output that was still less, for example, than full production had been during World War II.

The host country, Chile, relied on doing its best to create

---

[12] There was a good deal of controversy about just exactly what role the new Copper Department would play in pricing and marketing. Cf. *Panorama Económico*, September 24, 1954, and May 27, 1955; *Annual Reports*, Braden Copper Company, 1955–1960.

as many *estímulos automáticos* as possible. Expectations of success were high—the figure of one million tons output, double the capacity in World War II, was frequently mentioned.[13] More cautiously, a prestigious group of economists, businessmen, and political leaders (Comisión Especial del Círculo de Economía) suggested that the new legislation be judged on the basis of whether, under it, the companies acted dynamically enough to maintain or increase the Chilean share of the world market.[14]

Under the *Nuevo Trato*, Anaconda and Kennecott contracted no new obligations. They were not required to promise any specific commitments. With General Ibáñez's latter-day turn to the right before 1955, and with the subsequent election in 1958 of the conservative Jorge Alessandri to a six-year term as President, political risks seemed reduced to a historical minimum.

In short, Chile was coming a long way to create, economically and politically, the much-heralded "good investment climate". If the liberal model of foreign investment, relying solely on the incentive of private profits, were to maximize benefits to Chile, it would certainly do so in the decade following 1955.

III

In the late 1950's and early 1960's, even after Anaconda's new mine, El Salvador, replaced the mine at Potrerillos, the *Nuevo Trato* came to be considered a "failure" by almost all segments in Chilean society.

The truth was that the effects of the new mining code were complex, and gave some real benefits to both sides. The reason why the outcome was unnecessarily costly for Chile, however, and did not conform to even the most cautious domestic anticipations, lay in the model on which the legislation was based—the model of a simple firm maximiz-

[13] Cf. *Historia de la ley 11.828*, Vol. 2, October 27, 1954, p. 621.
[14] Cf. *Panorama Económica*, October 8, 1954; November 11, 1955; and November 25, 1955.

ing profits in a single country. Vertically integrated international corporations do not shape their strategy the way classical theory represents decision-making in simple firms. The result for Chile consisted of frustrated expectations, a needlessly unequal distribution of benefits, and a renewed sense of *dependencia*.

How one evaluates the effects of the *Nuevo Trato* in Chile would depend on what expectations were used as a measuring rod: if expectations were based on rhetoric about the automatic stimulus of a good investment climate, then the results of the *Nuevo Trato* could be labeled a failure. If expectations were based on the downward course of production in 1953–1954, or on what would have happened if no new legislation had been passed at all, then clearly the results of the *Nuevo Trato* were quite good. If expectations, finally, were based on what harder bargaining, more realistic analysis, and a better host-country strategy might well have achieved, then clearly the results of the *Nuevo Trato* left much to be desired.

What were the effects of the New Deal on the Chilean copper industry, and why was the legislation so relatively weak in its impact?

Production

With regard to the vast new production that Chileans expected, or were led to believe, would restore their share of the world market, the situation was complicated by the fact that the Potrerillos mine (Anaconda) was becoming exhausted and its output replaced by bringing a new mine, El Salvador, on-stream nearby.

In 1959, 1960, 1961—when the overwhelming criticism of the *Nuevo Trato* began to take place—Chilean yearly production was not in fact significantly different from what it had been at the end of World War II, despite Anaconda's new mine, El Salvador, which had come into full production in 1959 (see Table 5).

In terms of share of the world copper market, in 1945

Chile produced 22%; in 1960, it produced 14%. The figure would have declined much further if Chile had depended upon the actions of Anaconda and Kennecott alone. During the period of the *Nuevo Trato* (1955–1964) the small and medium mining sector increased its output by 250%, from 42 to 106 thousand metric tons per year. By the early 1960's Chile was the sixth largest producer of copper in the world,

TABLE   5

Output of *Gran Mineria* as Percentage of World Market

Average Annual Output of Gran Mineria (Chilean subsidiaries of Anaconda and Kennecott) (thousand metric tons) [15]		*Percentage of World Market* (total Chilean production)
1940 to 1945	433.5	18%
1945 to 1950	414.1	20%
1950 to 1955	345.5	15%
1955 to 1960	437.5	16%
1960 to 1965	505.4	15%

even before the *Gran Mineria* of Anaconda and Kennecott was counted.[16]

Many Chileans compared how their country fared under the *Nuevo Trato* with the experience of their rival to the north, Peru, which had initiated a similar major attempt in the mid-1950's to attract foreign investment into copper.[17]

[15] Official Codelco statistics.

[16] Not all of the medium and small mines were owned or operated by Chileans. Some of them belonged to US or European companies (including Anaconda). Nor were the medium and small mines governed by the *Nuevo Trato* mining legislation. The *Gran Mineria* referred to mines with an output above 75,000 tons per year— namely, Chuquicamata and Potrerillos or El Salvador of Anaconda, and El Teniente of Kennecott.

[17] The Chilean and Peruvian mining codes are not directly comparable. For example, the Peruvian code included a depletion allowance but required a certain amount of profits to be reinvested in Peru. Chile

In 1955, Peru's share of the world market was 1.5%; by 1960, it was 5.0%. In absolute amounts, Peru's output had risen almost 140 thousand tons, while Chile's output fought to maintain the same level.

There were clear differences in how the two companies in Chile reacted to the new legislation (see Table 6). Ana-

TABLE 6

Output of Individual Subsidiaries in Chile

Production of Chilex [18] (Anaconda at Chuquicamata mine) (thousand metric tons)	*Production of Andes* (Anaconda at Potrerillos and El Salvador)	*Production of Braden* (Kennecott at El Teniente)
1940 to 1945 215 per year	84 per year	139 per year
1945 to 1950 210	61	128
1950 to 1955 164	43	139
1955 to 1960 236	41	160
1960 to 1965 264	80	158

conda officials had used abundant rhetoric to describe how a larger cash flow would automatically stimulate any rational enterprise to increase investment and production. To a large extent they were claiming as a general law what they were planning to do as a single company. It is less certain to what extent Kennecott executives extolled the wisdom of how good investment climates automatically produce great investments—in any case, they were not disposed to act in Chile. Passing legislation that almost

had no depletion allowance but no reinvestment provision either. Peru had a system of "total returns" from hard currency sales; Chile had the system of "partial returns". See Jack N. Behrman, "Taxation of Extractive Industries in Latin America and the Impact on Foreign Investors", in Raymond F. Mikesell, ed., *Foreign Investment in the Petroleum and Mineral Industries* (Baltimore: Johns Hopkins Press, 1971).

[18] Official Codelco statistics.

doubled Kennecott's profits, without contracting for any new obligations from Kennecott in return, could only be called a pure gift to the corporation.

Refining

The *Nuevo Trato* was even more disappointing in the "natural" response it elicited from the foreign copper companies with regard to refining.

In 1951, the percentage of refined copper (electrolytic and fire-refined) produced by the foreign companies in Chile was 89%; in 1961, the percentage had declined to 45%. The decline was both relative and absolute. In 1951, 319 thousand metric tons were refined; in 1961, 216 thousand metric tons (see Table 7). The average refined ton-

TABLE 7

Refinery Production of Anaconda and Kennecott subsidiaries [19]

	Total Electrolytic and Fire-refined (1,000 metric tons)	Total Blister (smelted but not refined)	Percentage Refined	Percentage Blister
1950	299	46	87%	13%
1951	319	41	89%	11%
1952	319	55	85%	15%
1953	211	115	65%	35%
1954	177	145	55%	45%
1955	242	151	62%	37%
1956	240	203	54%	46%
1957	222	214	51%	49%
1958	186	231	45%	55%
1959	260	238	52%	48%
1960	226	254	46%	53%
1961	216	266	45%	55%
1962	246	264	48%	52%
1963	241	267	47%	53%

[19] Markos Mamalakis, "The American Copper Companies and the Chilean Government, 1920–1967: Profile of an Export Sector", Economic Growth Center, Yale University, Discussion paper No. 37, September 22, 1967, p. 115.

nage from 1950 to 1955 was 245 thousand; the average refined tonnage from 1955 to 1960 was 207 thousand.

Anaconda did not add electrolytic refining capacity at
either of its mines (as it had promised prior to the passage
of the legislation).[20] But once again it was the Kennecott
subsidiary, Braden, that had the least interest in investing
in refinery capacity or even in maintaining the company's
former level of refined output in Chile. From 1950 to 1955
Braden produced an average of 131 thousand metric tons
of fire-refined copper; from 1955 to 1960, the average declined to 85 thousand metric tons. The slope of the decline
was even more striking than the averages indicate—in 1950,
Braden refined 143 thousand metric tons; in 1960, 79 thousand metric tons; by 1963, 62 thousand metric tons.

As a bitter irony for the Chileans, Kennecott announced
in New York—not long after the last speech on "climate of
investment" had ended in the Chilean Congress—that Europeans were indeed demanding more electrolytic copper
for their electrical needs, and that therefore Kennecott was
spending more than one hundred million dollars on a giant
new refinery precisely to treat Chilean copper . . . in
Maryland.[21]

Investment

The tepid effect of the *Nuevo Trato* in attracting huge new
amounts of capital into the Chilean copper industry was
also reflected in investment figures (see Table 8). In fact,
even these figures appear more favorable than they actually

[20] Anaconda executives at Andes indicated in interviews during February 1970 that after the passage of the *Nuevo Trato* the smelter and
refinery at Potrerillos were scrapped and plans made to build new
processing facilities at Chañaral on the coast. Those plans were subsequently dropped for being too expensive. Later, when Allessandri
placed a tax on exports of non-refined copper in 1961, Anaconda felt
"stimulated" to reconstruct the 1925 smelter and refinery at Potrerillos
to treat El Salvador's output. The figures on refinery output come from
Mamalakis, *op.cit.*

[21] *Annual Report*, Kennecott, 1956.

were—since new investments after 1955 were allowed to be depreciated at the vastly accelerated rate of 20% per year.

In the case of Kennecott, once again the *Nuevo Trato* appeared to have little effect whatsoever.

TABLE 8

Gross Investment of Anaconda and Kennecott in Chile
(million dollars)

	Total	*Andes* (Anaconda)	*Chilex* (Anaconda)	*Braden* (Kennecott)
1945 to 1950	34	0	30	5
1950 to 1955	115	0	107	8
1955 to 1960	169	104	51	13
1960 to 1965	83	14	41	27

[22] Official Codelco statistics.

To offset the effect of accelerated depreciation after 1955, Mario Vera Valenzuela, *La política económica del cobre en Chile* (Santiago: Universidad de Chile, 1961), uses net investment figures:

Net Investment
(Gross Investment minus Depreciation) (million dollars)

	Total	*Andes* (Anaconda)	*Chilex* (Anaconda)	*Braden* (Kennecott)
1945 to 1950	7	(—12)	19	0
1950 to 1955	84	(— 8)	89	3
1955 to 1960	105	93	6	6
1960 to 1965	(—35)	(—42)	(—6)	14

SOURCE: Official Codelco statistics.

Such figures later became the center of the allegation that the *Nuevo Trato* had been a "failure", since net investment in the ten years prior to the legislation ($91 million) was actually greater than in the ten years subsequent to it ($70 million).

Mario Vera goes so far as to claim that investment in the period 1945 to 1955 (which included Anaconda's $130 million plant for sulphides at Chuquicamata) was in some sense a "normal" rate of investment.

There are two flaws in these arguments that seek to condemn the *Nuevo Trato* totally. First, the use of net investment figures must be handled more carefully. The effect of gross investment minus depreciation where both figures are high is not the same as the effect

Nuevo Trato *Legislation of 1955*

Revenues

Tax revenues increased very favorably for Chile after 1955. This was due, however, to substantial increases in world prices in 1955 and 1956 in comparison to the weak Chilean sales in 1952 and 1953, rather than to large new production (see Table 9).

TABLE 9

Total Tax Revenues from Anaconda and Kennecott
(direct taxes plus estimates of indirect taxes through fixed exchange rates) [23]
(million dollars)

	Total	Andes (Anaconda)	Chilex (Anaconda)	Braden (Kennecott)
1945 to 1950	148	12	86	48
1950 to 1955	180	10	91	79
1955 to 1960	468	19	223	225
1960 to 1965	441	8	221	216

This meant a great inflow of foreign exchange for the government. But it was more appealing for Chileans to make the simple calculation of high prices times the huge increases in production that they had expected after 1955 (but which never materialized), than to make the sad calculation of high prices times the weak sales of 1952–1953 if they had not passed any legislation.

---

of gross investment minus depreciation where both figures are low, even though the arithmetic result, the "net investment", may be the same in the two cases. In the first case, a large amount of capital has flowed "through" the system to build it up and modernize it. In the second case, little capital has flowed "through" the system.

Second, it is hard to justify an argument that there is ever any "normal" rate of investment where new mines or refineries come as large commitments from discrete decisions. Only the reinvestment of some fraction of depreciation to maintain existing facilities could (perhaps) be justified as a "normal" rate of investment.

[23] Official Codelco statistics, and Statistical Appendix to this volume, p. 266, for computation of indirect tax through artifical exchange rates.

Thus, whether the *Nuevo Trato* could be judged a failure or not depended heavily upon the expectations of what should have happened after the new legislation was passed and the new "climate" created.

But of one result produced by the *Nuevo Trato* there could be no doubt. The new mining legislation approximately doubled the average yearly profits of Anaconda and Kennecott operations in Chile. The returns on operations in Chile became two or three times as profitable as the other operations of Kennecott or Anaconda in other parts of the world.

Why, after the favorable impact of the *Nuevo Trato* on their rate of earnings, did Anaconda and (especially) Kennecott not respond more dynamically? The companies did not seem to obey the classical model of corporate behavior and react automatically to the promise—indeed, the assurance—of higher profits.

The "failure" of the huge multinational corporations to behave in accordance with what to Chilean businessmen and economists seemed like reasonable expectations led directly to the renewed growth of economic nationalism and the explosive reaction against *dependencia*.

IV

The increase in profits, profit rates, and cash flow to the Anaconda and Kennecott parent companies after the *Nuevo Trato* was spectacular (see Table 10).

TABLE 10
Profits of Chilex and Braden [24]
(after taxes)

Chilex (Anaconda)	1950 to 1955	$14.4 million per year
	1955 to 1960	$29.4 million per year
Braden (Kennecott)	1950 to 1955	$11.2 million per year
	1955 to 1960	$20.0 million per year

[24] Official Codelco statistics.

If Braden had in fact expanded production so as to drive its tax rate toward the 50% level, as Anaconda did, the after-tax profits and profit rate would have increased even more substantially[25] (see Table 11).

TABLE 11
Average Profit Rate of Chilex and Braden[26]
(as a percentage of average book value during the period)

Chilex (Anaconda)	1950 to 1955	9.1% per year	or 18.8% per year
	1955 to 1960	13.4% per year	or 22.0% per year
Braden (Kennecott)	1950 to 1955	25.5% per year	
	1955 to 1960	37.9% per year	

The third major mining company, Andes, which was Anaconda's smaller subsidiary, was given extraordinarily favorable treatment under the new mining legislation as the company replaced Potrerillos with the new El Salvador mine.[27] According to the Annual Reports of Andes, the $80 million that was invested in the buildings, machinery, and equipment required for the new mine was allowed to be charged against income at the rate of 20% per year; almost all the costs of actually developing the mine itself were allowed to be treated as "deferred charges for mine development" and deducted as soon as income started to be produced (instead of being capitalized); and the $25 million undepreciated balance from the exhausted Potrerillos mine was permitted to be transferred to the new books and depreciated at normal rates.

[25] Cf. *Annual Reports*, Braden Copper Company, 1955–1961.

[26] Official Codelco statistics on book value as reported by the companies and audited by the Corporación. For the basis for the alternative calculation for Chilex, see Chapter 2, footnote 17.

[27] This account is based on the *Annual Reports* of the Andes Copper Company (1954–1965), and on interviews with officers of Anaconda and of the accounting department of the Corporación del Cobre (1970).

This resulted in high accounting charges against before-tax income. Consequently, although the mine came on-line at full capacity in 1959, Andes showed almost no profit and paid almost no taxes between 1957 and 1965.

The depreciation provisions of the *Nuevo Trato* were so generous, in fact, that Andes had to petition the Chilean government to stretch the period for total depreciation beyond five years, or else be allowed to accumulate accounting losses that could be carried forward against future income. The generosity of the *Nuevo Trato* also proved to be an embarrassment to the company in labor relations—since wage contracts had been signed with an innovative profit-sharing plan, but the company was not showing any bookkeeping profits!

Chile had found out in 1951–1953 that a "bad investment climate" sharply discouraged foreign activity in the copper industry. Now they found out, to their dismay, that a "good investment climate" did not by itself sharply encourage foreign activity.

This was all the more frustrating and mystifying because Chilean operations appeared to be the most profitable activity Anaconda and Kennecott were engaged in anywhere at any stage of the copper business (see Table 12).

An economist would be quick to point out that average returns are not marginal returns—that, because the return per year on all Chilean assets is higher than elsewhere, the next incremental investment in Chile will not necessarily bring a higher return than the next incremental investment elsewhere. But if average returns over a ten-year period are higher in Chile than outside of Chile and if they appear to be rising as the company undertakes new projects in Chile, then there is good reason for assuming that returns at the margin are greater in Chile than outside.[28]

[28] This analysis is based on the assumption, confirmed in interviews with officers of Anaconda and Kennecott, that both companies had promising new discoveries of ore in Chile and/or could have expanded output at existing facilities with a comparable return on the expendi-

TABLE 12
Relative Return on Assets in Chile and Elsewhere [28]
(per year)

	1950 to 1955	1955 to 1960	1960 to 1965
Anaconda			
return on Chilex assets	9.1%	13.4%	9.7%
(alternative computation of assets)	18.8%	22.0%	14.2%
return on non-Chilean assets)	6.3%	6.9%	3.0%
Kennecott			
return on Braden assets	25.5%	37.9%	19.0%
return on non-Chilean assets	13.0%	13.3%	7.6%

But Anaconda's and Kennecott's investments were not flowing into Chile in search of those higher rates of return. Rather, their capital was flowing elsewhere (see Table 13).

The *Nuevo Trato* had reduced tax rates and accelerated depreciation, had increased cash-flow and speeded it to the parent, to produce a "good investment climate" in Chile. But the foreign companies were investing instead in other countries, other stages, other industries.

With the *Nuevo Trato*, Chile opened wide its door to welcome foreign investment in the copper industry, and, to its surprise and chagrin, large sums flowed out. The country wanted new capital for its own development; instead it seemed to be exporting capital to finance the "development" and diversification of the multinational corporation.

---

ture of new capital. The example of the new mine, El Salvador, showed plainly how lavish the treatment for new projects would be.

[29] Calculated on the basis of figures from the Corporación del Cobre and from the *Annual Reports* of Anaconda and Kennecott.

TABLE 13
Investments in Chile and Worldwide [30]
(million dollars)

	1945 to 1950	1950 to 1955	1955 to 1960	1960 to 1965
Anaconda in Chile	30	107	155	55
Anaconda world-wide	71	277	329	261
Kennecott in Chile	5	8	13	27
Kennecott world-wide	53	67	190	161

V

How would the classical model of the simple firm that served as the basis for the *Nuevo Trato* have to be modified to explain the dynamics of Anaconda and Kennecott in Chile?

According to classical economic theory, private firms try to maximize profits. They invest funds where those funds can earn the greatest marginal return on the investment. "If your country takes pains to create conditions in which foreign investors can find good, secure returns on their operations—that is, if your country creates a 'good investment climate'—you can receive the benefits of a healthy inflow of foreign investment. Your aim should be to offer foreign investors a higher rate of return on their activities (discounted for relative risk) than alternatives available elsewhere." In its most basic form, that might be called the conventional theory of foreign investment. It seems simple, and it makes some sense. It underlies the thinking of many

[30] Official Codelco statistics and the *Annual Reports* of Anaconda and Kennecott.

US investors today—or they think it underlies their thinking[31]—and it was, as we have seen, the basis for Chile's basic postwar mining legislation, the *Nuevo Trato*.

Why, if the conventional theory seems so sensible, may it be wrong as a strategy for a host country when dealing with large, complex corporations? If the philosophy behind the *Nuevo Trato* was wrong, if the figures given for relative return on investments were right, then the multinational corporations did indeed seem like alien and irrational creatures, unresponsive to national enticement or control, following an internal logic of their own.

There were three basic factors that would have to be taken into consideration to understand the behavior of multinational copper corporations and the apparent "failure" of the *Nuevo Trato* mining legislation: first, the companies follow a strategy of maximizing returns to their corporate system as a whole, and not to each individual stage or country where they have operations; second, such a strategy of maximizing returns to the system as a whole is sufficiently long-term, or involves sufficient preference for stability and security of income, as to include diversification by product and/or by geographical region;[32] third, the decision for new investors to move into an unknown region or stage of the industry involves substantial information and decision costs that must be offset before the possibility of investment can even be considered.

With regard to the first factor, a model of foreign investment that seeks to predict or explain the activities of multinational enterprise must specify that the justification for

[31] See, e.g., the report of US National Foreign Trade Council in *Boletín Minero*, June 1952; Raymond, "Chilean Mining's History and Future"; National Industrial Conference Board, *Obstacles and Incentives to Private Foreign Investment, 1962–1964* (New York, 1966).

[32] Diversification by product and/or by geographical region may not merely reflect judgments about long-term profitability or security, but also be undertaken to take maximum advantage of accumulated managerial expertise or of certain aspects of financial accounting or tax regulations.

any individual investment depends upon the capacity of that investment to make some contribution to the system as a whole. In such a situation, it is almost impossible to know exactly to what extent the value of an investment to a corporation may be represented by marginal profitability.[33] For example, profits declared at one stage may depend in large part on expenditures made at another stage in the industry—e.g., funds invested in wire fabrication may prevent Anaconda from meeting monopoly power downstream from mining and thus protect the profits being generated at the mining stage. In other cases, the reduction of risks for the system as a whole may be the aim of the investment—e.g., Kennecott may invest in aluminum as a hedge against substitution, or in the coal industry to diversify sources of income, or in a copper mine expansion in Arizona to build up domestic sources of supply—even though new operations in Chile might actually show a higher realized rate of return on investment.

In constructing an alternative model for the behavior of complex corporations, the only way to measure the effect of a single investment for the system as a whole—and thus to compute its "real" return—is to try to calculate what the difference would be to the corporate whole if the investment were not made. How much better off is the parent corporation to be somewhat protected if aluminum keeps eating into copper's uses, or if a dock strike cuts off imports from foreign mining operations? These are the relevant calculations that corporate management must make to judge "real" return on investment from any particular stage, or particular country, or particular product. The actual

---

[33] As Chapter 2 pointed out, the apparent profitability of a particular stage or a particular region can be made to appear artificially large or small through the manipulation of transfer pricing or intersubsidiary financing. Since these techniques were not important in shifting profits into or out of Chile, they are not the focus of attention here. The criticism of the classical model offered here has to do with corporate investment strategy, not internal accounting.

amount of extra profit realized by an incremental investment in Chile was only a small part of a much more complicated strategy for global investment.

The difficulty of matching apparent return-on-investment with actual location-of-investment is likely to be particularly severe in natural resource oligopolies—where oligopoly members customarily have control over more reserves than they need to maintain their share of the market, or to expand in line with global demand. In such a situation, the marginal present value of an additional investment in production may be very low—or, in fact, may be negative if it upsets the informal pricing and marketing arrangements within the oligopoly.

It would be misleading to imply that Anaconda or Kennecott were not acting "rationally" because their behavior in Chile did not correspond to expectations based on the classical model of the firm. Similarly—contrary to the judgment of prominent North American analysts who have criticized Chilean copper policy—there is no justification for suggesting that the Chilean government would have been acting "irrationally" if it had disregarded the classical model of the simple firm in framing its mining legislation of 1955.[34] Rather, the proper implication must be that the classical model of the simple firm maximizing its marginal return in one product in one country—investing in new production until marginal cost equals marginal price—cannot by itself account for the behavior of large, diversified, multinational companies, or provide a guide for host country policy.

How should Chile in 1955 have approached the foreign corporations to get them to maximize their operations and profits within its taxing jurisdiction? The corporations had the potential to offer benefits that the country valued highly. For the moment, the balance of power was tilted to their side. Some substantial concessions, therefore, would have had to be offered to Anaconda and Kennecott for Chile to

[34] Reynolds, *Essays on the Chilean Economy*, and Baklanoff, "Taxation of United States-Owned Copper Companies in Chile."

get what it wanted. But what was needed were concessions that acted as an incentive for the corporations to take action that would not otherwise be taken, rather than as a reward for general good behavior. Careful negotiations structured to give the foreign companies an inducement to do what the host country wanted would have had a better chance of success than a mere display of generosity.

The basic asymmetry in the strategies of the foreign copper companies and Chile—namely, that the companies were interested in maximizing returns to their global corporate systems while the country was interested in maximizing returns in one country and at one stage of operations—meant that the invisible hand that harmonizes interests in classical theory was much too invisible. In a sense, the Socialist Senator Raúl Ampuero was correct when he claimed that "our interests and the interests of the foreign copper corporations are in permanent contradiction".[35] But his conclusion that only nationalization could possibly serve the national interest did not follow. What did follow, given Chilean technical and organizational capabilities at that time, was that cautious negotiation with a clear specification of the new obligations of both sides would have served Chile best in 1955.

This was particularly true when one considers the second factor mentioned above—that the country was dealing with companies that had high corporate preferences to diversify out of the copper industry or out of Chile, or both. As Chapter 2 pointed out, both Anaconda and Kennecott were under strong pressures throughout the 1950's to use available corporate funds to diversify out of exclusive activity in the copper industry—that is, to diversify into other fields as a hedge against the cyclical nature or the decline of the copper industry. Kennecott was building up an equity position of nearly $100 million in Kaiser Aluminum. Anaconda was making heavy financial commitments to construct its

[35] Ampuero, in *Historia de la ley 11.828*, Vol. 2, January 19, 1955, pp. 1293–1298.

own aluminum smelter in Montana and integrate backward to the raw material. Kennecott also entered the iron foundry business by acquiring and expanding the Quebec Iron and Titanium Corporation in the 1950's, and bought into the coal business by acquiring the Peabody Coal Company in the 1960's. What Kennecott really hoped for, but was never able to achieve, was an opportunity to diversify into the petroleum industry.[36]

In addition, stockholders and creditors of both Anaconda and Kennecott were putting pressure on management to budget investment for increased copper production *outside* of Chile—that is, to create a more diversified geographical base for the companies. Anaconda frequently had to apologize to security analysts for having so many of its assets (39% in 1955–1960) concentrated in Chile, and for deriving so large a proportion of its consolidated income (47% in 1955–1960) from Chilean operations. The company spoke frankly about its priority of building up a domestic ore base in the United States. A fundamental part of Anaconda's postwar investment strategy was aimed at developing the Butte (Montana) mines, at great expense, to help correct its own corporate "dependence" on Chile.[37]

In short, the real or perceived reduction in risk accruing to diversification or geographical dispersion was high in management calculations in comparison to a marginal difference in return on investment between Chile and the next best alternative.

[36] For Kennecott's corporate investment strategy, see the *Annual Reports*; McDonald, "The World of Kennecott", *Fortune*, November 1951; Rush Loving, Jr., "How Kennecott Got Hooked with Catch–22," *Fortune*, September 1971; and James L. McCarthy, "The American Copper Industry, 1947–1955", *Yale Economic Essays*, Vol. iv (Spring 1964).

[37] For Anaconda's corporate investment strategy, see the *Annual Reports*; Isaac F. Marcosson, *Anaconda* (New York: Dodd, Mead, 1957); Thomas O'Hanlon, "The Perilous Prosperity of Anaconda", *Fortune*, May 1966; "Anaconda: The Domestic Problems of an International Giant", *Forbes*, December 15, 1968; and McCarthy, *op.cit.*

Thus, no matter how "good" the investment climate in Chile might seem or how low the discount for risk might be pushed, Anaconda and Kennecott managements showed preferential commitment of attention and financial resources to areas and activities outside of Chile. In such a situation it is unlikely that a marginal increase in profit rate would by itself capture corporate imagination and induce the devotion of time and capital necessary for huge new projects. Straightforward *quid pro quo* bargaining proposals, on the other hand, would add a cost for inaction to the reward for action as a stimulus to corporate activity.

The profit motive, private enterprise, and the good investment climate, which brought to Senator Bücher's mind the image of water racing downhill, had for the established copper companies in Chile more of the dynamics of water backing uphill.

One way to approach the dynamism of rushing water might have been to use the new mining legislation of 1955 as part of an active international campaign to attract other major producers into Chile. This effort would have involved consideration of the third factor mentioned above—that the decision to make a new foreign investment in an unknown country involves substantial information and decision-making costs that have to be overcome before the investment can be considered. In three volumes of hearings in the Chilean Congress on the *Nuevo Trato*, there is no evidence that even after the decision was made to offer major incentives and generous concessions to foreign copper investors any active steps were taken to attract new companies.[38] There was little realization in Chile that even huge foreign corporations run by Senator Aldunate's "most able and talented men in North America" would have to be actively induced to expand their horizons.[39] Rather, once a "good

[38] *Historia de la ley 11.828,* Vols. 1–3, 1954–1955.

[39] On the costs of acquiring new information before undertaking a foreign investment, see Yair Aharoni, *The Foreign Investment Process* (Boston: Division of Research, Graduate School of Business Administration, Harvard University, 1966).

investment climate" was written into Chilean mining law, the country sat back passively to watch something called the "profit motive" go to work. Routine reports about the new mining legislation appearing haphazardly in trade journals, plus smiles on the faces of Anaconda and Kennecott executives, were supposed to stimulate entrepreneurs in New York, Hamburg, and Tokyo to fly to Antofagasta and set out for the mountains or the desert.[40]

There was an ambivalence in the Chilean attitude. The Congress made a decision, painful to many groups, to increase the profits, benefits, and concessions given to foreign-

[40] In fact, Anaconda and Kennecott may well have been engaged in an active effort to discourage or block the entry of competition into the Chilean mining industry. Testimony was introduced before the Chilean Senate in 1954 that both German and Japanese groups had made initial attempts to enter into mining production in Chile, but that the North American companies successfully dissuaded them. (*Historia de la ley 11.828*, Vol. 1, September 16, 1954.)

The United States government may also have discouraged initiatives from Western Europe and Japan. In 1952 the Paley Report (United States, President's Materials Policy Commission, *Resources for Freedom*, Washington, D.C., 1952, 5 vols.) was released, warning of a supposed decreasing self-sufficiency for the United States in crucial raw materials. The US Senate Minerals, Materials and Fuels Economic Subcommittee began to investigate "the accessibility of the critical raw materials" to the US during wartime. In 1954 that subcommittee, headed by Senator George W. Malone, recommended a US policy based on Western Hemisphere self-sufficiency. Senator Malone stated: "We belong to the Western Hemisphere. Our security comes to be threatened in the case of any European or Asiatic country acting in this area to gain military, political, or economic control of it. Therefore, our broadest cooperation among the nations of the Western Hemisphere constitutes an immediate and compelling need. The spirit of the Monroe Doctrine which has 130 years of existence constitutes the established principle on which such cooperation should be based. And this principle is applied in equal form to British, Dutch, French, Soviet and all other countries of Asia and Europe."

This view was widely considered in Chile to be the official US policy toward mineral development in South America. Cf. *Historia de la ley 11.828*, Vol. 1, January 19, 1955, pp. 1267–1272; *Panorama Económico*, No. 116, February 11, 1955; and *Engineering and Mining Journal*, August 1954.

ers, but then it did not push to use those benefits and concessions to the fullest extent possible to bring in new investments and new investors. The Congress made a painful acknowledgment that it needed a foreign presence in its midst, an expanded foreign presence, to run the copper industry, but it was hesitant to invite more than the two traditional "imperialists" to Santiago. There was no sense that five or six foreign capitalist giants might be easier to bargain with, in competition with each other, than the two traditional producers.

In summary, the rhetoric about the automatic stimulus of a good investment climate obscured the motives of both sides and brought in no new actors. The *Nuevo Trato* aroused false expectations and created new frustrations. In 1960, two years after the new production constructed under the legislation came on-line, the Chilean share of the world market was back at the low point it had reached in 1950–1951 under the old tax rates and the threat of the sales monopoly. The US recessions of 1957–1958 and 1960–1961 stimulated new Chilean concerns about the capacity to import (even though the absolute level of revenues was of course higher than in 1949), and in 1960 the conservative Alessandri government began to push up the tax rate again.

By the late 1950's and early 1960's the *Nuevo Trato* was widely looked upon in Chile as a "failure". The period of the "good investment climate" had come to be considered a disastrous setback in the march away from *dependencia*.[41] With the repudiation of the *Nuevo Trato*, that march was resumed.

[41] In Chile the period of liberal incentives could not be associated with a massive mining boom in the minds of domestic conservatives and state governors—in contrast to the cases of Canada, Australia, Peru, Brazil, and (most recently) Indonesia.

CHAPTER 5

From Chileanization to Nationalization: Success and Revenge in the Movement away from *Dependencia*

The growth of economic nationalism in Chile began with frustration at the feelings of *dependencia* after the Second World War and reached an initial peak with the sales monopoly of 1952—as a first unsuccessful attempt to end that *dependencia*.

A second phase in the growth of economic nationalism began with the failure of the sales monopoly and ended with the rejection of the *Nuevo Trato* and its philosophy of foreign investment. Disappointment with the results of the *Nuevo Trato* revived the sense of frustration at having large, vitally important foreign corporations in the midst of the affairs of the country, foreign corporations whose internal decisions were crucial to the course of domestic development but whose behavior seemed both mystifying and exploitative.

The third phase in the growth of economic nationalism began with the Christian Democratic program of Chileanization and ended with the nationalization of the large US copper companies. The take-over of Kennecott and Anaconda was initiated—firmly but cautiously—by the Frei regime. The final nationalization of Anaconda and Kennecott and Cerro was finished—audaciously and inefficiently, but irreversibly—under Allende. Domestic control of the copper industry is in all likelihood one of the few achievements of this period whose legitimacy will effectively survive the bloody struggle over Chile's new constitutional order. This chapter will trace the movement from Chileanization to nationalization. Chapter 8 will outline some of the difficulties as well as the achievements of the post-nationalization period.

119

Eduardo Frei began in 1964 as the candidate of moderation, with a strategy of "progress through negotiation"— indeed, in a political slogan that would fall leadenly on North American ears, the Christian Democrats summed up their approach as *progreso contratado*. Their policy would be pragmatic rather than dogmatic, cooperative rather than —in a phrase that would fall leadenly on Chilean ears— *zero-sum*.

The Frei Chileanization program achieved substantial benefits for Chile. Huge new investment funds were brought to the domestic industry to increase mining, smelting, and refining capacity. Chilean-dictated pricing policy during the Vietnam War resulted in unprecedented levels of foreign exchange flowing into the national treasury. The terms of trade were reversed. The capacity to import was expanded. In contrast to the *Nuevo Trato*'s failure, this attempt at "progress through negotiation" was, by any but the most stingy standards, clearly a success.

Yet Frei's own administration ended with the nationalization of Anaconda. And it ended with all three candidates for the next administration pledging to uphold, if not extend, the policy of nationalization.[1]

Following the election of Dr. Salvador Allende in 1970, the new marxist President moved swiftly with broad public support on copper policy. A Chilean Congress dominated by the non-marxist opposition passed without a single dissenting vote a constitutional amendment directing the nationalization of all the large foreign copper companies. With solemn Chilean declarations about the international right of exercising national sovereignty and with exuberant Chilean feelings of expropriating the expropriators, Anaconda, Kennecott, and Cerro were taken over.

---

[1] Salvador Allende and Radomiro Tomic (the Christian Democratic candidate) both wanted to expand the policy of nationalization. Alessandri was the only candidate whose position was equivocal. For one of the clearer statements of his program, see *El Mercurio*, February 7, 1970.

There were two basic factors underlying the movement from Chileanization to nationalization: (1) increased Chilean confidence in the domestic ability to run the copper industry at the production stage and (evidently) to set copper policy on the international level as well; and (2) a continuing—indeed, accelerated—loss of political support for the US copper companies among domestic groups of the center and right in Chile. Their net effect was a projection of only small costs to set against huge benefits for nationalization of the *Gran Minería*—a projection that was persuasive to a broad spectrum of Chilean opinion.

As a result, in a moment of Chilean confidence and corporate vulnerability, the country moved once and for all to end the condition of *dependencia*.

I

In formulating and carrying through the Chileanization program in the mid-1960's, Eduardo Frei could draw on the expertise of a widening pool of Chilean *técnicos*—lawyers, administrators, and economists—who had experience in running large enterprises and, in some cases, competence in monitoring the behavior of the copper industry itself.

This was in marked contrast to the situation at the time of the first Chilean sales monopoly during the Korean War, or at the time of the writing of the *Nuevo Trato*.

In 1952, as the commercial monopoly directed by the Central Bank began to falter, the Chilean Congress had called on the Comptroller General of the Republic, as an independent auditor, to present a report on the condition of the domestic copper industry.[2] The Comptroller General responded with a sworn statement that except for the foreign management of the companies nobody, including himself, had any idea of what was going on in the industry or had ever had the basis for making a judgment! There was

[2] See the commentary on this report in *Historia de la ley 11.828*, Vol. 1, September 15, 1954, pp. 3734 *et seq.* For earlier comments, see *Panorama Económico*, January 16, 1953.

no audit of how much the foreign companies were actually producing, shipping, storing, paying in taxes, earning as profits, or receiving as prices.[3] The Ministry of Mines, he asserted, published exactly what figures the companies gave it to publish, and had no others. The Internal Revenue Service, the Office of Ports and Customs, the Commission on Foreign Trade all published figures. All the figures were different. And, he claimed, they could not be reconciled.

The Comptroller General had to admit that his office too would have to go to Anaconda and Kennecott to get the figures to do the study to check the figures of the companies!

If Chile in the early 1950's did not have the facilities set up to monitor, accurately and authoritatively, even what was happening in the domestic industry, it is not surprising that the capacity to analyze international oligopoly strategy was even less finely developed. In the debates surrounding the *Nuevo Trato*, decisions involving hundreds of millions of dollars were made or rejected at the highest levels of the Chilean administration on the basis of information copied from a stockbroker's opinion received by chance in the mail from New York. When Senator Ignacio Palma, for example, tried to persuade his colleagues from the floor of the Senate as to how to reconstruct the nation's mining legislation, he waved in his hand a stock analysis by Loeb, Rhoades & Co. as definitive evidence about the global strategy of Anaconda and Kennecott.[4]

[3] One of the first attempts to improve this situation was the study of mineral taxation commissioned by Felipe Herrera, then Minister of the Treasury, and carried out by Félix Ruiz, *Tributación directa e indirecta a las grandes empresas de cobre* (Santiago: Sección Estadística del Banco Central, August 1953).

[4] *Historia de la ley 11.828*, Vol. 1, September 16, 1954, p. 3970. Ironically, the brokers in question argued that Anaconda and Kennecott felt a priority to use available funds to diversify out of Chile. If the Senate had drawn the proper conclusions from this (as argued in Chapter 4)—and had not relied on the rhetoric of the "automatic incentive" of the "profit motive" that would supposedly pull the

Certainly even then there were some prominent members of the Chilean Congress—such as Senators Videla Lira, von Mühlenbrock, Duran, Palma, Tomic—who had experience in domestic business and in international negotiations. But their knowledge tended to be impressionistic, and their experience haphazard. As late as 1955 it was clear that able and sophisticated Chileans were trying to make decisions affecting the growth and welfare of their nation on the basis of almost no independent information, with little expertise, and with no institution devoted to the accumulation and verification of what few data were available.

The *Nuevo Trato* law of 1955 took a major step forward in providing an institution to develop Chilean competence in monitoring the copper industry. As a rearguard action in 1954, the more critical opponents of the *Nuevo Trato* succeeded in attaching a provision to the legislation for a Chilean "Copper Department" to watch over the actions of the foreign companies.[5] Once established, the Departamento del Cobre began by collecting statistics on production, prices, taxation, profits, dividends—statistics supplied primarily by the companies or gathered from international trade journals. Gradually, new efforts were made to check and verify, to compare year by year, the figures that were collected. A bureaucracy (of lawyers, engineers, accountants, businessmen, and economists) with some expertise was built up, and it became familiar with analyzing and making sense of the companies' balance sheets and income statements. It had a responsibility to supply information to

companies' capital into Chile—Chile would have been saved millions of dollars.

[5] This position was argued most strongly by the Falangistas and Radicals in the debates of 1954–1955, *Historia de la ley 11.828*, *passim*. See also the well-reasoned statements by Jorge Fontaine in favor of a strong Copper Department, in *Panorama Económico*, May 27, 1955, and August 5, 1955. The editorial position of *Panorama Económico* in favor of extended powers for a Copper Department can be found in the issues of September 24, 1954, and March 4, 1955.

the Congress and the Executive, and since the Department's "experts" could be used to challenge the figures or the arguments of the companies, Anaconda and Kennecott had an (unenthusiastically greeted) vested interest in keeping the institution informed about what was happening in the industry.[6]

The Copper Department was important in putting pressure on the foreign companies to expand local procurement; it lobbied for more Chilean personnel in responsible positions in the US companies; and it took a capricious interest in sales policy.[7] While Jorge Alessandri was President (1958–1964), the government sided with the companies (against its own Copper Department) in almost all important disputes.[8] The initiatives of the Department tended to be muzzled rather than encouraged, since President Ales-

[6] Unfortunately there is no study of the historical development of the Departamento del Cobre or its successor, the Corporación del Cobre. The material here has been compiled from interviews with members and former members of these two institutions, from the *Annual Reports* of the Kennecott and Anaconda subsidiaries in Chile, from the *Boletín Minero*, and from *Panorama Económico*, as well as from congressional discussions in *Historia de la ley 16.425*, Vols. 1–3, 1964–1966.

There were parallel improvements in data-gathering and in the accumulation of expertise in the Ministry of Mining itself, and in the National Mining Society (Sociedad Nacional de Minería) under Hernán Videla Lira and Francisco Cuevas Mackenna.

[7] Although Braden, for example, fought pressures from the Copper Department to make local purchases in many specific instances, the company adopted a policy of local procurement after the *Nuevo Trato* was passed. Braden reported that local purchases grew from $4 million in 1955 to $20 million in 1969, from 57% of operating expenses in 1959 to 70% in 1968. *Expropriation of the El Teniente Copper Mine by the Chilean Government*, Kennecott Copper Corporation, 1971, p. 6, and *Annual Reports*, Braden Copper Company, 1955–1966.

On sales policy, one on-going dispute arose from the hostility of the Copper Department to long-term sales commitments (for delivery at a price determined by market conditions at the time of delivery). Such corporate practice represented an "entanglement" to the Chileans, similar to being "captive production".

[8] *Annual Reports*, Braden Copper Company, 1958–1964.

sandri did not believe in government "interference" in private enterprise. But by the time President Eduardo Frei reconstituted the Copper Department as the Corporación del Cobre, he could pull together from within and without the old Department a number of talented and, more importantly, experienced Chilean personnel who felt at home using most of the standard data in the copper industry, analyzing many of the important problems, explaining and interpreting most of the behavior of the mining companies.

Alejandro Hales, who as Minister of Mines directed the nationalization of Anaconda under Frei in 1969, had also been Minister of Mines under President Ibáñez and had helped draw up the legislation creating the Copper Department in 1955. Javier Lagarrigue, who was one of Frei's most skillful negotiators with the companies, had been chief of the commercial section and later a vice-president in the Copper Department.

Clearly, not all of the *técnicos* who contributed to the formation of Frei's copper policy had backgrounds within the Department.[9] Others came from state-run industries or positions in private business. Raúl Sáez, an economist who had been head of the National Electricity Company (ENDESA) and a member of the Alliance for Progress Committee of Nine, led the negotiations in 1964 with the US companies.[10] One of his principal co-workers, Flavian Levine, had been president of the National Steel Company (CAP).

To be sure, not all of the bright young *técnicos* with skill and experience in analyzing the behavior of the copper industry worked for the Frei government or supported the

[9] According to *Panorama Económico* (March 1969), the campaigns of 1958 and 1964 put large strains on the *técnico puro o objetivo* aspect of many academicians who wanted to give active support to the political positions of various candidates. As a result of the drain of *técnicos* into the Frei administration, *Panorama Económico* was not published from 1964 to 1969.

[10] For Sáez's defense of Chileanization, see Raúl Sáez, *Chile y el cobre* (Santiago: Departamento del Cobre, January 1965).

125

Chileanization program. Mario Vera Valenzuela, an economist from the Instituto de Economía of the University of Chile, who had written the most detailed and sophisticated Chilean critique of the results of the *Nuevo Trato* legislation, was highly critical of Frei's Chileanization legislation.[11] As advisor to the National Copper Workers' Confederation and to leftwing political parties, Vera argued strongly for nationalization.

The pool of domestic talent and expertise could provide a basis for sharpening the country's bargaining position with the companies, and Frei used his advisors to this end. But more was changing than mere bargaining position. Increased Chilean competence meant that the perception of the foreign "contribution" was reduced at the same time that a group interested in taking more control was created. At a minimum the companies would be expected to put more and more of their own talents, resources, and expertise at the service of the host country just in order to maintain a position in Chile. To a growing number of talented Chileans, increased Chilean competence reduced the perception of loss and heightened the perception of gain if the foreigners were "replaced". The companies could be more than "pushed against"—they could be pushed out. Nationalization became more than a credible threat. It became a credible, and appealing, alternative.

At a moment when the companies had just finished a large lump investment and would not be willing to make any further commitment for some time, they would be particularly vulnerable. If this coincided with a moment when

[11] Vera's analysis of the *Nuevo Trato* is contained in his *La política económica del cobre en Chile* (Santiago: Universidad de Chile, 1961). His critique of Frei's program can be found in frequent articles for *Cobre*, the magazine of the National Copperworkers' Union. His proposals for nationalization are most thoroughly stated in *Una política definitiva para nuestras riquezas básicas* (Santiago: Prensa Latinoamericana, 1964).

Both Socialists and Communists used Vera's work in the debates on Chileanization, *Historia de la ley 16.425, passim.*

most domestic groups identified their own interests with the expulsion rather than the preservation of the foreign presence in the industry, the result for the companies would be sharper than a serpent's tooth.

These two moments began to coincide at the end of Frei's administration.

II

Eduardo Frei insisted that the Chileanization program for copper was the main plank (*viga maestra*) of his plan for the nation. Upon achievements in copper policy would depend success in financing agrarian reform, urban welfare, and economic development. During the campaign, Frei revealed that he intended to seek a definite commitment for substantial increases in Chilean production through stiff negotiations with the North American companies—he would fulfill through legal contract what the *Nuevo Trato* had unsuccessfully promised nearly ten years before. He also affirmed that he would seek some sort of Chilean participation in the ownership of the mines, although exactly what form this participation would take was left deliberately vague.[12]

Frei hoped for a supportive response from the companies, rather than confrontation. He was claiming to be the best alternative to the threat of communism and marxism. He had the wholehearted approval of the United States government and the funds of the Alliance for Progress behind him. And he expected that the copper companies would indeed want to contribute to the success of his program and his administration.

Doubtless, the narrow defeat of the marxist Allende in 1964 was an occasion of joy and relief for the North American copper companies. But the bargaining position of the new Christian Democratic administration was not necessarily as strong as the initial enthusiasm for the Frei vic-

[12] For a good comparison of Frei's and Allende's programs, see *Cobre*, July 6, 1964.

tory seemed to indicate. Chile's twin aspirations for increased copper production and for equity participation could be played off against each other by the companies in any tight bargaining situation. It was by no means clear that the corporate boards of directors for Anaconda and Kennecott (and now Cerro) would easily decide to begin long-term capital commitments during the regime of a six-year President who could not succeed himself.

Thus, it was a stroke of good fortune for the newly elected regime when, even before Frei took office, Kennecott met with his representatives and, to their surprise, told them Kennecott wanted to sell a majority share of the Chilean subsidiary.[13] In conjunction with the sale of 51% of the equity, Kennecott proposed a program to expand production at El Teniente by over 50%—from a capacity of about 180,000 tons per year to about 280,000 tons—and to reconstruct the living arrangements for most of the mineworkers. Kennecott would arrange for the bulk of the financing of this program itself, and would stay and manage the new joint venture through the difficult period of expansion and on for at least ten years.

The details of the Kennecott offer startled (and irritated!) Anaconda.[14] Anaconda itself had been prepared to put together some kind of conventional expansion program. But the idea of sharing The Anaconda Company's sov-

[13] The Chileanization of El Teniente was the most spectacular part of the Frei program when he announced it to the nation on December 21, 1964. Frei's negotiators had actually met first with Cerro and arranged minority participation (25%) for the Chilean government in the new medium-sized Andina mine. Then the negotiators met with Anaconda, where they found stiff resistance to any proposals of joint-ownership. The negotiations with Kennecott came last. Cf. Raymond F. Mikesell, ed., *Foreign Investment in the Petroleum and Mineral Industries* (Baltimore: Johns Hopkins Press, 1971), ch. 15.

[14] This account is based on interviews with the most senior Anaconda officials in New York (July 1970). Anaconda was finally persuaded to accept minority ownership by the Chilean government (25%) in the small, new Exotica mine.

128

ereignty over internal operations with a government—any government—offended the company's basic philosophy of the separation of business and government. Consequently, the top management resisted from the start any suggestion of offering equity participation in their major operations, especially majority participation, to Chile.

Thus, the Kennecott offer took everybody by surprise. In Washington it was greeted as an act of statesmanship in accord with the spirit of the Alliance for Progress. The Kennecott decision to sell 51% of El Teniente, the world's largest underground mine, set the tone of the Chileanization program and gave the new Chilean administration an immediate image of success.

Why had Kennecott decided to sell?

III

The Braden Copper Company, Kennecott's subsidiary operating El Teniente, had never been an aggressive copper miner in Chile.[15] The company had lived since the 1920's as a *rentier*. The mountain of rich copper ore at El Teniente had seemed inexhaustible, and the company invested just enough out of depreciation each year to keep production running relatively smoothly. Between 1930 and 1965, for example, Kennecott had a net capital disinvestment of —$5 million in Chile, while Anaconda had a net capital investment of +$93 million. Anaconda had undertaken two major expansion programs during that period, including the opening of the new El Salvador mine, while Kennecott had done no more than hold its own. The production capacity

[15] This interpretation is based on interviews with the leading Kennecott officials in New York and Santiago. It is confirmed in two analyses of Kennecott's corporate strategy: John McDonald, "The World of Kennecott", *Fortune*, November 1951; and Rush Loving, Jr., "How Kennecott Got Hooked with Catch–22", *Fortune*, September 1971. It is considerably different from the tone of the company's defense of its behavior in Chile: *Expropriation of the El Teniente Copper Mine by the Chilean Government* (New York: Kennecott Public Relations Department, 1971–1973), 6 sections.

of El Teniente in 1964 was approximately the same as it had been in 1937.[16] There was little active exploration for new ore-bodies and no indication of a desire by the Kennecott parent that Chilean operations be significantly increased.

Kennecott's attitudes began to change in 1959–1960. In 1955 the company had had no concrete plans for the development of new productive capacity in Chile, nor was it required to develop such plans under the *Nuevo Trato* mining laws. By the late 1950's, however, it was increasingly difficult for El Teniente even to maintain production at existing levels. Water and electricity were in short supply, transportation and haulage were difficult, and workers' housing was getting older and more dilapidated. The company could not keep production up enough to avoid the variable surtax that could push the total rate as high as 75%.

To Kennecott's economic difficulties were added political difficulties generated by the lack of response to the *Nuevo Trato*. The company's management accepted the fact that left-wing political groups had always been ideologically hostile to foreign capitalist domination of the copper industry. Increasingly, Kennecott officials felt, their company was receiving what they called "bad publicity" from right-wing political groups and the business sector in Chile.[17]

Then, in 1959–1960, exploratory drilling indicated that the basic El Teniente ore-body was much larger than previously realized.[18] Kennecott management began to con-

[16] The company defense states that Braden's annual copper productive capacity was 16,000 tons in 1916 and increased to 180,000 tons by 1967 for a 4.9% annual growth rate. This defense ignores the fact that productive capacity was not far below 180,000 by the middle 1930's— a capacity it barely maintained for the following thirty years.

[17] This account is based on interviews with the top Kennecott mining officials in New York and Santiago. Executives in corresponding positions in Anaconda had been privately distressed with the behavior of Kennecott and its failure to respond to the *Nuevo Trato*. They blamed Kennecott for the "bad name" the companies were getting in Chile in the late 1950's.

[18] *Annual Report*, Braden, 1959 and 1960.

sider the possibility that all of their problems could be solved with one large expansion program—production could be increased substantially, the tax rate could be reduced, and "bad publicity" about the failure of the *Nuevo Trato* could be stilled. This program was called the Codegua Project.

Yet within two years all plans for the Codegua Project were dropped. Why?

Kennecott was unwilling to undertake the large financial commitment necessary for the expansion project without what it considered effective twenty-year guarantees of inviolability. But, with the disintegration of domestic support for the foreign copper companies, the company could not get such guarantees, even during President Alessandri's conservative administration. Kennecott finally concluded that even if guarantees were passed by Congress, they would mean little.

The new element that was responsible for the deterioration in support for the US copper companies was the Alliance for Progress and the resentment it caused among conservative political and business groups.

The Alliance spoke in strong terms about the need for social change in Latin America, and demanded a meaningful land reform before US funds would be dispensed. The next chapter will analyze in detail the behavior of the Chilean right as it reacted to the Alliance for Progress and the threat of land reform. In brief, the response of conservative political and economic groups was to use the companies' failure under the *Nuevo Trato* as a scapegoat for the development problems of Chile—while denying the allegations about domestic maldistribution of income, about local monopolies, about the need for social reform. In fact, as the threat of land reform became more menacing, the strategy of the conservative parties became more Machiavellian. They proposed the nationalization of Anaconda and Kennecott in an effort to hold them as hostages to gain concessions on land reform.

131

President Alessandri in 1961 was able to patch over the splits in his cabinet, where the Minister of Mines, Enrique Serrano, a Conservative Party member, was leading the attack on the companies. With Alessandri's help, the first right-wing plan to hold the companies as hostage was finally blocked before it got to the Congress; but so was the legislation for Kennecott's large Codegua expansion program.[19] And, in the uproar over the Alliance and the companies, bills were passed that increased taxes on Anaconda and Kennecott by 10%–12%.

If it was previously possible to overlook the relatively mild attack on the US copper companies from the right wing over the "failure" of the *Nuevo Trato*, by now the pattern was clear. Long-term guarantees for operations in Chile—risky even in the best of times—were losing their meaning. Kennecott realized this. Anaconda did not. Shortly after the first outburst against the Alliance and the US copper companies (the Bulnes-Serrano crisis) Kennecott dropped its plans for the Codegua Project and began to entertain the idea of selling 51% of its Chilean operations to the government.[20]

IV

This was the basis for the paradox in the Kennecott decision to enter into partnership with the Chilean government: the joint-venture and expansion program were an effort to build domestic support and to improve the corporation's public image in Chile; they were also an effort to pull back from Chile and defend a deteriorating position through international rather than domestic ties.

[19] *Annual Report*, Braden, 1961.

[20] *Ibid.* This analysis is also based on interviews with leading Kennecott executives in Santiago and New York. They explained the difference in corporate approaches as a function of Anaconda's belief that it could keep manipulating the politics of Chile behind the scenes as it had always done in Montana (and as they supposedly did not).

The Kennecott program was not simple to analyze:[21] the company would sell 51% of its Chilean operations to the Chilean government; it would arrange the financing for about $203 million or 85% of the huge increase in capacity; it would manage the new joint company for ten years or more, and supervise the completion of the expansion project as well as the arrangements for selling the increase in output.

Kennecott asked, in return for this, payment of more than twice book value for 51% of its property and a reassessment of the "worth" of the remaining assets at a multiple substantially higher than that; it wanted an immediate reduction in the tax rate on its share of the returns; it wanted a Chilean commitment for more than half of the capital needed for the expansion, and more for related social overhead expenses; and it wanted a formal twenty-year government guarantee for the entire project.

Yet Kennecott was not in fact bringing one new corporate dollar into Chile or raising a single *escudo* locally in the company name. The parent was counting on the Export-Import Bank of Washington, under some pressure from enthusiastic Alliance officials in the US State Department, to provide $110 million of the $230 million required for the expansion. The rest of its share of the financing would consist of the Chilean payment ($80 million, plus interest) for 51% equity in the new joint venture, which Kennecott would loan back to the new company. The Chilean government would then contribute an additional $27.5 million.

21 Cf. *Historia de la ley 16.425*, Vols. 1–3, *passim*; Sáez, *Chile y el Cobre*; Kennecott *Annual Reports* and *Letters to Stockholders*; and interviews with Kennecott executives in New York and Santiago.

This is an analysis of the initial proposal for El Teniente. Later, as this chapter points out, an additional $45 million was raised by selling contracts for future output to Japanese and European customers.

Both Chile and Kennecott claimed credit for "contributing" the $80 million that Chile paid for a 51% interest and Kennecott loaned back to the new joint venture.

The value of Kennecott's operations in Chile would increase substantially. From a balance sheet perspective, Kennecott would still be a 49% owner of a company worth about four times as much ($286 million) as it had been ($69 million) before. From a cash-flow perspective, Kennecott would be receiving 49% of the proceeds from an operation exporting almost 64% more output at a tax rate reduced from over 80% to 44%. The Chilean government would guarantee the $110 million loan from the Export-Import Bank of Washington, and the $80 million loan from Kennecott. These arrangements were calculated, negotiated, and approved as being profitable for Kennecott at a copper price of 29¢ per pound (with 1964 mining costs) before copper prices in the 80¢–90¢ per pound range during the Vietnam War turned mining operations into an old-fashioned bonanza.

Kennecott hoped that the sale of majority interest in El Teniente would create public support for the company's continued presence in Chile—or at least reduce public antagonism. But Kennecott was taking no chances with what seemed like clearly deteriorating domestic alliances. The company wanted to protect its position in Chile as far as possible through international alliances of both a governmental and a non-governmental nature.

Kennecott management had never placed enough trust in the ability of the US State Department or the US Congress to provide a rapid and effective response in case of expropriation to have confidence in the Hickenlooper Amendment.[22] Therefore, the company decided it would have to protect its Chilean holdings through means other than merely hoping for direct diplomatic pressure. Kennecott was not sure how secure its position could be made, but the company was determined not to pass away in silence.

To line up supporters who would come to the company's

[22] Based on interviews with Kennecott officials in New York and Santiago.

aid in case of expropriation, Kennecott began by insuring the amount of the sale of equity ($80 million) supplied by Chile but committed to the joint project by Kennecott under a US AID Contract of Guarantee against expropriation (later assumed by the Overseas Private Investment Corporation). Thus, upon entering into the joint venture with Chile, the Kennecott parent had bypassed Congress and the State Department and arranged an immediate US government guarantee to pay an amount in case of expropriation larger than the net worth of its total Chilean operations had been prior to the reassessment of book value. At the same time Kennecott demanded that the sale amount and the Ex-Im Bank loan be unconditionally guaranteed by the Chilean state and made subject to the laws of the State of New York. These arrangements meant that Kennecott would have a general claim against the Chilean state should the Chilean operations be expropriated, and that the Ex-Im Bank, the State Department (AID), and the Congress would feel the effects of any nationalization simultaneously with Kennecott. The Ex-Im Bank would want its loan repaid by Chile as soon as the Kennecott management contract was broken; State (AID) would object to paying off a huge insurance claim; and these agencies plus Kennecott could join in mobilizing support for the Hickenlooper Amendment in Congress. Washington would not be able to ignore harm done to Kennecott's Chilean operations. The goal of Kennecott was to make any threat of nationalization result unavoidably in a face-to-face confrontation between the US and the Chilean governments.

Finally, to assure itself of an international reaction to any threat of nationalization, Kennecott raised the capital to cover a cost-overrun of $45 million for the joint project by writing long-term contracts for the new output with European and Asian customers, and then by selling collection rights on these contracts to a consortium of European banks headed by the Banca Comerciale Italiana ($30 million) and to a consortium of Japanese institutions headed by Mitsui & Co. ($15 million). This operation—similar to "factoring" in business finance or the selling of accounts receivable at a discount to a financial intermediary—was designed to bring international pressure on any nationalistic administration in Chile not to void the Kennecott management contract and not to repudiate the debt obligations of the El Teniente joint venture. Since repayment of the $45 million to the foreign banks depended upon faithful fulfillment of the long-term sales contracts to the customers, a crisis of confidence in the future of production (brought about by any threat to the Kennecott management contract, if Chile could not take over production dependably itself) would provoke outbursts from financial institutions as well as from customers in Europe and Asia.

"The aim of these arrangements," explained Robert Haldeman, executive vice-president of Kennecott's Chilean operations, "is to insure that nobody expropriates Kennecott without upsetting relations to customers, creditors, and governments on three continents."[23]

V

Anaconda, in contrast, was determined to maintain its corporate sovereignty intact and was prepared to undertake a major new commitment in Chile in its own name.[24] Chilean operations were to be increased by over 200,000 tons per year in new production. To finance this expansion, Anaconda would provide $72.55 million and the Export-Import Bank of Washington would provide $58.7 million. Since Anaconda refused to enter into any major joint association with the Chilean government, the only Chilean capital contribution was $3.75 million in payment for 25% of the equity in a small new mine near Chuquicamata named

[23] Interview, Santiago, May 27, 1970.
[24] Cf. *Historia de la ley 14.625*, Vols. 1–3, *passim*; Sáez, *Chile y el Cobre*; Anaconda *Annual Reports*; and interviews with Anaconda executives in New York and Santiago.

Exotica. And payment on the Ex-Im Bank loan was guaranteed by Anaconda, not Chile.

In return for these commitments, Anaconda was promised a tax reduction from an effective rate near 62% to about 52% on the returns from this substantially expanded output. Even this concession was not as straightforward as it seemed, however, since some prior benefits in the form of provisions for accelerated depreciation and rebates on refined copper were taken away. The result was that, in marked contrast to Kennecott, most of the advantages would accrue to Anaconda later in the 1970's, and not immediately.

A third company was included in the Chileanization negotiations—the Cerro Corporation—which wanted to open its first Chilean mine high in the mountains at Rio Blanco.[25] Cerro's approach was more similar to Kennecott's than to Anaconda's, and its financing was even more complex. The new Andina subsidiary of Cerro was expected to produce about 230,000 tons of 30% copper concentrate per year beginning in 1971. The original capital cost of the project was estimated at $89 million but later raised to $157 million. Cerro would provide $49.9 million, the Export-Import Bank $56.4 million, a group of Japanese customers (headed by Sumitomo Metal Mining Company) would provide $32.1 million, and Chile would provide $18.6 million. In all, 70% of the company's equity would be owned by Cerro, 30% by Chile. The Chilean government also committed itself to invest in a major electrical power station and supply electricity to the new company at favorable rates. The Chilean government guaranteed $35.4 million of the Ex-Im loan and $10.1 million of the Japanese loan. The tax rates on the profits of the new joint venture would be 15%, plus an additional 30% withholding tax on Cerro's dividends. About 67.5% of the initial output of concentrates would be covered by a 15-year contract to the Japanese smelters.

[25] Cf. *Historia de la ley 14.625*, Vols. 1–3, *passim*; Sáez, *Chile y el Cobre*; and Cerro *Annual Reports*.

Thus, there were clear differences between the approaches of Kennecott and Anaconda, with Cerro standing somewhere in the middle. Kennecott and Cerro were sharing equity ownership with Chile. They seemed to be participating more directly in the program of the Frei administration than Anaconda. They had the image of "Chileanization". Their deals were new and spectacular. They were "partners" with Chile. Yet they were doing everything they could to minimize the actual financial commitment that they were making in Chile, and to protect themselves against the risk of expropriation.

Anaconda, on the other hand, stuck to its traditional methods. The company was in fact providing more of its own resources for the new copper program than either of the other two companies. It was bearing the burden of the new expansion itself, in terms of both cost and risk, especially in the short run. In the longer run, of course, Anaconda would not have to split the benefits of the expansion program in the same measure as those companies that shared equity ownership with the host government.

Most importantly for the Anaconda management, there would be no outside Chilean directors sitting in on the board meetings of Anaconda's subsidiaries, except for the relatively insignificant Exotica. The necessary capital would be raised, as it always had been, through Anaconda's name in New York and guaranteed by the parent company directly. Anaconda would maintain its own sovereignty over internal decision-making intact.

This would be one of the central reasons why Anaconda would come under new Chilean attack even before the Frei administration had left office. The principal fault with the Anaconda strategy—straight equity investment, corporate sovereignty, foreign control—was not that it was more unjust or exploitative than other forms of foreign participation in natural resource development, but rather that it belonged to a system of rights and expectations that was (and is) rapidly disappearing.

138

VI

In total, President Frei's Chileanization program was calculated to increase aggregate copper production from about 630,000 metric tons per year to nearly 1,090,000 metric tons per year in the course of a six-year period. Compared with the results of previous administrations, this would represent a spectacular achievement. During the twenty years from 1945 to 1964, Chilean production rose only 160,000 metric tons, Frei reminded the nation, while his plan contemplated an increase of 460,000 metric tons in six years.[26]

Chilean experience, Chilean competence, and Chilean confidence were notably increasing at the production level. By the middle of Frei's administration (1966), exports from the small and medium mines (about 124,000 tons) made the country the fifth largest copper exporter in the world— greater than the total of all exports from Peru or the Soviet Union. At the large foreign mines, Chileans were taking over more and more of the mining and smelting and refining operations, including managerial responsibilities. The joint venture with Kennecott at El Teniente, employing 10,000 persons (including construction workers), was the most advanced in this respect. By 1968–1969 there were fewer than ten non-Chileans with responsibility for any

[26] In a fascinating cost-benefit analysis of the Chileanization program, Keith Griffin, *Underdevelopment in Spanish America: An Interpretation* (Cambridge, Mass.: MIT Press, 1969), ch. 4, concludes that nationalization in 1964 would have had more beneficial results for Chile than Frei's program, even if Chile had financed the expansion of the *Gran Minería* out of domestic savings. Because an increasing number of state enterprises were run entirely by Chileans, Griffin assigns a dubious value of zero to the "contribution" of the foreign mining companies in managing the massive construction projects or in introducing Chilean *técnicos* to industry practices. Griffin's analysis does not include the dynamic possibility, stressed here, that the optimal strategy for a nationalist may be to induce foreign companies to put operations successfully on-line and then tighten the terms—with the ultimate aim, perhaps, of taking them over.

activities having to do with mining, smelting, or refining—all the rest, including supervisory and executive personnel, were Chilean.[27] The Anaconda mines employed a larger number of foreigners, but there too the trend was toward Chilean supervision at all levels of operation.

The country was also building up its own competence in refining. To the older state works at Paipote, the National Mining Enterprise (ENAMI) in 1964 added a large new electrolytic refining plant at Las Ventanas with a capacity of 84,000 metric tons.[28] Frei began the process of expanding Las Ventanas to 120,000 metric tons per year of electrolytic copper, which would make ENAMI one of the largest state-owned smelting complexes in the world. The quality of ENAMI output was dependable and its reputation excellent, and both Kennecott and Cerro wrote contracts with the state enterprise to have portions of their own output refined there.

Members of Frei's government and technical administrators from the Chilean state bureaucracies participated in the affairs of the companies to an extent never before permitted. Detailed audits of Kennecott's Chilean operations were carried out by North American and Chilean companies, the results reviewed by representatives of the Copper Department, and a new appraisal value for El Teniente set. Chilean representatives went over the details of the engineering plans for the Kennecott, Cerro, and Anaconda projects, and Chilean as well as North American companies were contracted to carry out the construction. Chilean financial representatives were taken into the negotiations to obtain capital for Kennecott and Cerro from the United

[27] Based on interviews with the top Kennecott executives in Santiago in 1969–1970. Kennecott states that, of 10,000 employees in 1971, only two were American citizens (*Expropriation of the El Teniente Copper Mine by the Chilean Government*, p. 5).

[28] The original government smelter and refinery at Paipote had been planned by the Corporación de Fomento in the late 1930's but not completed until after the Second World War. The newer works at Las Ventanas had been constructed during the Alessandri regime.

140

States, Japan, and Western Europe, since the Chilean government was being asked to guarantee the international loans. Representatives from the commercial section of the Corporación del Cobre traveled with executives of the Kennecott Sales Corporation and the Anaconda Sales Corporation to Europe, Japan, and the United States to begin the process of selling contracts for future output.

Chilean participation in the inner workings of negotiations about construction, sales, and finance was a great advance for Chilean experience and Chilean confidence. A great deal of pride was certainly justified. Nevertheless, the huge expansion programs at the Anaconda, Kennecott, and Cerro mines were directed by the North American parent companies, financed through their reputations, and carried out under the supervision of US building and mining contractors. Host country "participation" largely meant watching at first hand the dealings of others more used to taking risks and probably less exposed to the consequences of miscalculation.[29]

[29] For example, in the expansion projects themselves, the feasibility of the engineering designs had already been passed on by the North American parent corporations, and North American construction companies had been charged with developing the detailed specifications before Chilean authorities were invited to review the plans or Chilean companies were given subcontracts for some of the construction. Even so, there was at least one major miscalculation. The Cerro Corporation with its contractors Parsons-Jurden and Morrison-Knudsen (Constructora Emkay, S.A.) made an initial calculation for the Rio Blanco venture at $89 million and in the course of construction had to raise the estimate to $157 million—for a cost over-run of nearly 100%. Cerro was able to persuade the Japanese customers and the North American financiers to go along with the new calculation. There was not even a ripple in Chilean politics. Surely it would be more difficult for a Chilean agency, acting as manager in developing a risky new enterprise, to persuade creditors to go along with or to survive domestic criticism of a 100% cost over-run.

The analysis of the Cerro cost over-runs is based on the *Annual Reports* of the parent. I have also had the opportunity to discuss the over-runs with various North American and Chilean mining engineers in Santiago.

There was nevertheless one important area in which Chile took direct control under Frei—in dictating international price policy. As the Vietnam War escalated from 1964 to 1966, the disparity between the US producers' price and the London Metals Exchange open-market price increased. The Johnson administration had opted not to impose formal price controls on the US economy, but the President jawboned the companies to keep their prices for primary copper from climbing too rapidly. This indirect pressure was backed by sales from the US stockpile, by mandatory setasides of production for the Defense Department, and finally by export restrictions to prevent domestic copper from flowing to the higher-priced markets in Europe and Japan. Thus, the North American price for copper remained at the beginning of the war near the 35¢–38¢ per pound level, while the LME price soared to the 65¢–90¢ range.

Anaconda and Kennecott kept their price for Chilean copper at the level of the US producers' price, and, at first, the Frei administration was persuaded to go along.[30] But since most Chilean copper was in fact being sold in Europe and Japan to consumers willing to pay a higher price, the Frei administration decided in 1966 to break the pattern of price moderation during periods of peak demand. The Chilean government took over direct control of price policy and by August was pricing Chilean copper directly at the high LME quotation. In June 1967 representatives of the Frei government met at Lusaka with their counterparts from Zambia, Peru, and the Congo, to form the In-

[30] President Lyndon Johnson sent Ambassador Averell Harriman to Santiago in 1966 to negotiate a sale of 100,000 tons to US fabricators at the US producers' price of 36¢ per lb. In return for this, the US government agreed to give Chile a $10 million loan, repayable over 40 years at less than 1% interest, and Anaconda was required to make an additional tax payment on this copper of $3.5 million to the Chilean government. Cf. *Historia de la ley 16.425*, and Thomas O'Hanlon, "The Perilous Prosperity of Anaconda", *Fortune*, May 1966, p. 119.

tergovernmental Council of Copper Exporting Countries (CIPEC). The LME quotation was adopted as the basis for all of the sales of this group, and plans were advanced for cutbacks in production, when necessary, to keep prices high.

The new Chilean price policy, combined with wartime demand and a long copperworkers' strike in the United States, resulted in enormous increases in copper revenues. From 1966 to 1970, Chilean tax revenues from the large foreign companies averaged $195 million per year in comparison to revenues during the Alessandri administration averaging only $80 million per year. Such spectacular results seemed to prove the wisdom of carrying out what the country had wanted to do all along—ditch the corporate producers' price system and go for all the market could bear.

By 1969 Chile had already increased copper production to 687,000 tons, and copper revenues to $216 million. The expansion programs of all three foreign companies, Kennecott, Anaconda, and Cerro, were well ahead of schedule, and due for completion in 1970 or 1971. Chileans were supervising more and more of their own mining, smelting, and refining. They were "participating" in the arrangement of international finance and marketing. And they were dictating pricing policy, with phenomenal success.

At El Teniente, the Kennecott hierarchy counted on the joint participation to be more a process of education for the Chileans into the management practices of Kennecott than a process of allowing Chilean control to spread over Kennecott. But education into the ways of Kennecott was in fact a means of breaking into those areas of expertise and experience that hitherto had been the monopoly of the foreigner. The potential to imitate Kennecott management could also be viewed as the potential to replace Kennecott management.

Many of those Chileans who watched from the inside the efficiency of North American management, the necessity of maintaining labor productivity, the risk of engineering an

143

expansion program and bringing new production on-line, the complexities of assuring long-term foreign sales, or the trust and dependability needed to arrange international finance doubtless felt that the foreigners' presence was a valuable asset, at least in the short run. But those Chileans who had a modest view of their own growing competence and those who had an enthusiastic view of the obvious national successes were not always the same people. Members of the Congress and the press who could observe only the phenomenal results of the new Chilean-dictated pricing policy, or the rapid completion of the expansion program, or the maintaining of efficiency as Chileans took over more and more supervisory roles argued that the foreign presence was contributing less and less while the benefits from replacing the foreigner in the copper industry were growing more and more.[31]

This might be the rare historical moment, many argued, when, through an act of national will, the country could end its condition of *dependencia* forever.

VII

The 1969 attack on Anaconda began from within the Christian Democratic Party. In April, Congressional Dep-

---

[31] A representative popular view on Chilean capabilities can be found in *Clarín*, March 25, 1970, in an editorial by "Castor" entitled "Tenemos que nacionalizar el cobre".

Panorama Económico, however, was more cautious in appraising likely Chilean administrative behavior after the foreign copper companies were nationalized. The editors were afraid that the industry would be run "politically" rather than "purely commercially" (No. 246, July 1969).

Contributing to the general mood of domestic optimism, however, Chileans could point at the same time to the competence of other state-run enterprises outside of the mining area. Senator Rafael Tarud, for example, cited the State Development Agency (CORFO), the State Electricity Administration (ENDENSA), the State Steel Enterprise (CAP), the State Telephone and Telegraph Agency (ENTEL), the State Petroleum Company (ENAP), and the State Airlines (LANCHILE) as examples of excellent national administration, run by Chilean workers and managed by Chilean *técnicos*.

uty Narciso Irureta denounced mining claims that Anaconda had filed for 80,000 hectares (or an area significantly
larger than the state of Delaware) in the northern Chilean
desert.

This incident sparked a general "re-evaluation" of the
country's relations with the companies. The demands and
the scope of such a re-evaluation quickly spread. Other
members of the Christian Democratic Party, besides
Irureta, delighted by the success of the Chilean-imposed
pricing policy, wanted to use this uproar to impose a surtax
on copper profits in order to capture more of the benefits
for Chile. The switch to the LME price peg, combined with
the tax cuts provided in the Chileanization agreements,
meant that a large stream of the earnings generated by the
Chilean maneuver were flowing as profits to Anaconda and
Kennecott. In 1968 alone, for example, Kennecott had received after-tax profits from its 49% interest in El Teniente
equal to almost 40% of the (old) book value of all the company's investments in Chile.

What about the twenty-year guarantees of "inviolability"
that the Chilean Congress had given to the companies?
Rebus were no longer *stantibus*, argued the Chilean lawyers—conditions (at least of bargaining power) had
changed. Since the original agreements had been calculated
on the basis of 29¢ (per pound) copper and since Chilean
policy was responsible for the shift to a price near 90¢, Frei
argued that his administration was not "violating" the
twenty-year guarantees by imposing a surtax. What choice
did the companies have? They had sunk their investment.
Output was expanding even more rapidly than expected.
The program was a success for everybody, but Chilean
public opinion insisted that the fruits should be enjoyed
more fully by the host country.

Neither Anaconda nor Kennecott protested too strenu-
ously, as a matter of fact, against the reasoning of the Frei
administration on the surtax.[32] For years prior to the invest-

[32] Against Congressman Narciso Irureta, Anaconda defended its new
claim on between two and three thousand square miles in northern

ment Kennecott had attached transcendent importance to the twenty-year government guarantee. But now that the investment was largely sunk and the operations were a roaring success, Kennecott and Anaconda rapidly consented to pay the surtax.

But in this round of "readjustment" the foreign copper companies were once again dominating the headlines. Conservative and Liberal Party leaders, in the midst of a bitterly contested Agrarian Reform, were under heavy constituent pressure not to support the US investors. Some groups within the Christian Democratic Party were joining the Communists and the Socialists and the Radicals in declaring that now was the time for nationalization. Chilean production was up, the Chilean share of the world market was up, copper prices were high, and Chileans could run the mines on their own!

When Frei demanded that negotiations be reopened with Anaconda, he actually pressed only for Chileanization, or 51% Chilean control with compensation, similar to the arrangement with Kennecott. But Anaconda did not want to make a new bargain after it had just completed a large corporate commitment. It refused to submit to Chileanization. It was afraid that this process of pushing and giving would just go on until it was expropriated. So it asked to be nationalized with compensation. The agreements were announced on June 26, 1969.

Frei called the nationalization of Anaconda Chile's Second Independence. Alejandro Hales, the Minister of Mines who had worked out the arrangements for nationalization, wept in public, saying that he had fulfilled a lifelong dream.

Chile with equanimity in public, but admitted in private that the move had been a "mistake in public relations".

Anaconda argued that the company had laid claim to the vast salt flats in the north to try to organize a joint chemical venture with Dow Chemical. Chileans suspected, however, that the claims were staked out to prevent other miners from moving into the area.

Workers were found who gave up their salaries and peasants their produce to help pay the compensation for Anaconda.[33]

But it was clear that the Final Battle was yet to be won.

VIII

Shortly after taking office in 1970, the new marxist President, Dr. Salvador Allende, introduced the long-awaited bill for complete nationalization as a final solution to the problem of *dependencia*. It provided for an immediate take-over of all the Chilean subsidiaries of Anaconda, Kennecott, and Cerro with compensation to be paid over a thirty-year period—compensation that was more than offset for the first two companies by a deduction for the "excessive profits" that had been earned since the beginning of the *Nuevo Trato* in 1955.

The nationalization legislation was passed unanimously as a Constitutional Amendment by the Congress on July 16, 1971.

As for Kennecott's strategy of self-protection, pressures on the Allende government to assume the international obligations of the El Teniente joint venture did come from all the directions that the company had mapped out in advance.[34] The customers who had bought long-term con-

[33] Cf. *Tercera de la Hora*, July 1, 1969. The self-conscious attempt to show grass-roots sacrifice for the nationalization of Anaconda, reminiscent of the nationalization of US petroleum companies by Cárdenas in Mexico, was not very successful.

[34] Cf. "Chile's Threatened US Property Seizure May Drain Federal Insurance Unit's Funds," *New York Times*, February 2, 1971; "Chile's Move Spurs US to 'Get Tough'", *ibid.*, September 30, 1971; "Chile Assailed by Rogers for Compensation Stand," *ibid.*, October 14, 1971; "Six Concerns Embroiled in Seizures Are Called in by Rogers," *Wall Street Journal*, October 25, 1971; "US Tells Chile Seizures Could Endanger Aid to Needy Nations," *New York Times*, October 16, 1971; "Chile to Nationalize Foreign-Owned Firms Legally, Allende Says", *Wall Street Journal*, October 30, 1971; "Chile, Reserves Low,

tracts for Chilean copper in Europe and Japan and the international financial institutions that had lent money to El Teniente on the basis of those contracts were putting pressure, through their governments, on the Group of Ten in Paris to make assumption of the old obligations a condition for refunding the Chilean debt. The US government, under pressure from Anaconda and Kennecott and from Congressional supporters of the Ex-Im Bank and the Overseas Private Investment Corporation (which had taken over the AID foreign investment insurance program), was pushing to make immediate compensation a requirement for rolling over the Chilean debt. Kennecott, on its own, was using the unconditional guarantees that the Chilean government had given for the original sale amount to obtain writs of attachment in the US Federal Courts against all Chilean property in the State of New York, including the jets of LANCHILE when they landed.

In response to this accumulation of pressures, President Allende announced in October 1971 that his government would directly assume the international obligations of the nationalized El Teniente company. It would honor the long-term sales contracts with customers in Europe and Japan. And it would take over the debts that the nationalized company had contracted with the Ex-Im Bank of Washington, with the Banca Comerciale Italiana, and with Mitsui & Co. Payment to the latter two creditors would clearly depend upon faithful fulfillment of the original long-term production contracts with customers in Europe and Asia. But the Allende government simply ignored the Kennecott management provision contained in the contracts, and pledged to supply the output itself.

Finally, four months later, in February 1972, Dr. Allende

Will Seek Renegotiation of Payments on Her $3-Billion Foreign Debt," *New York Times*, November 10, 1971.

I have also benefitted from interviews with representatives of the US copper companies and of the Chilean government.

went all the way and announced that his government would pay compensation to Kennecott equal to the sale amount that had been unconditionally guaranteed by the Chilean state. Despite the pledge of the Socialists of "Ni un centavo!" in compensation, Kennecott was to receive $80 million plus interest from the Allende administration.[35]

Thus, the Allende government successfully unraveled most of the transnational web spun by Kennecott.[36]

With payment pledged to cover the Chilean state guarantee to Kennecott, the company was obliged to drop the writs of attachment levied against Chilean property in New York. This pledge of payment to Kennecott also removed the threat of bankrupting the new Overseas Private Investment Corporation with a huge claim. With OPIC safe and

[35] "Chile Says She Will Pay $84 Million to Kennecott," *New York Times,* February 26, 1972. After several payments, the Allende government before its overthrow in 1973 again suspended payments.

For a commentary on the legal position of the Allende administration, see Eduardo Novoa Monreal, *La batalla por el cobre* (Santiago: Quimantu, 1972).

[36] Kennecott claimed that, in addition to the $80 million in debt, it had an uncompensated equity holding in El Teniente valued at approximately $178 million. ("Memorandum Governing International Law Principles" by Covington & Burling, *Expropriation of El Teniente,* New York: Kennecott Public Relations Department, 1971.) On this basis it sued in various European countries to block payments for Chilean copper from final customers. The Chilean tribunal had ruled that Kennecott was entitled to compensation for the book value of its equity interest, but that reductions for excess profits and deficiencies more than offset any compensation.

To side with Kennecott's suit for the commercial value of its equity in a nationalized mine, courts in France or Germany or Italy would have had to overrule the Chilean determination of excess profits, overrule the claim of deficiencies in installations, and (perhaps) overrule the claim in Spanish law that private corporations do not gain possession of unmined reserves through a concession agreement that grants only rights of exploitation.

A more important impact of the threat of legal action against customers is the pressure it puts on consumers to choose that country only as supplier of last resort. For more on this matter, see Chapter 7.

the Ex-Im Bank being repaid by Chile, Congressional interest dissipated.

Kennecott's strategy had, however, enabled the company to expand very profitably in the late 1960's with no new risk to itself and leave, after the nationalization in 1971, with compensation greater than the net worth of its holdings had been in 1964—despite the occurrence of the worst eventuality the company had envisioned.[37] From 1964 to 1970 Kennecott had received approximately $115 million in profits from Chile on an investment with an initial net worth of $69 million, and had left with what appeared to be at least $93 million in compensation ($80 million plus interest).

Anaconda, in contrast, which had not spread its risk or protected itself through a strategy of building transnational alliances, lost its old holdings, lost the new capital it had committed during the Frei regime, and was nationalized in 1971 without any hope of compensation. The company had applied for partial coverage on its new investments during the Frei period through a stand-by arrangement with AID. But after Anaconda was finally pressured into selling 51% of its Chilean operations to the Frei government in 1969, this insurance was apparently allowed to lapse.[38] The notes in payment for the sale of the majority interest in 1969 were not made unconditional obligations of the Chilean state but guaranteed only by the Corporación de Fomento (Corfo) and the Corporación del Cobre (Codelco), two subagencies of the Chilean government.

Despite Anaconda's huge losses, the Hickenlooper Amendment was not applied. That unhappy company, with writs of attachment that could only harass the activities of

---

[37] On the spread of transnational strategies similar to Kennecott's through the natural resource field, see my article, "Transnational Strategies of Protection and Defense by Multinational Corporations: Spreading the Risk and Raising the Cost for Nationalization in Natural Resources," *International Organization*, Vol. 27, No. 2 (Spring 1973).

[38] Overseas Private Investment Corporation, *Annual Report*, 1971, p. 34; and "U.S. Foreign-Investment Insurer Seeks Profit Rise, Takes Tough Line on Anaconda", *New York Times*, December 6, 1971.

Corfo and Codelco, with a disputed claim to any US government insurance, and with long-term contracts and debts made in its own name, had few options for mobilizing either national or international support. Payments for the nationalized properties of Anaconda were cut off under Allende and the company received no promise of compensation. The only reasonable course for Anaconda's board of directors—which it took—was to fire the entire top management and hire a new set of executive officers who could do their best to forget about Chile.

With regard to Cerro, Chile negotiated an amicable arrangement to buy the Andina subsidiary at approximately book value and Cerro helped the state finish bringing the mine successfully on-line.

Once Chile had assumed the contracts and debts owned in Europe and Asia, the private and public creditors in those regions faced a choice similar to that of accepting the shaky promise of an on-going concern or of trying to preside over a bankruptcy. The European and Asian customers whose long-term contracts for Chilean copper had been sold to raise capital for Chile were given a pledge of preferential delivery. The financial institutions in Italy and Japan that had bought those contracts and supplied the Chilean joint venture with investment capital were pledged payment. The Allende offer of settlement made the hope of stable production in a stable Chile the least risky alternative for the Europeans and Asians. The Nixon administration did continue to fight in Paris for the principle of full payment for expropriations as a condition of refunding the Chilean debt, but the Group of Ten refused to go along.[39] Chile's

[39] Cf. "Debt-ridden Chile Is Reported to Get Soviet Offer of $50-million in Credits", *New York Times*, January 16, 1972; "Nixon Announces a Tough US Stand on Expropriation", *ibid.*, January 20, 1972; "Chile, $3-Billion in Debt, Asks Creditors to Accept a Moratorium on Payments", *ibid.*, January 20, 1972; "Plea by Chile to Delay Debt Payment Is Slated for Discussion in Paris", *Wall Street Journal* January 26, 1972; "Allende Confers with Foreign Officials on Debts",

major public creditors were not anxious to see that country's dwindling foreign exchange reserves flow with priority to Anaconda and Kennecott. The United States had to acquiesce in a credit agreement that did not mention the principle of full compensation for expropriated properties. The country had at last, irreversibly, taken complete control of its domestic copper industry.

There would be no more "inherent conflict" between the powerful foreign corporations acting according to their own "narrow" corporate strategies and the Chilean government wanting to act according to the "broader" dictates of national development.

Within the horizon of its perception of foreign investor–host country conflict, Chile had at last pulled itself out of a condition that had plagued the nation for more than a century.

Dependencia would be replaced by *independencia*.

New York Times, April 15, 1972; "US Joins in Credit Accord with Chile", *ibid.*, April 21, 1972.

The Nixon Administration, however, continued to oppose loans for Chile from the World Bank, the Inter-American Development Bank, and the Export-Import Bank. See James Petras and Robert LaPorte, "Can We Do Business with Radical Nationalists?—Chile: No", *Foreign Policy*, No. 7 (Summer 1972); and *idem*, "An Exchange on Chile," *Foreign Policy*, No. 8 (Fall 1972).

Chile successfully negotiated a rescheduling of 1971–1972 maturities with the Group of Ten in Paris, but went into default again in 1973. Immediately after the coup, the Group allowed the junta a moratorium until 1974. "Chilean Debt Talks Put Off by Creditors," *Washington Post*, October 3, 1973.

CHAPTER 6

A Model of the Relations Between the Host Country
and Foreign Investors: Balance of Power, National
Interest, and Economic Nationalism

For twenty-five years after the end of the Second World
War Chile mounted a drive, never long abated, to close in
on and ultimately to take over the large foreign copper
companies whose operations played such a central role in
the development of the national economy. When President
Eduardo Frei began the nationalization of Anaconda, he
exclaimed: "This is the greatest battle that Chile has ever
won. . . . A Second Independence!" When President Salvador Allende finished the nationalization of Anaconda,
Kennecott, and Cerro, he affirmed: "The recovery of Basic
Resources is a sovereign decision reflecting the feelings of
all Chilean people . . . [an] indispensable requirement imposed by the economic development and the social processes of the country." A high Kennecott official in Santiago
reflected: "Nationalization was inevitable. It was only a
question of time!" One of Anaconda's chief counsels, using
legal terminology, remarked, "We used to be the fuckor.
Now we're the fuckee!"

How should one begin to understand the dynamics of
economic nationalism or analyze the course of the movement away from *dependencia*? Unless one considers the
push of economic nationalism in Chile to be the result of
sporadic emotions and random waves of anti-foreign feeling, a satisfactory analysis demands some attempt to relate
in a systematic way the interests, feelings, and visions of
major Chilean groups to the course of relations with the foreign copper companies.

Various hypotheses have been advanced, within Chile as
elsewhere, to explain the relations between foreign and do-

mestic groups in terms of "neo-colonialism", "center-periphery domination", or "the consolidation of underdevelopment". Such theories predict that the Chilean experience could never have taken place. None of them can account for the slow but cumulative shift in the balance of power during twenty-five years, away from the foreign copper companies and toward the host country. Over the long term, the national interest in development and the national concern for sovereignty propelled successive administrations to close in on the foreign-dominated industry and bring it under ever tighter control.

Other attempts have been made, in academic and business circles, to characterize foreign investor–host country relations in terms of "joint maximization", "mutual advantage", "fundamental harmony of interests". Theories built on such characterizations are static; they ignore the exercise of power and tend to confuse the postponement of conflict with its dissipation.

This chapter will place the Chilean experience with copper within the framework of a more satisfactory model of the evolution of the balance of power between foreign companies and underdeveloped countries.[1] The model developed here accounts for the instability of concession agreements as a function of abrupt shifts in risk and uncertainty, and explains the cumulative transfer of power away from the foreign corporations as resulting from the host country's moving up a learning curve of negotiating, operating, and supervisory skills.

Once the framework for the evolution of the balance of power between the host country and foreign investors has been sketched, we must examine how actual policy toward

---

[1] The model will first be developed in terms of large natural-resource investments where substantial lump-sum commitments must be sunk under conditions of great uncertainty. Modifications of the model to cover other industries, where there are more continuous and incremental changes, will be discussed later in the chapter.

the foreign companies is determined. To accomplish this, it is necessary to discard the state-centric abstraction called the "host country" and to look at policy as the outcome of the interplay of domestic groups trying to maximize their own particular interests as well as the larger national interest.[2] Such an analysis will explain the actual course of the relations with the foreign companies. But without the general framework against which to measure the actual policy, it would be impossible to judge, however roughly, the extent to which actual policy approximates the potential to pursue the national interest. As will be seen, this is not a search for a unique "best" policy against which actual host-country behavior can be measured. Rather, the balance of power framework is intended to help the analyst recreate the array of options open to policy-makers within the horizon of domestic knowledge and experience available at each stage of relations with the foreign investors, and to measure domestic performance against those options.

The use of the balance of power model developed here provides a better explanatory approach to analyzing the politics of economic nationalism than do the paradigms of "reactionary alliances" or "mutual advantage". It suggests an alternative definition of international exploitation—namely, a policy outcome in which the national interest is clearly not being pursued because domestic actors crucial to the decision-making process are using payoffs to foreign investors to advance their own private good at the public

[2] For other attempts to move beyond the state-as-unitary-actor approach to analyzing public policy formation, see Graham Allison, *Essence of Decision* (New York: Little, Brown, 1971); Morton Halperin, *Bureaucratic Politics and National Security Policy* (Washington, D.C.: Brookings Institution, 1974); Stephen Krasner, "Are Bureaucracies Important?" *Foreign Policy*, No. 7 (Summer 1972); Jessica Einhorn, "Effects of Bureaucratic Politics on the Expropriation Policy of the Nixon Administration: Two Case Studies, 1969–1972" (unpublished Ph.D. dissertation, Department of Politics, Princeton University, 1973).

expense. Such an outcome can be tested for and measured.[3] Despite clear instances of exploitation in the Chilean case, however, the balance of power model accurately predicts that the domestic perception of the costs of economic nationalism will decline over time—even among those most ideologically allied with the foreign corporations. In addition, it indicates that the sense of injustice in the host country is likely to be more acute in the case of large natural resource concessions[4] than in other types of agreements, and

[3] Preliminary suggestions on behalf of this definition of "exploitation" were developed by Edith Penrose, "Profit Sharing Between Producing Countries and Oil Companies in the Middle East", *Economic Journal*, June 1958, and *New Orientations: Essays in International Relations* (New York: Humanities Press, 1970).

For a further elaboration of how to identify and measure "exploitation," see my paper, "A Model of National Interest, Balance of Power, and International Exploitation in Large Natural Resource Investments", in James Kurth and Stephen Rosen, eds., *Testing the Theory of Economic Imperialism* (New York: Heath, 1974).

Exploitation by this definition, then, does not exist without "complicity" on the part of domestic elites. Exploitation may include specific pressures or bribes from foreign groups, but it need not. This model explicitly does not identify asymmetry of power *per se* between host countries and foreign investors as a basis for "exploitation", but rather only the refusal of domestic elites to act in the national interest to the extent that they have the power to do so. As will be seen, the history of the evolution of large natural-resource concession agreements suggests that there are abrupt shifts in the relative balance of power between host countries and foreign companies, and that both can take advantage of the asymmetries of power. This model assumes that it is in the national interest to attempt to maximize public benefits, direct and indirect, from the foreign-dominated primary export sector. Finally, this definition of exploitation does not yield a unique value when the cost of the exploitation is measured. Rather, exploitation can be shown to have a range of more and less probable values, depending on the options forgone to satisfy private domestic interests.

[4] The generic term "natural resource concessions" has been used throughout this work even though many countries call the agreements by some other name. Chile, in fact, does not use the term "concession agreements" for mining. What is meant is that there is a special category of activity associated with the primary export sector, not

that there is an objective basis for this sense of injustice. Furthermore, the balance of power model developed in this chapter suggests that there is in fact a rational pattern of technology transfer, learning, and interest articulation beneath the apparent "waves" and "emotions" of economic nationalism.

Finally, this chapter combines the dynamic balance of power model with the analysis of actual policy formation to develop the beginnings of general theory of foreign investor–host country relations—that is, to specify what kinds of variables must be measured, in any particular case, to predict the extent of conflict or cooperation.

I

The most familiar frameworks for analyzing foreign investor–host country relations rely on game theory and bargaining models (especially the bilateral monopoly model).[5] The foreign investor has the skills, experience, access to markets, and finance that the country needs to develop its resource base. The country has the ore-bodies, the labor force, and the control over taxation that can be mixed in some proportion to produce an attractive opportunity to the investor. Unless the host government loves foreign in-

---

covered under the laws of general application in the country—a special tax regime, a special import arrangement, a special juridical category for "subsoil rights", frequently a special foreign exchange arrangement, and a special regulatory agency—corresponding to the "privileged" status that the sector occupies in the life of the host country.

[5] Cf. George Stigler, *The Theory of Price* (New York: Macmillan, 1961); Thomas Schelling, *The Strategy of Conflict* (London: Oxford University Press, 1963); Charles Kindleberger, *Economic Development* (New York: McGraw-Hill, 1965), and *American Business Abroad* (New Haven: Yale University Press, 1969); Raymond Mikesell, ed., *Foreign Investment in the Petroleum and Mineral Industries: Case Studies in Investor–Host Country Relations* (Baltimore: Johns Hopkins Press, 1971).

vestors no matter how they behave, on the one hand, or is anxious to keep foreigners out no matter what the cost, on the other, then the terms under which a foreign investor will be allowed to enter the country and operate there constitute a problem in joint-maximization.

As both the foreign investor and the host government try to increase their returns from the industry, each side has threats to make and benefits to offer. The struggle centers on the relative distribution of revenues that are being generated or that potentially could be generated in the industry. This is not a zero-sum game, since the absolute level of returns is a function of the relative shares. Some kinds of collaborative strategies can increase the size of the pie to be divided and increase the absolute returns to all parties. The host government must weigh the benefits of demanding a larger share of the existing revenue against the prospect of a larger absolute amount (but a smaller share) of revenue if the investor can be induced to expand operations. The foreign investor must weigh his prospects for further profits on the original investment against the chance for larger profits on expanded operations.

This kind of explicit bargaining characterized relations between the large US copper companies and the Chilean government, as it does large natural resource concessions elsewhere, each time major new corporate commitments were sought—just after the Second World War, with the passage of the *Nuevo Trato* in 1955, and at the time of Chileanization beginning in 1964. In each instance, major concessions demanded by the foreign companies were promised by Chile in return for the companies' expanding or maintaining operations at a certain level.

The bargaining models or game theory approach do indicate that some sort of negotiating process is going on, but they are not dynamic enough to show underlying trends or cycles in bargaining strength. For a preliminary approach to understanding the fundamental trends or cycles in the bargaining relations between foreign investors and host governments, one must add considerations about the role of uncertainty.[6]

The foreign investor starts from a position of monopoly control over the capacity to create a working operation out of a potential ore-body—a monopoly control that only a few alternative competitors could supply at a broadly similar price. There is always a great deal of uncertainty about whether the investment can be made into a success and what the final costs of production and operation will be. The government would like to see its natural resource potential become a source of revenue and employment, but the government cannot itself supply the services needed from the foreign investor and is even less qualified than the investor to evaluate the risk and uncertainty involved.

The conditions under which a foreign company will agree to invest must initially reflect both his monopoly control of skills and his heavy discounting for risk and uncertainty. The host government may want to get as much as possible from the new venture. But the strength of the bargaining is on the side of the foreign investor, and the terms of the initial concession are going to be heavily weighted in his favor.[7]

---

[6] Studies that incorporate the role of uncertainty in the evolution of bargaining relations include: Raymond Vernon, "Long-Run Trends in Concession Contracts", *Proceedings of the American Society for International Law* (April 1967), pp. 81–90, and *Sovereignty at Bay* (New York: Basic Books, 1971); Louis T. Wells, "The Evolution of Concession Agreements in Developing Countries", Harvard Development Advisory Service, March 29, 1971; and T. H. Moran, "The Evolution of Concession Agreements in Underdeveloped Countries and the U.S. National Interest", U.S. Senate Foreign Relations subcommittee on multinational corporations (testimony and report), Washington, D.C., July 1973.

[7] Extreme disparity in bargaining power will exist at the initiation of any concession agreement, independent of the character of the bargainers. No matter how "nice" an investor the foreign company is, the board of directors would probably consider themselves irresponsible to commit a large sum of money with such great uncertainty unless they anticipated that the payoff would be big. Thus, writers who argue

159

If an investment is made and the operation is not a success, other ventures will require the same or greater enticements.

But once an investment is made and the operation is a success, the whole atmosphere that surrounds the foreign–host relationship changes. The old doubts are forgotten, and the terms of the concession no longer correspond to the "realities" of the situation. A gamble with large risks has been won, and the host government is unlikely to want to keep paying premiums that reflect those risks for long. In the natural resource field, uncertain investments are frequently turned into bonanzas, and the distribution of benefits from such ventures invariably has the appearance, in retrospect, of the strong (company) cheating the weak (country). In a certain sense, this is true—since concession agreements are always written in terms very favorable to the foreigner—but it need not remain true for long. If a perception of injustice is not felt after a time by the government that originally negotiated the agreement, it can easily be created by the opponents of that government. And with the investment sunk and successful, the host country is in a position to bring pressure for renegotiation. In the perception of the foreign companies, the host country (now strong) can begin to cheat them (now weak).

At the same time that the first mines are successfully opened, uncertainty about the existence of ore-bodies and about the structure of production costs has been reduced

---

that behavior as a "good corporate citizen" can alleviate the tension generated by the investment process would have a very weak case with respect to large natural-resource concession agreements. "Good corporate citizens" are not relieved of the problem of discounting for risk. Similarly, the character of the host government—whether composed of fierce nationalists or of weak bribe-takers—will not alter the fact that the company is in a position to demand generous treatment.

The need for the company to commit substantial funds at great risk, and thus to take full advantage of the initially large asymmetries of power, means that the subsequent host-country perception of injustice may be greater than in other types of foreign investments.

for subsequent investors. The government can drive a tougher bargain with later entrants, and this in turn increases the leverage in demanding revision of the original concessions to put them in line with the later agreements.[8]

In short, with the reduction of uncertainty the bargaining strength inevitably shifts from the foreigners toward the host government. The latter finds itself with the power to force "renegotiations", "adjustments", "surtaxes", "back-taxes", "recomputations", to reflect this shift in the balance of power.

Empirically, since the end of the Second World War, few successful concession agreements in developing countries— in ferrous and non-ferrous metals, petroleum, sulphur, and natural gas—have remained long unaltered.[9]

In mining and drilling industries where investment for new production or processing facilities must come in large discrete lumps, the shifts in bargaining power are repeated before and after each new major corporate commitment. Before the investment for new production capacity, a new smelter, or a new refinery, the relative weight of bargaining

[8] In oligopolies that invest in close follow-the-leader patterns as an insurance policy against risk of losing their share of the market, the leverage is very great indeed.

[9] For case studies in these industries, see Edith Penrose, *The Large International Firm in Developing Countries* (London: Allen & Unwin, 1969); Michael Tanzer, *The Political Economy of International Oil* (Boston: Beacon Press, 1969); Mikesell, ed., *Foreign Investment in the Petroleum and Mineral Industries*; Harvey O'Connor, *The Empire of Oil* (New York: Monthly Review Press, 1955) and *World Crisis in Oil* (New York: Monthly Review Press, 1962); E. Lieuwen, *Petroleum in Venezuela: A History* (Berkeley: University of California Press, 1954) and *Venezuela* (London: Oxford University Press, 1965); Robert I. Rhodes, ed., *Imperialism and Underdevelopment: A Reader* (New York: Monthly Review Press, 1970); Miguel Wionczek, *El nacionalismo mexicano y la inversión extranjera* (Mexico City: Siglo veintiuno editores, 1967); Vernon, *Sovereignty at Bay*; Louis T. Wells, "The Evolution of Concession Agreements in Developing Countries"; Zuhayr Mikdashi, *Business and Government in the Extractive Industries* (forthcoming, 1974); Marvin D. Bernstein, *The Mexican Mining Industry, 1890–1950* (Albany, N.Y.: SUNY Albany, 1965).

strength tilts in favor of the foreign investor; after the operation is successful, it begins to tilt back toward the host country.

A schematic representation of this changing balance of power between foreign investors and the host government would look like Diagram I.

Diagram I

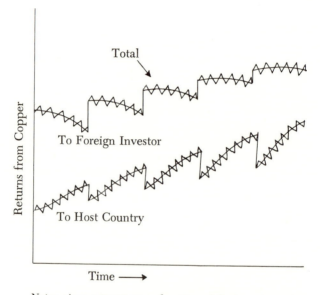

Note: since returns are a function of final market prices, the curves will not be smooth.

II

A model of the balance of power between the host country and foreign natural-resource investors would be incomplete, however, if uncertainty were the only independent variable. The experience of most Third World nations with rich endowments of raw materials requires introducing the idea of a host-country learning curve.[10]

A country that has no history of large natural-resource concessions begins in all likelihood, with a very inexact knowledge of the extent of its mineral or petroleum wealth, and has very little independent capacity to check the feasibility studies or exploration reports presented by foreign investors (or even by foreign consultants). There has been no occasion to build up a bureaucracy informed about standard business practices in a particular industry, or familiar with the terms of concessions in other countries.[11] In many cases a host government may not be experienced enough in handling transnational corporate accounting (transfer prices or intersubsidiary financing) or international tax provisions to make the negotiation process very meaningful. In much of the Third World before the Second World War—even in regions not formally colonized—initial investments in resource extraction were undertaken with only the most primitive attempts at bargaining. When the international oil companies first approached General Vicente Gomez of Venezuela or King Ibn Saud of Saudi

[10] There is also a process of corporate "learning", which was represented in Diagram I by suggesting that resource availability and production costs become clearer to the foreign company over time. One may also hypothesize a long-term corporate learning curve with regard to the social and political environment offered by the host country. Such a concept was introduced in Chapter 5 in the analysis of the contrasting copper-company perceptions of domestic vulnerability in Chile.

For evidence of a host-country learning curve from the petroleum, copper, tin, iron ore, bauxite, and sulphur industries, see the sources listed in footnote 9.

[11] Even today it is extraordinarily difficult (but *not* impossible) to obtain the details of concession agreements across many countries. The repeated suggestions of UN or World Bank members to set up a central reference service have never borne fruit. Yet, as argued here and in Chapter 8, such a reference service could have an enormous benefit for host countries.

Arabia, they were invited to draft their own petroleum legislation. In Chile, as Chapter 3 pointed out, Anaconda and Kennecott were rewarded for their risks in the Atacama Desert or Andes mountains in the early twentieth century with concessions that entailed almost no taxes or other obligations. Early international investments in tin, bauxite, zinc, and iron ore were made under much the same conditions. The possibility of earning foreign revenues from unknown mineral deposits was considered a windfall, and primitive forms of tax collection—frequently royalty payments—were the reward collected by governments ill-equipped to judge adequately how far they could push against the companies.[12]

Successful ventures, however, provide an incentive for the host country to develop skills and expertise appropriate to the industry. Beginning with elementary attempts to tighten the bargaining process, the country starts to move up a learning curve that leads from monitoring industry behavior to replicating complicated corporate functions.

The incentive to chip away at the foreigner's monopoly on skills and expertise is magnified as demands for a larger share of the revenues grow and as claims on those revenues multiply. When the oil companies first established themselves in the Middle East or the mining companies in Africa and Latin America, the fiscal needs of the host governments were little more than the personal expenses of their followers and the patronage of their political clientele. But as the Second World War and de-colonization brought social mobilization, urbanization, and import-substituting industrialization to these regions, the idea of playing the game of joint maximization more aggressively with the foreign

---

[12] Royalties (or excise taxes) in oil-exporting countries now, however, play a special role in oligopoly discipline. See M. A. Adelman, *The World Petroleum Market* (Baltimore: Johns Hopkins Press, 1972); and Penrose, *The Large International Firm in Developing Countries.*

companies began to become a crucial political issue. In Chile, the first readjustments of the original mining agreements were slow and cautious. With massive social requirements for additional revenues, however, the need to search for means to maximize the returns from the mining sector became built into the structure of domestic political and economic group interests. Relations with the foreign copper companies began to take on the character of more explicit confrontation and negotiation, with a national resolve to build up bargaining capacity. As Chile, like other host countries, chipped away at ignorance and mystery, the esoteric value of the foreigners' services declined. The swings in the balance of power became more sharply defined, and shorter. And there was a cumulative shift in relative strength toward the host country.

Even those governments most effectively manipulated by the foreign companies have not been immune to such pressures, and did not hesitate to respond to them when the balance of power was favorable. After Mossadeq nationalized the Anglo-Iranian Oil Company in 1951 to finance the First Iranian Development Plan, he was overthrown. But state revenues from the petroleum sector have not stopped rising, nor have domestic pressures allowed them even to remain level, for any two-year period since the subsequent agreements with the Iranian Oil Consortium were negotiated in 1954. The profit split between Iran and the Consortium climbed from 68%–32% in 1954 to about 80%–20% by 1970. In Venezuela, even the dictator (General) Pérez Jiménez, who overthrew the more "nationalistic" Rómulo Betancourt in 1950 with the promise of helping the foreign oil companies, found that he needed ever more revenues to finance urban construction and industrial growth. He provoked a crisis in the international industry in 1956 by withcalling options held by the established producers and auctioning off large concessions to new companies more willing than the old ones to expand output. Successor governments

165

in Venezuela pushed the host-country share of petroleum revenues above 70% in the 1960's with a national commitment to "sow the petroleum" for development.[13]

The value of incremental revenues to sustain growth and/or to dissipate social tensions in countries that are undergoing rapid development and social mobilization is too high, and the political temptation too great, to allow foreign companies undisturbed collection of their monopoly rents. For a country where additional foreign exchange revenues can boost the economic growth rate to 10% per year, the true social return on the increment available for investment is above 20%, while a postponement of that increment for five years reduces its value by half. For a country (with a high or a low economic growth rate) where there is a threat that stagnation may bring social turmoil—or merely electoral displeasure—political elites must make a calculation even more heavily weighted toward developing skills in the present. In short, the development process magnifies the benefits that can be gained by improving the ability to push against foreign companies, and magnifies the costs that will be borne by leaders unable or unwilling to push.

This produces a powerful stimulus to strengthen domestic capabilities and reduce domestic weaknesses. As knowledge about industry operations is accumulated—as secrecy is dispelled and domestic confidence is gained—the monopoly position of the foreigner, even in his peaks of strength, is eroded.[14] The result is a cumulative shift in power away from the international corporations toward the host country.

Consequently, as the host country moves up a learning curve of bargaining skills and operating experience, its re-

[13] Cf. Penrose, *op.cit.*; Mikesell, ed., *Foreign Investment in the Petroleum and Mineral Industries*; O'Connor, *World Crisis in Oil*; Lieuwin, *Petroleum in Venezuela: A History* and *Venezuela*.

[14] In most natural resource industries the increase in domestic skills has coincided, since the end of the Second World War, with greater opportunities to hire independent consultants and technicians to strengthen the host-country side.

lations with foreign investors in the industry do not merely swing back and forth. Rather, the balance of power looks more like the schematic representation in Diagram II.

Diagram II

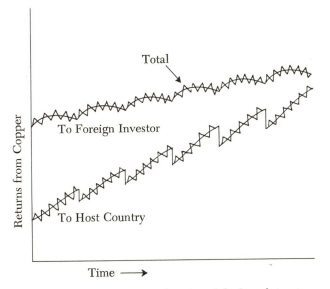

Note: since returns are a function of final market prices, the curves will not be smooth.

At the extreme end of the curve, the country may acquire skills sufficient to operate the industry directly. As the host develops this ability to imitate or duplicate the functions of the foreigner, the cost of nationalism rapidly diminishes. What was only the rhetorical dream of "recovering control of the natural wealth" and "restoring sovereignty over national development" comes at last within reach.

The tendency to ignore short-run swings in the balance of power between foreign investors and the host country, as well as to overlook the long-run cumulative shift in the balance of power toward the host country, renders the conventional use of bargaining theory very misleading. It freezes the examination of host country–foreign investor relations at only those points where the foreign investor is in the strongest bargaining position—namely, where large, explicit, new commitments are made and formal bargains are struck. But the instances where host governments give full and formal consent to the terms of a new bargain occur precisely at the points where the country is yielding of necessity to terms of an adversary at his strongest—just as the instances of "readjustment" in between formal agreements, and the cumulative tightening of all agreements, reflect a process in which foreign investors have to yield of necessity to terms of an adversary gaining strength.

The static bargaining framework offers an implicit standard of rationality to the joint-maximizer: "Choose the best alternative available to you when you negotiate, and be satisfied that you have acted rationally". But a choice that was rational at a time of extreme weakness is not likely to seem satisfying at a time of great strength. Within the conventional joint-maximizing framework, only the foreign corporations are portrayed as acting "rationally" (and "morally"[15]) with proper respect for sanctity of contract, while host countries suffer from "spurts" or "waves" of economic nationalism in which they act emotionally and irrationally—i.e., they break contracts. Foreign investor-host country relations appear as a series of calm consensual

---

[15] To the static tendencies of most bargaining models are frequently added, without justification, the implicit moral assumptions of contract theory: once a bargain is struck, it must be honored because it represents a contract between freely consenting individuals. This subjects the use of bargaining models to the same criticism that has traditionally been leveled against contract theory—that it overlooks inequalities of power at the moment of making the bargain (as long as one of the parties has not been put under explicit physical duress by the other), and refuses to recognize subsequent changes in the balance of power as justification for invalidation or renegotiation of the original contract.

agreements marred by outbursts of emotional and "irresponsible" behavior on the part of the host country between agreements.

In fact, joint maximization is a process of on-going mutual adjustment in which foreign investors act in accord with their own best interests when they are in the strongest position and accede to necessity when they are weak and exposed while host governments accede to necessity when they are weak and act in accord with their own best interests as they gain strength.

There is no mystery why foreign investors respect contracts that are inevitably written heavily in their favor. There should be no mystery why host governments may try to "readjust" contracts, when possible, in their own favor. The so-called bursts or waves of emotion and economic nationalism are no less "rational" ways of testing the strength of the country's bargaining position than the formal contract with the ritual 20–40–99-year guarantee of "inviolability" is a way of celebrating the foreign investors' moments of strength.

III

Even the most elaborate and dynamic model of the changing balance of power between foreign investors and a host government, however, will be useful only as a framework for analyzing the actual course of relations in any given historical situation and as a standard against which to measure actual host-country performance.

Copper policy has not been formed in Chile, or in any other country, by a single decision-maker called a "host country". Rather, policy has been the outcome of the struggle of diverse groups, of successive administrations and their adversaries, to maximize their own power, position, or wealth as well as to advance their own conceptions of the national interest through manipulation of copper policy.[16]

---

[16] For references to recent attempts to analyze the politics of policy formation, see footnote 2.

The schema in Diagram II represents an ideal sequence that relations with foreign investors would go through if a single actor, trying to maximize revenues by gathering all his skills and using all his relative bargaining power over time, were omnipotent in determining domestic copper policy. In fact, the actual distribution of returns to Chile, compared with the ideal schema, would look something like Diagram III.

What determines this actual distribution of returns in any particular historical situation? Why is one host government driven to push foreign investors as far as possible, while another is content to settle for a far smaller share of total revenues than it could get? That is to say, what accounts for deviations from how a host government would behave if it used its available strength in an attempt to maximize the direct or indirect benefits to the country from a foreign-controlled primary export sector, deviations that are clearly not attributable to ignorance or error?

To understand the course of relations between foreign investors and a host country in any specific case, it is finally necessary to discard the abstraction called "host country" or "host government" and look at the interplay of political and economic interests in the determination of domestic copper policy. How is opposition to a given agreement with foreign investors mobilized and through what groups does it spread? What creates a momentum to move in constantly on certain foreign investors and ultimately to take them over? What domestic or international alliances retard that momentum and protect those investors?

The remainder of this chapter will try to answer these questions for the Chilean case, and to test alternative explanations that account for foreign investor–host country relations in terms of "reactionary alliances" and "consolidation of underdevelopment". Then, drawing on the Chilean experience and using the balance of power model developed here, the chapter will conclude by attempting

Diagram III

RELATIVE DISTRIBUTION OF RETURNS

(Factoring out Independent Fluctuations in Price of Copper)

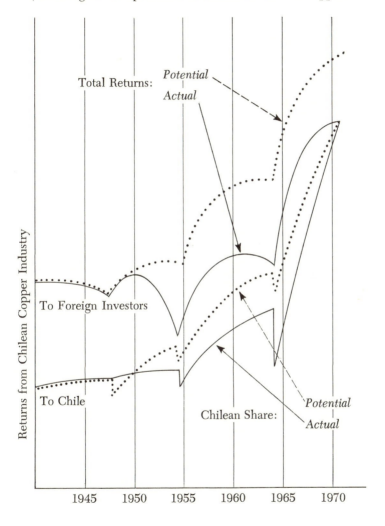

Returns from Chilean Copper Industry

Total Returns: *Potential*
Actual

To Foreign Investors

To Chile

Chilean Share: *Potential*
Actual

1945   1950   1955   1960   1965   1970

to lay the groundwork for a general theory of economic nationalism.

IV

There have been numerous hypotheses, both implicit and explicit, to explain the relations between domestic groups in Chile and the large foreign copper companies. They have a common theme: that the international economic system binds foreign investors, especially natural resource companies, and the domestic right, domestic conservatives, and domestic capitalists together. This alliance is based on a community of interest, on common economic and political needs. Each wants the presence of the other to ensure its own position against the left, which would mobilize the masses to challenge their privileges. Development within such a system only takes place along lines that permit the underdeveloped "periphery" to complement ever more perfectly the developed "center".

At the end of the Second World War this model fit.

The Chilean right identified its own interests and its vision of the national interest with close alliance to the foreign copper corporations and the US government.[17] The Chilean Conservative Party claimed, unembarrassedly, that intimate ties to North American business were the best defense of "Western Christian civilization". The Liberal Party defended the principles of free enterprise for both foreign

---

[17] For the views of the Chilean right, I have relied on *El Diario Ilustrado*, newspaper of the Conservative and Liberal Party viewpoint; on *El Mercurio*, newspaper of the center right; on *Industria*, the monthly journal of the National Society of Manufacturers; and on *Memoria*, the annual report of the Santiago Chamber of Commerce. There is also an important issue of the business-economic journal *Panorama Económico*, November 1949, devoted to the topic "The Attraction of Foreign Capital". For a general history of the attitudes of the parties of the right and center toward foreign investment, one should consult Rubén Cabezas Pares, *Pensamiento Económico de los Partidos Políticos Históricos Chilenos* (Santiago: Editorial Universitaria, 1964).

and domestic business and identified a common interest in creating an economy as open as possible.

The Chilean left was hostile to alliances with the international capitalist "monopolies" and their imperialistic governments.[18] The groups that composed the left argued that national consciousness had to be aroused to prevent Chile from being made into an economic and political "colony". Even where foreign capital and technology were considered indispensable, the Communist and Socialist Parties asserted that they, unlike the right, would fight to acquire these on terms that would not "subvert our independence".

The left claimed that the community of interests between foreign business and the domestic right constituted a reactionary alliance against broad national development, a system of neo-colonialism whose dynamics served to keep the periphery as the supplier of raw materials to and a market for manufactured products from the industrial heartland. Foreign investments in extractive industries, wrote Julio César Jobet, one of Chile's best-known social historians,[19]

[18] This representation of the views of the Chilean left comes from the Communist newspaper *El Siglo* (before it was closed down by the government in 1948) and the Socialist newspaper *Última Hora*, as well as from books by authors cited below. For an interesting statement on foreign investment by Senator Salvador Allende, see *Panorama Económico*, November 1949.

[19] Julio César Jobet, *Ensayo crítico del desarrollo económico-social de Chile* (Santiago: Editorial Universitaria, 1955), p. 213.

Other expositions of the model of "reactionary alliances" and "development of underdevelopment" with regard to Chile include Hernán Ramírez Necochea, *Balmaceda y la contrarevolución de 1891* (Santiago: Editorial Universitaria, 1958) and *Historia del imperialismo en Chile* (Santiago: Austral, 1960); André Gunder Frank, *Capitalism and Underdevelopment in Latin America: Historical Studies of Chile and Brazil* (New York: Monthly Review Press, 1967).

Variations of this approach can be found, for example, in Paul A. Baran, *The Political Economy of Growth* (New York: Monthly Review Press, 1957); André Gunder Frank, *Latin America: Underdevelopment or Revolution* (New York: Monthly Review Press, 1969); Theotonio Dos Santos, *Dependencia y cambio social* (Santiago: Centro de Estudios Socio-Economicos, Universidad de Chile, 1970); and

in the early 1950's, "are imperialistic. They are devoted to the exploitation of our primary resources and never attempt to develop the internal economy on behalf of the national interest. Their exclusive aim is to create sources of supply for the industry they come from, from which they then send manufactured products, realizing a lucrative trade to the detriment of the colonial nation."

Such a formula was in fact not far different, given an obverse rhetorical shading, from the vision of the right. To Chilean conservatives, foreign investors were welcome to invest in raw materials, where the country's natural comparative advantage lay. Free enterprise in the domestic economy allowed the country to fit most advantageously into the international capitalist system. Those ties created through the encouragement of foreign investment brought the example of democracy closer to the nation, and provided a defense against revolution or subversion. Thus, the Chilean right, like the left, assumed that the relations between foreign investors and domestic groups would be dictated by an alliance of economic and political interests.

But, as Chilean economic growth came to depend ever more closely on the performance of the copper companies in the postwar period, such an alliance proved to be most fragile. Similarly, as the balance of power shifted from the foreign investors to the host country, such a model of the community of interests proved to be most inadequate.

At the time when the first movements were underway to establish postwar conditions in the Chilean copper industry in 1947–1948, however, there was ample evidence to inspire the view of close ideological, political, and economic ties among Chilean conservatives, the US mining companies, and financial groups influential with the US government in New York and Washington. The kind of relations Chile

---

James D. Cockcroft, André Gunder Frank, and Dale L. Johnson, eds., *Dependence and Underdevelopment: Latin America's Political Economy* (Grove City, N.Y.: Doubleday, 1972).

would have with North American investors was inseparably bound up with the attitude the country would adopt toward communism.

The Socialist paper *Última Hora* defined the situation in Hamlet's terms: "To be or not to be anti-Communist—that is the question!"[20]

Gabriel González Videla, a Radical, had been elected President in 1946 with the support of the Communist Party, and had accepted three Party members as ministers (out of a total of nine) in his cabinet. Following the election there was recurrent turmoil in the labor unions, including costly shutdowns in the copper and coal industries. "The communists," commented the American ambassador, "bent on creating economic chaos, unemployment and social disorders, concentrated their efforts on illegal strikes."[21] And, in the municipal elections of 1947, the Communist Party made impressive gains.

The situation was doubly delicate for González Videla's coalition government because Chile was trying not only to persuade Anaconda and Kennecott to invest funds but also to seek major loans from financial institutions in the United States to modernize the country's infrastructure and consolidate the industrial base built during the war. A special Chilean mission to look for foreign credits, headed by Guillermo del Pedregal, returned in May 1947 from an extended stay in New York and Washington, without the least apparent success.[22]

[20] *Última Hora*, May 14, 1947.

[21] Claude G. Bowers, *Chile Through Embassy Windows: 1939–1953* (New York: Simon and Schuster, 1958), p. 303.

This was a period of intense conflict within the Chilean labor unions among communists, socialists, and anarchists. In addition to Bowers, see Robert J. Alexander, *Communism in Latin America* (New Brunswick, N.J.: Rutgers University Press, 1957); and Federico Gil, *The Political System of Chile* (Boston: Houghton Mifflin, 1966).

[22] On the Pedregal Mission, see *El Diario Ilustrado*, May 1, 1947; *El Mercurio*, May 4, 1947; *La Nación*, May 17, 1947. Senator Hernán Videla Lira later gave a description of the problems of arranging

North American fact-finding missions, headed by the presidents of the Chase National Bank, Kennecott Copper, the World Chamber of Commerce, and Coca-Cola, were in turn visiting Santiago.[23] And spokesmen for the Liberal and Conservative Parties came out of these meetings announcing, with glee, that the elimination of the Communist Party from power was the condition for opening the flow of foreign capital into Chile.[24]

Although there is little public evidence about how far the US government and US business interests applied pressure on the González Videla government,[25] the Chilean right

---

credits in *Historia de la ley 11.828*, Vol. 2, January 19, 1955, pp. 1269 *et seq.*

Some US interest in supporting the Chilean drive to industrialize, however, was evidently felt among government officials in Washington. Ambassador Claude Bowers had written Assistant Secretary of State Spruille Braden in November (1946), saying: ". . . should we decide to refuse all credits to Chile for her industrialization the situation internally would become rather grave. . . . Chile has gone too far, interest here is too great, in the plans for industrialization to end it now." Braden had written in the margin, "We don't want to end it, but to do it soundly." *Foreign Relations of the United States, 1946* (Washington, D.C.: GPO, 1969), Vol. xi, p. 613.

[23] *El Diario Ilustrado*, April 20–23, 1947; *El Mercurio*, April 19–20, 1947; *El Siglo*, May 1, 1947.

The representative from Coca-Cola was James Farley, a close friend of President Harry Truman and an important figure in the Democratic Party.

[24] Statements of Joaquín Prieto Concha, president of the Conservative Party, in *El Diario Ilustrado*, May 1, 1947; of Enrique Cañas Flores, a Conservative deputy, in *El Mercurio*, May 1, 1947; of Hernán Videla Lira, Senator from the Liberal Party, in *El Mercurio*, April 15, 1947.

[25] Six months prior to the Pedregal mission, however, a secret State Department memorandum stated that: "[Assistant Secretary of State] Braden took advantage of his [Mario Rodríguez, Chilean Chargé d'Affaires] call on another matter to reiterate the Department's very serious concern with the El Teniente (Braden Copper Company) strike situation. . . . Mr. Braden impressed upon Señor Rodríguez the possible adverse effects on public opinion and Congress of precipitate action and subsequent settlement on terms that might prove tanta-

made it clear that they themselves would exploit the issue of communism in Chile to serve their own political interests. In the midst of the crucial international credit negotiations, the Liberal Party declared that the Communists in the government were running out of control and that, consequently, they were resigning from the coalition. This provoked a governmental crisis. At the same time, in a maneuver designed to be a self-fulfilling prophecy, the Conservative Party launched a drive to impress upon the public that foreign confidence would not be restored until the Communist Party was eliminated and labor discipline reestablished. The result for Chile was no new foreign credits and no new foreign investment.

As labor unrest continued in 1947 President González moved to the right. In October he announced that he had discovered secret letters showing that the Chilean Communist Party "were instruments of a worldwide plan to deprive the United States of primary materials in event of war".[26]

He dismissed the three Communist ministers from his cabinet, demanded extraordinary powers from the Congress to deal with strikes, and broke diplomatic relations with Russia, Czechoslovakia, and Yugoslavia. At the same time he subscribed to the Interamerican Treaty of Recipro-

---

mount to government intervention. In this connection, he mentioned that Kennecott's 90,000 stockholders are not without influence. Should the situation develop to the point of irrevocably damaging this U.S. private investment in Chile, the Department, the Eximbank, and the Government as a whole would be in a most embarrassing position for having simultaneously extended large loans to Chile." *Foreign Relations of the United States, 1946,* p. 613.

[26] *Memorias: Relaciones Exteriores,* Ministerio de Relaciones Exteriores (Santiago: Imprenta Chile, 1947), pp. 60–68.

González Videla subsequently visited the United States in 1950 and gave very strong support to the "West" in the Cold War, saying that communism was a threat to Western civilization (*Memorias: Relaciones Exteriores, 1950*). For a further account of González Videla's turn toward the United States in the Cold War, see Bowers, *Chile Through Embassy Windows: 1939–1953.*

cal Assistance, which promised mutual aid against armed attack or subversion, assured shipment of strategic raw materials to the United States in event of war, and obliged Chile to refrain from trading with Soviet bloc countries.

The following year González arranged passage of a "Law for the Defense of Democracy" that outlawed the Communist Party in Chile, ordered the removal of former Communist voters from the electoral roles, and permitted the administration to confine Communist leaders in remote parts of the country.

Thus, when Chile went back to the foreign banks and foreign investors in 1948, the government could promise to keep the left in order, to restore labor tranquillity, and, in addition, to reduce the tax burden in the copper sector. The climate for investment in Chile, reported the US Department of Commerce, "greatly improved in 1948 and is getting better every day".[27] The change brought results. Kennecott promised to maintain production at the levels of wartime capacity. But the big prize was Anaconda. The company announced early in 1948 that it would build a new $130 million complex to treat sulphides at Chuquicamata— the largest single investment in Chilean history.

There is no doubt that Chile's international image in the business world improved after 1947. Foreign loans to Chilean government agencies increased by a factor of four in the two years following the outlawing of the Communists, despite the fact that official reserves were declining substantially.[28] Even after the recession of 1949 had hit Chile

[27] As reported in *Última Hora*, May 1, 1949.

[28] The Chilean Central Bank published figures (*Balanza de Pagos*, 1951, p. 46) showing "Total Foreign Credits" as follows:

1945	$ 6,133,217
1946	$ 9,737,888
1947	$10,954,700
1948	$19,108,520
1949	$42,386,031

On the "grave situation" of declining reserves caused by slack demand for copper in response to the 1949 US recession, see *Memoria Anual*, Banco Central, 1949, p. 21.

with magnified force, the same agencies of the US government and the World Bank that had refused Pedregal in 1947 offered credits to the new conservative Minister of the Treasury Jorge Alessandri because the Chilean economy was now "in good hands . . . and the Chilean name has prestige in the United States".[29]

The Chilean right did not feel that the extreme political restrictions enacted in 1947–1948 were in any sense a kind of foreign "exploitation". Despite the enactment of a law that disenfranchised Chilean citizens and ended free political activity—a law that would come to be considered for twenty-five years (until the *golpe* of 1973) the worst national disgrace in a country dedicated to liberal democracy—the Liberal and Conservative Parties considered their particular political interests to be identical to the national interest.

But, having made the political payoff to foreigners that served their domestic designs as well, they reneged on the economic payoff.[30] Indeed, since the political concessions had been so generous, why make any economic concessions

---

[29] *Última Hora*, July 6, 1949.

[30] Guillermo del Pedregal and Cornelius Kelly, president of Anaconda, first announced that they had reached an agreement in principle about eliminating the artificial exchange rate in May 1947 (*La Nación*, May 17, 1947). That agreement was abandoned. Later, Jorge Alessandri also promised the elimination of artificial exchange rates when the new Anaconda investment in the sulphide plant at Chuquicamata was completed. There were some concessions made by Chile on the rate of conversion for the new investment, but the indirect tax on operations was not completely eliminated until the *Nuevo Trato* in 1955.

E. T. Stannard, president of Kennecott, complained about the process in which the US copper companies always found themselves under pressure to contribute more and more to the Chilean industrialization program. In conversations with Assistant Secretary of State Spruille Braden, "Mr. Stannard expressed himself strongly against the policy which this Government has followed in extending large Eximbank loans to Chile, and in acquiescing in the Chilean Government's fiscal policy of milking the copper companies more and more for foreign exchange with which to service said loans." *Foreign Relations of the United States, 1946*, p. 608.

to their foreign "allies" at all? Responding to self-interest in obtaining more foreign exchange rather than to an ideological community of interest, they did not reform the tax structure for Anaconda and Kennecott. Rather, once the corporate commitments were fixed and the balance of power had shifted in their direction once again, they watched with approval as the effective tax rate rose from a level of 50% at the end of the Second World War to over 70% in 1950.

V

The Chilean right might have included the groups most willing to exaggerate the political payoff to increase economic benefits from the foreign copper sector, but they were certainly not alone in pushing for a larger share of the revenues thus generated. Pressures to expand the fragile indigenous industrial base and to convince the public that the copper companies had to be forced to contribute more dynamically to such a process came from across the spectrum of Chilean society. It is possible to distinguish four broad groupings of individuals or organizations that played prominent roles in tightening control over copper policy: (1) academic "developmentalists"; (2) the "marxist left", especially the leadership of the Socialist and Communist Parties; (3) political leaders of the center as well as of the right; (4) non-political interest groups of Chilean industrialists. All four participated in the early postwar disputes about whether their country contributed "captive production" to a semi-integrated corporate system that retarded as well as stimulated broad domestic development. These were the groups that pressed for higher prices, higher revenues, and finally, for a Chilean state sales monopoly.

The first group, the academic "developmentalists", was the most explicit in trying to define and analyze the precarious relationship between Chile's possibilities for industrial development and the behavior of the foreign copper companies.[31] Academic "developmentalists" included economists, political scientists, and businessmen clustered around the new United Nations Economic Commission for Latin America (ECLA), around the Institute of Economics of the University of Chile, around the journal of economics and business called *Panorama Económico*. From the first issue of the magazine in March 1947, this group pointed to the importance of the apparent decline in their country's terms of trade. Often following ECLA's Raúl Prebisch, the members of this group foresaw the dangers of remaining a non-industrialized primary exporter. They became critical of the conventional doctrines of export-led growth. They advocated state intervention to "defend" the capacity to import and to promote industrialization. Some were academic economists or political scientists like Aníbal Pinto, Luís Escobar, Carlos Oyarzun, or later, Osvaldo Sunkel and Claudio Véliz; others, like Jorge Fontaine, one of the foremost early critics of corporate copper policy, went on to professional careers in the midst of the business world.[32] This group of "developmentalists" propounded the views of ECLA on trade and import-substituting industrialization. They organized seminars and published round-table discussions by businessmen, political leaders, and *técnicos* on the subject of development. And they trained the students who would take over leading roles in the public enterprises and state agencies of the 1960's and 1970's.

[31] For views expressed by the "academic developmentalists," see *Panorama Económico*; Aníbal Pinto, *Hacia nuestra independencia económica* (Santiago: Editorial del Pacífico, 1953), and *Chile: Un caso de desarrollo frustrado* (Santiago: Editorial Universitaria, 1959); and *Desarrollo económico de Chile, 1950–1956*, Instituto de Economía, Universidad de Chile, under the direction of Luís Escobar, Dean of the Faculty of Economics.

[32] See Fontaine's analysis of copper policy in *Panorama Económico* May 27 and August 5, 1955. Jorge Fontaine later went on to become president of the Confederación de la Producción y del Comercio, Chile's broadest organization for business, commerce, and agriculture.

Second, the development of the idea of *dependencia* and the reaction against control of Chilean copper policy by North American companies had origins among the "marxist left". Historians such as Julio César Jobet and Hernán Ramírez Necochea argued that the natural growth of the copper industry in Chile would have the same pernicious outcome that the nitrate industry had produced during the late nineteenth century—promoting a kind of economic expansion that benefited only the few traditional groups who were allied with the foreign exporters while hindering a broader process of vigorous domestic industrialization.[33] This theme was constantly repeated by political leaders in the Communist Party as well as in the various splinters of the Socialist Party. They felt that Chile had to struggle against the "inherent dynamics" of foreign investment in natural resources, which, if left undirected, would reduce the country to a hollow colony. For the "marxist left", the political and economic future of Chile depended upon industrial development, and the Chilean state had to force Anaconda and Kennecott to play a more dynamic part in supplying the needed foreign exchange. Following the Prebisch model of declining terms of trade, they argued that the "free trade" system in fact was allowed to function only when it served the international economic interests of the United States. Finally, the "marxist left", like the academic "developmentalists", wanted to break the condition of being "captive production" to the US companies by selling to the highest bidders in all markets, including Soviet-bloc markets.

Third, the declining postwar terms of trade, the recession of 1949, and the arbitrary price ceiling set for the Korean War provoked a harsh reaction from political leaders of the center and right. This movement toward monitoring and controlling the actions of Anaconda and Kennecott

---

[33] Jobet, *Ensayo crítico del desarrollo económico-social de Chile*; and Ramírez, *Balmaceda y la contrarevolucíon de 1891* and *Historia del imperialismo en Chile*.

came to be associated with those Falangistas who would later be at the heart of Christian Democratic policy-making —Senators Eduardo Frei, Radomiro Tomic, and Ignacio Palma.[34] They mistrusted the idea that a laissez-faire attitude toward the behavior of the international companies would provide an adequate basis for Chilean policy. They argued that a state agency equipped to bargain carefully with the companies, administer policy, perhaps even participate in management would be necessary to force the foreign companies to play a more dynamic role in Chilean development.

Similarly, Radicals such as Alberto Baltra and Julio Durán recognized the need for a firm export policy to give direction to Chilean industrial growth.[35]

But perhaps the strongest early criticism of the US copper companies in Chile, and the toughest positions recommended for Chilean policy, came from the Chilean right—from leaders such as Hernán Videla Lira and Mariano Puga Vega. As a Congressional Deputy in the Liberal Party in the 1940's, Mariano Puga was one of the first Chileans to try to collect comprehensive statistics on the domestic copper industry and draw relevant policy conclusions from them.[36] He later became Ambassador to the Organization of American States in Washington (1957–1958) and president of the Liberal Party (1962). Both in Santiago and in Washington he argued that the copper companies had to be made to generate more foreign exchange to serve the needs of his country.

[34] Cf. Frei in *Panorama Económico*, June 6, 1952; Tomic in *Panorama Económico*, November 11 and May 27, 1955; and Frei, Tomic, and Palma in *Historia de la ley 11.828.*

[35] Cf. Baltra in *Panorama Económico*, April–May 1949 and September 2, 1955; Durán in *Historia de la ley 11.828.*

[36] A collection of Puga's speeches and writings on copper policy from the 1950's and 1960's has been published in the volume, *El cobre chileno* (Santiago: Editorial Andes Bello, 1965). On the significance of Puga's early attempts at gathering data, see Aníbal Pinto, *Hacia nuestra independencia económica*, pp. 172–173.

Hernán Videla Lira—who was president of the National Society of Mining (1937–1965) as well as Senator from the Liberal Party and president of the Senate Mining Committee—was perhaps the most important figure in Chilean copper policy.[37] Videla was a great admirer of the United States, and showed steadfast respect for foreign companies in general. But, between the Second World War and the Korean War, he was one of the first to suspect that the relations between his country and the North American copper companies constituted a system of international exploitation that hindered the national development of Chile. He argued a position resembling that of Prebisch in Washington and New York as well as Santiago—not out of love for Prebisch's model of declining terms of trade or state-induced import substitution, but because of his own firm beliefs in classical free trade. He claimed, from the position of a political and economic conservative, that "arbitrary" and "artificial" pricing on the part of the multinational copper companies was a threat to Chile's sovereignty as a nation. Videla played a major role in demanding the concessions on price and marketing that were embodied in the Washington Treaty of 1951 and, later, in annulling those agreements and proceeding to set up the Chilean sales monopoly of 1952.

It is not sufficient to confine the analysis of the groups who contributed to the movement of economic nationalism after the Second World War to the diverse politicians of the left, right, and center, or to the outspoken ECLA-led academic group. A central role was also played by individuals and interest groups dedicated directly to the growth of the national manufacturing industry. The most important of these groups was the National Society of Manufacturers (*Sociedad de Fomento Fabril*); and the most important individual was the vigorous head of that organization, Dr. Walter Müller.

[37] Most of Videla's speeches and writings on copper policy can be followed in the *Boletín Minero*, official publication of the Sociedad Nacional de Minería. See also *Historia de la ley 11.828.*

184

Müller, like Videla or Puga, was generally considered a member of the "old upper classes" with agricultural and banking interests in the southern farming areas of Chile.[38] But he believed firmly that the country's future depended on the development of a broad industrial base. Müller was not at all anti-American, and he warmly encouraged foreign investment in the Chilean economy. As the president of the National Society of Manufacturers, he was the very symbol in Chile of private enterprise. But he saw clearly that national growth could not depend merely on local savings combined with begging for international credits, but rather must look to the expansion of foreign exchange receipts from copper. Müller was one of the first men active in Chilean public affairs to point out to Chilean businessmen,[39] as

[38] Dr. Müller's views on copper policy can be followed in *Industria*, the official publication of the Sociedad de Fomento Fabril.

Dr. Müller was consistently referred to, in interviews in Santiago, as being a member of the "old upper classes" or "traditional oligarchy", in sharp contrast to the newer single-business families that had grown up in the process of import-substitution during and after the Second World War. The *Diccionario Biográfico de Chile* points out that in addition to being president of the National Society of Manufacturers, Müller was also a director of the Sociedad Nacional de Minería, a director of the Banco Central de Chile, and a member of the Sociedad Nacional de Agricultura. He was also involved with several private companies. Like Videla and Puga, Dr. Müller or others in his family were members of Chile's two most prestigious social clubs, the Club Hípico and the Club de la Unión. From 1959 to 1962, during the administration of Jorge Alessandri, Dr. Müller was Chilean ambassador to the United States.

Thus, it would be difficult to claim that Müller (or Videla or Puga or other members of the Liberal and Conservative Parties) represented a new industrial class that was breaking with an old traditional oligarchy. They were in fact members of the "old traditional oligarchy" who by now had strong roots in industry as well as commerce, banking, and agriculture.

[39] This was the beginning of a pattern that would repeat itself in the Chilean experience: the older, established leaders of the traditional upper class would lead the newer, smaller businessmen of the "national bourgeoisie" in setting the attitudes toward the foreign copper companies. There was no discernible split on the question of foreign investment.

well as to US officials in Washington, exactly what was happening to the domestic capacity to import under the "free trade" arrangement. He argued that the corporate "system" that linked rich Chilean mines to rich industrial consumers was causing most of the pain in the growth of the Chilean manufacturing industry. Armed with this point of view, Müller used the manufacturers' periodical *Industria* as well as the podium of the economics faculty at the University of Chile, and led his strong interest group of industrialists to criticize the unregulated behavior of Anaconda and Kennecott in Chile. Müller was responsible for hammering out the agreement with the Santiago Chamber of Commerce and the National Agriculture Society in 1951 that permitted the entry of the Chilean state into regulation of copper pricing and marketing.[40]

These, then, were the four interlocking groups that created and led the first sustained challenge to US corporate domination of Chilean copper policy.

Certainly all of the groups and individuals that fomented the movement against *dependencia* were in some sense "nationalists"—but the movement cannot be passed off merely as an emotional "burst" or "wave" of nationalism, since many of the participants were strongly pro-United States and worked tirelessly for closer ties. This was true of the Liberals and Conservatives, Radicals and Falangistas. It was equally true of businessmen and academics such as Walter Müller, Flavian Levine, Jorge Fontaine. Even Salvador Allende spoke persuasively of the need to attract private US capital when it had unique benefits to offer within a socialist development plan.[41]

Certainly all of the groups involved in the postwar reac-

[40] Dr. Müller's earnest maneuvering to bring the support of the National Agricultural Society and the National Chamber of Commerce behind government intervention against the copper companies in 1950–1951 is shown in *Memoria*, Cámara de Comercio de Santiago, 1951, p. 35, and in *Industria*, April 1951, pp. 203 *et seq.*

[41] *Panorama Económico*, November 1949.

tion against *dependencia* felt that the country was being in some sense "exploited". Contrary, however, to the simple model of reactionary alliances and the "consolidation of underdevelopment", this feeling of exploitation grew from the process of development itself and not from a sense that the foreign presence in the copper industry was requiring Chile to remain a simple exporter of raw materials and importer of manufactured products. Any sense of exploitation was in fact a feeling of *relative* deprivation of the ingredients necessary for industrialization, not of *absolute* deprivation or the *suppression* of industrialization. This exploitation was felt more keenly and by more groups as industrial development through import substitution became built firmly into the domestic system.[42]

The general dissatisfaction with the behavior of the copper companies sprang from the feeling that the companies were not contributing dynamically enough to feed the growing needs of industrialization. It did not arise from antagonism towards foreign efforts to keep the Chilean market open to the importation of US manufactured goods. There was nothing in Chile resembling, for example, the Roca-Runciman Pact between Argentina and Britain in 1933, requiring privileges for English imports and English investments in return for entry of Argentine beef and wheat into the British market on Commonwealth terms.

The foreign exchange revenues from the copper industry were indeed used to finance imports from the industrial metropolis—what else could they have been used for?—but

---

[42] This is not to say that the Chilean path to industrialization was optimal, or that more (or less) central planning and state control would not have led to a more dynamic growth or a better distribution of income.

For analyses of the process of industrial development in Chile, cf. Oscar Muñoz, *Crecimiento Industrial de Chile, 1914–1965* (Santiago: Instituto de Economía y Planificación, Universidad de Chile, 1967); and Markos Mamalakis, "An Analysis of the Financial and Investment Activities of the Chilean Development Corporation: 1939–1964", *Journal of Development Studies*, Vol. 5, No. 2 (January 1969).

the domestic concern about declining terms of trade and a fragile capacity to import showed an appetite for hard currency that was being transformed, as the Instituto de Economía proudly documented,[43] into materials and machinery for national industry—not consumer goods.

All four of the groups that led the movement against *dependencia* looked to industrialization as the proper course for Chilean development. They held widely divergent views on free enterprise, labor unions, and relative distribution of income in Chilean society. But they joined in wanting to protect and expand the country's industrial base.

There was scant evidence in Chile of a split between a traditional oligarchy and a new "national bourgeoisie" over the treatment of the foreign copper exporters or over the question of imports versus import substitution. In the Chilean case—long before the Alliance for Progress crystallized conservative reactions against Anaconda and Kennecott— leaders of the traditional upper classes were at the head of the movement to close in on the foreign copper companies.[44] Hernán Videla Lira, Mariano Puga Vega, Walter Müller, leading the political and economic groups they represented, were leading Chilean public opinion, in demanding a more dynamic contribution from the US com-

[43] *Desarrollo Económico de Chile, 1950–1956*, Instituto de Economía, Universidad de Chile, pp. 70–80.

[44] The contention that many of the more prominent families in Chile's "traditional oligarchy" had diversified from commerce and agriculture into finance and industry is supported in the fascinating study by E. Ricardo Lagos, *La concentración del poder económico* (Santiago: Editorial del Pacífico, 1965). Further evidence has been discovered by Robert Kaufman—56% of all Conservative and Liberal Congressmen in this period were active in both urban and rural enterprises, and all the leaders of the National Society of Manufacturers were also owners of large *fundos*. (Robert Kaufman, "Chilean Political Institutions and Agrarian Reform: The Politics of Adjustment", Ph.D. thesis, Government Department, Harvard, 1967.)

For more analysis of the "traditional oligarchy" and the "national bourgeoisie", see footnote 78.

panies to aid in the process of domestic industrialization. These men were pro-American and pro-"Free World". They were anti-Socialist and anti-Communist. They wanted more foreign (US) investment in Chile and closer military ties to the United States. But they were no less convinced than the Chilean left that the corporate system that linked Chilean mines to industrial consumers was cheating them in their struggle to create a base for sustained national growth.

With political leaders of the Chilean right and center and conservative business leaders joining the Chilean left and the academic "developmentalists" in spreading the reaction to *dependencia,* alliances with foreign investors based on common ideology proved to be extraordinarily fragile as domestic economic interests seemed to diverge from those of the foreign copper companies in the 1940's and early 1950's. These four broad groups remembered the damaging experience with copper in World War II. They watched the declining terms of trade and lamented their weakened capacity to import in the early postwar period. They saw the severe effects of the 1949 recession in the United States transmitted with exaggeration into their own economy. And they concluded, in varying ways, that the country had to increase the use of its power vis-à-vis the foreign companies.[45] First, they allowed the tax rate in the copper sector to rise above 70%. Then, with the onset of the Korean War, they mobilized the domestic reaction to the Washington decision dictating a "low" price ceiling for Chilean copper.

The Washington agreement—a private collusion, as Chapter 3 explained, between the US government and the heads of Anaconda and Kennecott—seemed like the confirmation of the whole structure of *dependencia.* But, for once, Chile did not have to remain passive in the face of this

[45] For a fascinating analysis of the uses of anti-imperialism in the domestic struggles of diverse interest groups in Argentina, see Peter H. Smith, *Politics & Beef in Argentina: Patterns of Conflict and Change* (New York: Columbia University Press, 1969).

threat to its sovereignty, this threat to national growth and welfare. Even with no past experience in the workings of the international copper industry, it appeared to these four groups that the country could sell on the booming wartime open market of London and do better than the "unimaginative" marketing patterns maintained by the US copper executives for the benefit of their parent country and their traditional customers. Chile had to "defend" its capacity to import, "support" its terms of trade, exercise its self-interest instead of passively accepting crucial decisions that were made by others. Obeying the dictates of foreign corporate officials or the officials of their government, they concluded, was a threat to sovereign control over domestic development and prosperity; obeying the impersonal laws of supply and demand was not—so long as demand was high.

The perception of the contribution of foreign management to international marketing was low for these groups— even negative. The perception of the value of taking control from the foreigners was high.

Most important, after the postwar commitments of the copper companies had been fixed, the balance of power had swung to the Chilean side.

"I think that the moment has come," the conservative president of the Senate Mining Committee, Hernán Videla Lira, told his colleagues in the Congress in April 1952, "for our government to confront the only logical solution to our export problem—to get for all our copper sales a just price!"[46]

Two and a half weeks later President González Videla informed President Truman that Chile was withdrawing from the wartime materials agreement and would manage copper sales policy on its own.

VI

After the end of the Korean War, however, the balance of power moved rapidly back toward the foreign copper

[46] *Boletín Minero* (May 1952), p. 1161.

companies. The Chilean sales monopoly, exposed as an inexperienced and inefficient operation even during wartime demand, became an obvious failure when consumption tapered off. The Chilean Central Bank, as we have seen, could not market domestic copper output at a price above, or even equal to, the US producers' price.

To top off these problems, Anaconda announced, as Chapter 4 pointed out, that its second largest mine, Potrerillos, was becoming exhausted and would have to be closed down in the near future. Even if Anaconda and Kennecott kept operating at full capacity in the adverse Chilean environment, the loss of Potrerillos would mean a large drop in foreign exchange revenues.

The balance of power had clearly shifted back toward the foreign investors. And all sectors of Chilean society, including the marxist left and the academic developmentalists, conceded that some sort of new bargain would have to be struck.[47]

The economists and *técnicos* associated with the Instituto de Economía, joining with political leaders of the center and several prominent businessmen, tried to bring pressure on the Congress to make the negotiations clear and explicit.[48] They realized, as did the left, that substantial concessions would have to be made to the foreign companies, but they shared the suspicion of the left that such conces-

[47] Interviews with leaders of the Chilean Socialist Party (October 1972), for example, confirmed that, despite the rhetoric of nationalization in the mid-1950's, the various Socialist factions clearly realized that a deal with the foreign companies was the only way to increase production and keep the industry running.

[48] For the positions of political leaders of the center and left, see *Historia de la ley 11.828.* There were also numerous careful appraisals of the *Nuevo Trato* in *Panorama Económico,* 1954–1955. In particular, the legislation was submitted to critical analysis by a group of businessmen, politicians, economists, and labor leaders who called themselves the Comisión Especial del Círculo de Economía, including Radomiro Tomic, William Thayer, Américo Simonetti, Carlos Ruiz, and Ramón Silva Ulloa (*Panorama Económico,* October 8, 1954, and May 27–August 5, 1955).

sions might mistakenly be surrendered without their knowing what they were going to get in return.

Why did Chile not in fact maintain what momentum it could in trying to use the copper sector as the motor for domestic growth, albeit from a position of relative weakness vis-à-vis the foreign copper companies? Why was the *Nuevo Trato* the outcome of a negotiation that had no hard bargaining? The new mining legislation was written, as we have seen, to offer Anaconda and Kennecott literally all the concessions they asked for without demanding any specific commitments on their part. What needs explanation is why Chile gave away so much and asked so little in return.

To answer this, one must again look at the domestic interests of particular groups involved in influencing Chilean public policy. This time, too, the crucial groups were from the right.

The idea of the *estímulos automáticos*—that a good investment climate in Chile would automatically bring forth a huge flow of investment and more vigorous activity from the foreign copper companies—was the invention of the right. But it would be a mistake to think that their tireless efforts to write the legislation according to this formula were inspired merely by ignorance and error. Rather, the liberal construction of the *Nuevo Trato* was important to conservative political and economic groups in Chile because of the role it was expected to play in their counterattack against state intervention in their own affairs.[49] They were mount-

[49] The evidence indicates that the Liberal and Conservative Parties expended very little intellectual effort analyzing the probable outcome of their recommendations for copper policy—as shown by their naive projections about doubling production and their almost disastrous approach to international tax policy.

In the enthusiasm for raising profits as a means of stimulating economic activity, Conservative Party representatives such as Senator Larraín Vial argued that Chilean taxes on the copper companies should be lowered to about 31% to compete with the depletion allowance of US and other countries. Senator Palma of the Falangistas informed the Senate, however, that under the Foreign Tax Credit provisions of

192

ing a public campaign to move the new President (General) Carlos Ibáñez to the right. They were convinced that the *Nuevo Trato* was crucial as a model to counteract the "structuralist" approach to inflation and domestic development. The structuralists, following Raúl Prebisch, argued that the government must intervene in the Chilean economy because traditional landholding and business groups did not respond adequately to profit incentives.[50] In reaction to this threat, the Liberal and Conservative Parties, and many non-political business interest groups, were trying to move the Ibáñez administration away from the General's agrarian-labor Peronist predilections, away from the structuralist position, away from the specter of land reform, and away from selective credit controls, selective price controls, and the creation of state enterprises.

Two of the leaders who set the theme—that the foreign copper companies, like domestic companies, would serve the national interest better if profit rates were allowed to rise unchecked and if enterprise were freed from state interference—were Jorge Alessandri and Hernán Videla Lira. Alessandri, president of the Confederation of Production and Commerce, Chile's largest business organization, when the debates on the *Nuevo Trato* were raging in 1954–1955,

---

the US Internal Revenue Code the difference between the Chilean rate and the US rate (47%) would merely flow to the US Treasury when it was remitted. The Chilean reduction would benefit neither the US companies nor Chile. This came as a revelation to the Ibáñez administration as well as to the rest of the Congress. Francisco Cuevas Mackenna, Minister of Hacienda, admitted that he had planned to set the Chilean tax rate on copper at 37.5% precisely so that it would be lower than the US rate (*Historia de la ley 11.828*, Vol. 1, September 16, 1954, pp. 3909–3966; and Vol. 3, February 1, 1955, p. 4182).

[50] For discussions of the structuralist position that go beyond the analysis of terms of trade contained in Chapter 3, see Albert Hirschman, *Journeys Toward Progress* (New York: Doubleday, 1965); and Robert L. Ayres, "Economic Stagnation and the Emergence of the Political Ideology of Chilean Underdevelopment", *World Politics*, Vol. xxv, No. 1 (October 1972).

welcomed the legislation as a step toward cutting back on state intervention in Chile. For him, the *Nuevo Trato* was praiseworthy because of its general principle of allowing the free play of free men in free enterprise.[51] Videla, a classical liberal, told his audience in 1954 that he was inspired by Eisenhower's movement ("corresponding to reality") away from governmental controls in the United States.[52] He argued that now Chile too should free itself from the artificiality of state intervention and rely on free trade and the stimulus of private profits for foreign as well as domestic companies.

The campaign from the right was broad and forceful. *El Diario Ilustrado*, the influential newspaper representing the views of the Liberal and Conservative Parties, supported the *Nuevo Trato* with the same line of argument:[53] the new mining legislation certainly would help Chile, the editors claimed, by giving benefits and guarantees to the foreign copper companies in the expectation that they would expand production. But even more important than this, they concluded, the mining law would be a good model (*buena*

[51] See, for example, "La intervención estatal en la economía", *Industria*, May 1955; *El Diario Ilustrado*, May 5, 1955; and "La situación económica nacional", *Industria*, August 1955.

[52] See the speeches of Hernán Videla Lira before the Chilean Senate, April 14 and May 5, 1954, reprinted in *Boletín Minero*, March–April 1954, pp. 1940 *et seq*. Other major speeches of Videla on the *Nuevo Trato* legislation can be found in *Boletín Minero*, January–June, 1955; in *Panorama Económico*, February 11, 1955; and in *Historia de la ley 11.828*.

Videla, however, wanted a more precise statement of projected company investments than the *Nuevo Trato* required. (*Historia de la ley 11.828*, Vol. 3, February 3, 1955, p. 1659.)

[53] *El Diario Ilustrado*, lead editorial, May 4, 1955.

El Mercurio also supported the legislation and paid special tribute to Roy H. Glover when he was rewarded for his work in getting the *Nuevo Trato* passed by being promoted to chairman of the Board of Directors of Anaconda. Glover was commended by *El Mercurio* for "personally directing the difficult and delicate tasks of working out the *Nuevo Trato* with our government" (May 28, 1955).

orientación) for public opinion. The emphasis that the *Nuevo Trato* gave to freedom and security for private enterprises pointed the true path to the solution of Chile's major domestic problems.

Similar arguments that Chilean businessmen should support the battle for the *Nuevo Trato* for the foreign copper companies as part of their own struggle in national politics were expressed by the presidents of the Chilean Chamber of Commerce, the National Society of Manufacturers, and the Institute of Mining Engineers.[54] Popular conservative associations like the Rotary Club de Santiago were treated to special speeches of support for the principle of the *Nuevo Trato* legislation.[55]

If one were to define "exploitation" as the difference between what the country could have obtained from its primary export sector using the alternative bargaining strategies available to it and what the country finally achieved, then the right's overwhelming pressure to push through the *Nuevo Trato* constituted complicity in such exploitation.[56]

[54] *Memoria*, Cámara de Comercio de Santiago, 1954; exposition of the new acting president of the Sociedad de Fomento Fabril, Domingo Arteaga, *Industria*, July 1955; Hernán Elgueta Guerín, president of the National Association of Importers, *El Diario Ilustrado*, May 5, 1955; Instituto de Ingenieros de Minas, statement in *Industria*, February 1954.

[55] The speech of César Fuenzalida Correa to the Santiago Rotary Club was reported in *Boletín Minero*, January–June 1955.

[56] In another paper, "A Model of National Interest, Balance of Power, and International Exploitation in Large Natural Resource Investments", in James Kurth and Stephen Rosen, eds., *Testing the Theory of Economic Imperialism* (New York: Heath, 1974), I have argued that one can measure "exploitation" as the cost to the country of giving payoffs to foreigners to advance the purely private interests of domestic groups at the public expense. The result is not a unique value for exploitation, but a range of more and less probable values based on a reconstruction of what bargains might have been struck if the complicity (trading public benefits for private gain) had not taken place.

In the Chilean case, I have conservatively reconstructed five alterna-

Just as they were willing to arrange a large political payoff to foreigners to serve their own particular domestic interests in 1947–1948, so now they arranged an economic payoff to serve their needs at the public expense. In the 1947–1948 period the country exaggerated the political concessions to avoid paying the economic costs of enticing new investment. In the 1954–1955 period, the country paid the economic costs to gain nothing.

There is a problem here in separating out ignorance and error from complicity. Probably many of the representatives of the Conservative and Liberal Parties that were so strong in Congress actually believed their own rhetoric about "good investment climate" and would not have written the *Nuevo Trato* exactly as they did if they had known

tive bargains that the evidence indicates might plausibly have been negotiated in the absence of the "good investment climate" campaign of the right. I have assumed that return of control over sales and pricing and the restructuring of the tax regime were *sine qua non* for beginning any negotiations. I further estimated, pessimistically, that Anaconda could under no conditions have been persuaded to do more than replace the depleted Potrerillos mine with El Salvador, and that neither Anaconda nor Kennecott could have been persuaded to build any new electrolytic refining capacity in Chile. Finally, I assumed, on the basis of evidence from the Congressional hearings on the *Nuevo Trato*, that the Ibáñez government would have been hoodwinked into granting the elaborate concessions in accounting procedure for new mine development that the companies wanted no matter what. The five alternative bargains, then, were all based on these assumptions.

The two most plausible of the five were that Kennecott could have been persuaded to increase its production capacity from 160 thousand tons per year to 280 thousand tons per year in return for cutting the tax rate from 80% to 47% (the lowest rate possible in view of the US Foreign Tax Credit); or that if Kennecott had not wanted to make any bargain under any circumsances, the tax rate on El Teniente could have been raised to 90% (still yielding a 7% return on assets).

These two alternative bargains yield gains to Chile—that is, measures of exploitation—in comparison to what actually took place under the *Nuevo Trato* of $44 million and $67 million respectively in the first five years.

196

just how disastrous the results would be. But in their eagerness to argue that low profits, high taxes, and state intervention were the causes of their own tepid economic performance, they were negligent in looking closely at the implications of their proposals for the foreign copper sector. And they ignored prominent dissenters from their own ranks who argued that their projections and promises about foreign behavior were self-deceptions.

For a brief period, then, in the second half of the Ibáñez administration and through the election of Jorge Alessandri in 1958, the celebrated community of interest between foreign investors and domestic conservatives again had a firm basis in reality. When the results of the *Nuevo Trato* broadly became judged a failure in the late 1950's, however, the right joined the left and the center in condemning the behavior of the foreign companies. From them came the complaint that the large international copper companies, with more guarantees and privileges than any local business,[57] failed to perform as vigorously in an atmosphere of free enterprise as the country had a right to expect. Even President Alessandri himself publicly expressed his disappointment that the copper companies, especially Kennecott, did not have more of a "disposition" to respond to the stimulus of higher profits that he had done so much to arrange.[58]

With the mood of disillusionment spreading among groups of the left, right, and center, a new element was introduced into the determination of relations with the large foreign investors that hastened the last major swing in the pendulum of power.

That new element was the Alliance for Progress.

[57] There is no doubt that the foreign copper companies had more formal governmental guarantees and more privileges with regard to foreign exchange and duty-free imports than local businesses. Their tax rate, however, was consistently higher than rates on domestic enterprises. No data were ever advanced to show whether their actual profit rate was higher or lower than various local business activities.

[58] *Cobre*, No. 5, January 1963.

VII

To understand Eduardo Frei's political difficulties in passing the carefully constructed Chileanization legislation and the subsequent rapid movement against the companies even in the face of the success of the new agreements, it is necessary to go back and look at the changing pattern of domestic pressures on the right after the announcement of the Alliance for Progress.

The Cuban Revolution and Castro's announcement that he was a marxist-leninist were traumatic events for the Chilean right, as for conservative sectors throughout Latin America. Jorge Alessandri had beaten Salvador Allende by only the narrowest of margins (32% of the vote for Alessandri, with 29% for Allende and 21% for Frei) in the presidential race of 1958, and, after a promising beginning, economic growth under Alessandri was declining. The stimulus of private profits during his administration was not producing dynamic Chilean development. There was inflation, stagnation, unemployment, and a skewed distribution of income. In the countryside, Chile ranked, along with pre-1952 Bolivia, among the countries of Latin America with the most unequal distribution of land—significantly worse than Argentina, Brazil, or pre-revolutionary Cuba.[59]

[59] Bruce Russet, using a Gini Index to measure inequality of land distribution, found Chile as well as pre-revolutionary Bolivia to be at the top of a list of 47 South American, Asian, and European countries. The index for Chile was 98.8, for Argentina 86.3, for Brazil 83.7, for pre-Castro Cuba 79.2. "Inequality and Instability: The Relation of Land Tenure to Politics", *World Politics*, Vol. XVI, No. 3 (April 1964), p. 455.

Robert Kaufman found that in Chile approximately 12% of the active rural population received 66% of total agricultural income ("Chilean Political Institutions and Agrarian Reform: The Politics of Adjustment", Ph.D. dissertation, Government Department, Harvard, 1967).

Solon Barraclough reports that prior to the Agrarian Reform, large estates covered 79% of Chile's agricultural land surface—the highest concentration of the six Latin American countries for which data are available (Argentina, Brazil, Colombia, Ecuador, and Guatemala).

There was easily reason to suppose in the early 1960's that Chile might become "another Cuba".

One might expect that a common fear of communism and revolution would drive domestic conservatives and foreign investors closer together, would renew alliances on the basis of political and economic ideology.

In Chile, it did not. Throughout the 1960's, the hostility of the Chilean right to the foreign copper companies grew and intensified, especially among the rank and file of the Liberal and Conservative Parties (as well as among sectors of the Radical and Christian Democratic Parties), to the point where conservatives helped lead the movement for nationalization. The reason for this new hostility was the Alliance for Progress and its insistence on Agrarian Reform.

The announcement of the Alliance in Washington was meant to sound a note of sympathy on the part of the United States for "sweeping social change", the "breaking-up of the old latifundias", assaults on the "power of the traditional oligarchy". At the same time, the United States was suggesting that most of the proposed change and development would be carried out by private capital, both domestic and foreign, through the encouragement of free enterprise.

Some writers representing the right and center of Chilean society stressed that the Alliance's encouragement of private enterprise would provide "security" within which "reform" could take place.[60] For others, however, even the mention of "social change" and "land reform" had too unsettling an effect.

"Agricultural Policies and Strategies of Land Reform", in Irving Louis Horowitz, ed., *Masses in Latin America* (New York: Oxford University Press, 1970).

[60] The position of *El Mercurio*, in articles as well as editorials, was consistently more receptive to the Alliance for Progress at its initiation than that of the writers for the *Diario Ilustrado*. Cf. editorials in *El Mercurio*, July 6 and July 9, 1961. *El Mercurio* also played down the fear and outrage within the Chilean right. Later, it also became very hostile to the Agrarian Reform.

The first storm broke on Sunday, July 2, 1961. On that morning *El Diario Ilustrado*, the newspaper of the right, "invited" the powerful Conservative Party Senator Francisco Bulnes Sanfuentes to write a guest editorial entitled "Chile Versus the Alliance for Progress". There is no need for social change in Chile, Senator Bulnes argued,[61] since the country has had many social laws on the books for more than 50 years and has been reforming itself from within. It would be better for the United States to quit stirring up our economic and social problems. What the country does need is huge new investments in copper production. The *Nuevo Trato* has been a failure—merely the granting of exaggerated concessions to the companies in return for almost nothing. Therefore, if the companies cannot be made to launch a huge new program and let the proceeds flow to develop Chile as the Alliance envisions, the government should nationalize them!

I am not anti-North American and have demonstrated this on more than one occasion, Senator Bulnes concluded, but I must comply with my duty to speak frankly what is on the minds of many Chileans. In the name of the defense of the Christian and Western world, the Alliance for Progress must be prevented from degenerating into the rhetoric of demagogues!

This was an explicit attack on the copper companies as well as the Alliance. It was the beginning of an effort to make Anaconda and Kennecott receive the blame directed at the right for the problems of development—rather than allowing the blame to rest on the poor distribution of income in Chile, the domestic monopolies, the unequal distribution of land. It was also the beginning of a threat—the companies, as Frei would later find out, would be held hos-

---

[61] *El Diario Ilustrado*, guest editorial, "Chile frente a la Alianza del Progreso" by Senator Francisco Bulnes Sanfuentes, July 2, 1961.

The newspaper knew what it was getting into, since Senator Bulnes had already tried out these opinions, with rousing success, on a convention of Young Conservatives.

tage to put pressure on the government to modify the Agrarian Reform required by the Alliance for Progress.

Meanwhile, another member of the Conservative Party, Enrique Serrano, who was Alessandri's Minister of Mines, was busy pressing the attack and making the threat credible. The problems in Chile's development, he reiterated, were due to the copper companies, not to a traditional landed oligarchy. In accordance with the development "goals" envisioned by the Alliance for Progress, Serrano announced a compulsory program under which Kennecott and Anaconda would be required to increase production by 15% every three years and to refine at least 90% of the copper production in Chile.[62]

The result was a crisis for the companies and for Alessandri's government. Charles Brinkerhoff, the chairman of Anaconda, left his home in the middle of the 4th of July weekend and flew to Santiago, where he went directly to see President Alessandri.[63] The newspapers were reporting a major cabinet reshuffle in the government while Alessandri was trying to reestablish control over his administration and over his supporters in Congress. In an elaborate attempt to quiet the uproar, Alessandri finally said he would not ask Serrano to resign, and the president of the Conservative Party, Hector Correa Letelier, said that he would not withdraw Conservative support for the administration in the Congress.[64] But the Serrano plan for obligatory copper company "contributions" to the development program demanded by the Alliance for Progress remained.

[62] Serrano formally presented his plan before the National Society of Mining on July 21, 1961, with coverage by all the major newspapers, especially the *Diario Ilustrado*. For the Serrano plan, see also the *Annual Report* of Kennecott's subsidiary, Braden, 1961.

[63] One may follow the course of this crisis in all the Chilean newspapers and in UPI dispatches to the United States. Anaconda's concern was confirmed in an interview with Mr. Brinkerhoff in New York, July 1, 1970. Kennecott's concern was shown in the *Annual Report* of Braden for 1961.

[64] Cf. *El Diario Ilustrado*, July 5, 6, and 7, 1961, front page.

And the attack from many members of the Chilean right continued. The following Sunday the front page of the *Diario Ilustrado* declared that the United States was meddling in unimportant problems (like land reform, tax reform, and social change) instead of doing its proper job, namely, saving Latin America from communism.[65]

President Alessandri was able, with difficulty, to patch over the splits in his cabinet. Before the end of 1961, Serrano was quietly replaced by another Conservative minister, Julio Chana, who, in the words of the Kennecott subsidiary, "avoided defining his position as that outlined by his predecessor".[66]

The Bulnes-Serrano incident, however, seemed to have started a process that the leaders of the right, because of pressures from their constituents, could not abandon even if they wished. At the annual meeting of the Conservative Party held just before the first Punte del Este Conference in July 1961, the proceedings were interrupted by an ovation for Serrano, and the major speech by party president Correa included a strong attack on the companies that was greeted enthusiastically by the members.[67]

Serrano's plan was blocked, as Chapter 5 pointed out, before it got to the Congress, but so was the legislation for

[65] *El Diario Ilustrado*, July 9, 1961. See also the editorial in *ibid.* on July 22 which claimed that "copper has been Chile's second opportunity after nitrates to develop with foreign capital as a base. But, despite the concessions given by the *Nuevo Trato*, the hoped-for new investments never materialized. Our percentage of world production keeps declining and the companies will not invest enough to keep up, let alone recover, the 1945–1949 Chilean share of the world market."

[66] *Annual Report*, Braden, 1961.

[67] *El Diario Ilustrado*, July 17, 1961.

Rubén Cabezas Pares reports that Senator Juan de Dios Reyes of the Conservative Party made an equally critical attack on the companies that included the proposal that they be nationalized. *Pensamiento económico de los partidos políticos historicos chilenos* (Santiago: Editorial Universitaria, 1964), pp. 145–150.

Kennecott's large Codegua expansion project. Anaconda frankly thought that its management could recreate ties of domestic support with Chilean business groups and members of the Liberal and Conservative, Radical and Christian Democratic Parties. Kennecott—which had never had as satisfactory links with local economic and political interest groups, and which had a poorer "public image" in Chile on account of its mediocre investment behavior—began to think of selling Braden.

The agrarian program proposed and begun by the Alessandri administration was in fact a miniature land reform that did little to disturb social relations in Chile. But neither Alessandri nor Frei (nor even Allende) would ever again find the conservatives defending the companies or arguing for any copper program except nationalization.

VIII

In the election of 1964, Eduardo Frei received the support of the Conservative and Liberal Parties in the final stages of his campaign against the marxist Allende. He won the election with an absolute majority of the vote, a rare feat in more than a century of Chilean electoral politics. In the following Congressional elections of March 1965 the Christian Democratic Party achieved an even more spectacular showing. Christian Democrats captured 82 of 147 seats (56%) in the House, and held 13 out of 45 seats in the Senate.[68]

Yet even after his substantial electoral victories, the new President's Chileanization program, the *viga maestra* of his

---

[68] The Christian Democrats could initiate legislation in the House, but needed one-third of the Senate to sustain its passage (which they did *not* have). This put the right (with seven senators) in a potentially strategic bargaining position. On legislative procedure in the Chilean Congress and the relation between the Copper Program and Agrarian Reform, see Robert Kaufman, *The Politics of Land Reform in Chile* (Cambridge: Harvard University Press, 1972), pp. 171–182.

àdministration, took nearly three years to pass through the Congress. Many of the "developmentalists", the academic economists and *técnicos*, worked in the Frei administration itself and supported the Chileanization proposals. The Communists and Socialists opposed the legislation, as was anticipated, and pressed instead for nationalization. The "surprise", to many outside observers, came in the opposition to Frei's program on the part of the right-wing parties and interest groups that was accompanied by hostility to the copper companies and calls for nationalization.

The Conservative Party was the group that once again drew the crucial lines of battle: the central issue, according to the official statement of the Conservatives,[69] was the "right of property" as guaranteed in Article 10 of the Constitution of Chile. The North American companies were claiming that they could not invest in Chile, the statement declared, unless they were given 20-year guarantees of inviolability for their capital. This demand was being written into the Chileanization legislation. Yet the Agrarian Reform bill, which was also pending before the Congress, would allow the government to expropriate landlords' property at the government's discretion and at a possible "damaging" price. Thus, the Conservative Party concluded, the government would be giving guarantees of "inviolability" to the property of foreigners while moving (under pressure from the United States) to withdraw the Constitutional inviolability of the property of its own citizens. There could be no copper program, the Conservatives declared, without substantial modification in the Agrarian Reform.

Consequently, Arturo Olavarría has suggested that during nearly three years of political maneuvering from 1964 to 1967, whenever President Frei wanted to talk with the Conservatives about the copper program, he sent the Minis-

[69] Statement of the Conservative Party, July 28, 1965, presented by its president, Bernardo Larraín Vial, and reprinted or reported in the newspapers.

ter of Justice ("inviolability of private property") and the Minister of Agriculture to see them—never the Minister of Mines![70]

The Conservative Party, which had the largest constituency of landowners, was most explicit in its strategy of holding the destiny of the copper companies in suspension until modification could be negotiated in the Agrarian Reform. But the concerns of the Conservatives were also preoccupying members of the Liberal, Radical, and even Christian Democratic Parties, many of whose members were themselves large landlords. In October 1965, for example, *El Diario Austral* of Temuco (in the rich agricultural south) reported that the entire Christian Democratic leadership of that important city had resigned over disputes with the party headquarters in Santiago about the Agrarian Reform.[71]

To the outside world, however, it was the Liberal Party that dropped the bombshell on the US copper companies. On August 12, 1965, the prominent Liberal Party Senator Julio von Mühlenbrock publicly demanded the outright nationalization of the copper companies and placed a legislative proposal to that effect before the Congress. The stocks of Anaconda, Kennecott, and Cerro dropped in New York, and, although von Mühlenbrock announced his decision as a matter of "personal conviction" only, the *Wall Street Journal* commented that the defection of the Chilean

[70] Arturo Olavarría Bravo, *Chile bajo la democracia cristiana* (Santiago: Editorial Nacimento, 1966), Vol. 2, pp. 190 *et seq.*

[71] *Ibid.*, Vol. 1, pp. 382 *et seq.* Robert Kaufman reports that ownership of land was an important part of the social background of 64% of Liberal deputies (1961–1965), 43% of the Conservatives (1961–1965), 11% of the Radicals (1961–1965), 18% of the Christian Democrats (1965–1969), and none of the Socialists and Communists. In addition, right-wing politicians estimated that from 25 to 40 (of 82) Christian Democratic deputies as well as several cabinet members partially sympathized with their criticisms of the land reform program. (*The Politics and Land Reform in Chile*, pp. 80, 93.)

right wing to the position of the Communists and Socialists was a hard blow indeed to copper prospects in Chile.[72]

For a year and a half more, the Chileanization program sat in Congress while the struggle over Agrarian Reform and the attendant rights of property continued.[73] The companies by now had only the party in power, the Christian Democrats, and their economic and technical advisors to defend them. The Communists and Socialists were claiming that the country had already developed the skills and expertise necessary to run domestic mining operations, and that the country had a moral responsibility to take international marketing functions away from those capitalist groups that were occupying the Dominican Republic when Chileanization was proposed (1964), and invading Vietnam while the program was being debated (1965–1966). The Radicals were opposed to the corporate system of control over markets and prices, and they could show with increasing justification (as the open market price soared above the US producers' price) that Chileans could manage policy better on their own. And the Conservatives and Liberals on the right were proposing nationalization.

Despite this opposition, President Frei, blessed with an

---

[72] *Wall Street Journal*, August 13, 1965 (Pacific Coast edition).

[73] The best sources on the course of the Chileanization program are the hearings in the House and Senate, *Historia de la ley 16.425*, and the concurrent newspaper accounts. I have also relied on Arturo Olavarría, *Chile bajo la democracia cristiana*; the *Annual Reports* of Braden; and Mikesell, *Foreign Investment in the Petroleum and Mineral Industries*, ch. 15.

Despite the fact that the US copper companies were being held hostage in return for a softening of the Agrarian Reform, the US government did not back down in its pressure for social change. Ambassador Ralph Dungan took such an activist role in pushing for concrete domestic reforms in Chile that several prominent Conservative leaders suggested that he be declared *persona non grata*, for interfering in internal Chilean affairs. See statement of the executive board of the Liberal Party, *El Mercurio*, January 7, 1966, and lead editorial, *Diario Ilustrado*, January 8, 1966, in reaction to an interview with Dungan in *Ercilla*, January 5, 1966.

enlarged Christian Democratic majority in the lower house of Congress and using consummate skill in reform-mongering, was able to maneuver his Chileanization legislation through both houses of Congress. With ample use of patronage and perhaps other forms of persuasion, Frei undermined Radical Party opposition.[74] In addition, there were reports that he did give some concessions to the right on land reform as a means of gaining support for Chileanization from among members of the Liberal and Conservative Parties and his own Christian Democrats, but the evidence is ambiguous.[75] At last, he attached the Chileanization bill as an amendment to the popular annual wage-readjustment bill of 1966, and it passed.

But the passage of the general Chileanization legislation (Law 16,425 of January 25, 1966) by no means signaled an end to the opposition of the right. Frei still needed approval of the specific investment programs of the individual companies, and, as the prospect of Agrarian Reform became more real, the hostility from the right became acute.

The Frei regime realized that to have an authentic land

[74] United Press International reported from Santiago that the Christian Democrats had agreed not to rearrange the governmental bureaucracy so as to damage the Radicals' power base among the civil service in return for Radical support of the copper program.

Olavarría, *op. cit.*, Vol. 1, pp. 350 *et seq.*, suggests that the Christian Democrats voted for Senator Hermes Ahumada Pacheco of the Radical Party to be Provisional President of the Senate in return for his agreement not to bind the Radicals to vote against the copper program as a matter of party discipline.

[75] *El Siglo* reported that Frei made a personal compact with leaders of the Conservative and Liberal Parties in early 1966 that with the rising LME price for copper he would give them a "good" system of payment for expropriation if they would speed their agreement on the copper program. Cf. Olavarría, Vol. 2, p. 179 *et seq.*, and Kaufman, *The Politics of Land Reform*, pp. 175–176.

Olavarría also reports that the Chilean right was more disposed to cooperate with Frei after he moved the army against a strike at Anaconda's El Salvador (with eight deaths), prosecuted the leaders of the mining union, and stood up to a left-wing call for a national strike (Vol. 2, p. 170 *et seq.*).

reform, it could not afford to expropriate thousands of square miles of ill-used or poorly managed farm land at what the landowning class would consider "commercial prices". If the administration did, it faced the prospect of ending up as many felt President Alessandri had—with few farms expropriated, and hundreds of friends of the party in power waiting in line to sell their worst land to the government for cash at prime prices.

Article 10 of the Chilean Constitution, which guaranteed the "inviolable rights of private property", was interpreted to require immediate compensation in cash at the most favorable commercial prices for any property taken over by eminent domain.[76] Frei wanted to be able to expropriate farms at prices more closely related to what they were producing, and pay out a part in cash and the rest in long-term government bonds.[77]

In a highly inflationary economy like Chile's, where the readjustment of principal for government bonds depends upon the will of parties and congresses, the power to expropriate without paying cash is a very sensitive issue. Throughout 1966 there was an open and carefully conceived effort on the part of prominent conservatives with landed interests to spread the fear of Agrarian Reform among small single-business families in industry and trade.[78] Prominent leaders on the right argued that if Ar-

[76] For a respected standard commentary on the *Constitución Política de la República de Chile*, 1925, see Mario Beraschina Gonzáles, *Constitución política y leyes complementárias* (Santiago: Editorial Jurídica de Chile, 2nd ed., 1958).

[77] For an explanation of the rationale behind the Constitutional Reform of Article 10, see the analyses of Professor Francisco Cumplido of the Law Faculty of the University of Chile, as reported in *El Mercurio* and *El Diario Ilustrado*, December 3, 1964, *et seq.* The intent was to shift from the liberal ideology of property rights in the 1925 Constitution towards re-defining the "social character" of the rights of property within the context of the broadest needs of the community.

The evolution of Frei's approach to compensation is traced in Kaufman, *The Politics of Land Reform*, ch. 3.

[78] That is, to the so-called "national bourgeoisie". Interviews with leaders of the Sociedad de Fomento Fabril at the time of this incident

ticle 10 were changed for purposes of Agrarian Reform, a situation would be created in which, in the extreme case, property existed only at the whim of the executive and could be expropriated without meaningful compensation. Thus, the argument that the Agrarian Reform threatened the whole system of private property, and that with property threatened there was no stability or security for any enterprise in Chile, could be made to seem powerful and frightening.

Early in 1966, the president of the National Society of Manufacturers, D. Fernando Smits, spoke in these terms as he gave a warning about Frei's programs to the annual meeting of members.[79] He argued that the leadership of the manufacturers' organization was very worried about the future of any private enterprise in Chile if the Agrarian Reform brought with it a Constitutional Reform concerning the rights of property.

As the Constitutional Reform of Article 10 moved along

---

revealed that the effort was directed at the relatively "new" industrial bourgeoisie (often Jews, Arabs, Germans, Italians, Spaniards, with small family firms) that had grown up during and since the Second World War in the process of import-substitution.

This campaign suggested that there was some delineation that could be called "traditional oligarchy" and new "industrial bourgeois". But most of the prominent members of the "traditional oligarchy" had themselves diversified into manufacturing and finance, and were leading the newer and smaller industrialists against the companies, rather than defending foreign investors against an industrial bourgeois–industrial labor alliance.

The view that the "national bourgeoisie" did not regularly play an independent role in Chilean politics, but rather followed the lead of the traditional oligarchy is supported by evidence from Dale Johnson, "The National and Progressive Bourgeoisie in Chile", in James Cockcroft, André Gunder Frank, and Dale L. Johnson, eds., *Dependence and Underdevelopment* (Garden City, N.Y.: Doubleday, 1972); and Maurice Zeitlin and Richard Earl Ratcliff, *Landlords and Capitalists* (New York: Harper and Row, forthcoming).

[79] D. Fernardo Smits, "Sin Derecho de Propiedad No Puede Existir Progreso ni Democracia", reprinted in *Industria*, Nos. 3–4, 1966.

farther through the Congress, feelings grew even more intense.

The climax came in November 1966 at the Hundredth Anniversary of Antofagasta. President Frei and his ministers were assembled on the platform, while the acting president of the National Manufacturers' Society, Ernesto Pinto Lagarrigue, a man of great prestige in the Chilean right, served as speaker to inaugurate the industrial fair of the city. To the President's face, in public, Sr. Pinto attacked the whole course of the President's program to change the rights of property.

Very seldom in the entire history of Chile, said Sr. Pinto, had conditions made it so difficult to decide whether or not to invest as it was today.[80] The Constitutional Reform of Article 10 would allow the Executive arbitrarily to revoke the existence of private enterprise (with the suggestion of "tyranny"). The proposed change to the Constitutional rights of property must not be approved.

There was a large sense of shock following the speech. President Frei and others considered the attack a personal insult to the Presidency.[81] Clearly it was a call to all businessmen as well as landowners to repudiate the President's program out of fear of political tyranny in the economy.

According to leaders of the National Society of Manufacturers in 1966, the Frei government clearly recognized that the Agrarian Reform program was fundamentally jeopardized if broad business and commercial sectors joined wholeheartedly in the campaign against it. The National Society of Manufacturers refused to apologize for the incident or to retract what Sr. Pinto had said, but one of its suborganizations (the Associación de Industriales Químicos) did both.

[80] The speech was reprinted and distributed by the *Sociedad de Fomento Fabril.* Later, it was also reprinted in *Industria,* Nos. 11–12, 1966.

[81] Cf. *El Mercurio,* November 16, 1966; *El Diario Ilustrado,* November 17, 1966.

The Frei government took the position that it would no longer ration its credit and its capital through the manufacturers' society—an action that nearly destroyed the usefulness of the society as an organization.[82] With private credit in the inflationary Chilean economy tightly and selectively controlled by the government, and with such a large proportion of investment capital (approximately 50%) coming from the government, there was no real possibility that the small and medium-sized businesses could dare to join actively in the fight against Agrarian Reform.

Once again, Frei won out. The Constitutional Reform of Article 10 became law on January 20, 1967. On April 20, Law 16,624 established the final legal basis for the investment programs involved in Chileanization of copper. And on July 16 President Frei signed the Agrarian Reform into law in a large ceremony in the Plaza de la Constitución.

As Chapter 5 pointed out, the companies were in a strong position—before they committed themselves—to demand major concessions in the tax rate, in government investment and government guarantees, and in revaluation of net worth (for Kennecott). Frei had to make generous concessions, but his careful approach to the negotiations insured that the country would get a major expansion of capacity in return. Also, he realized, once the new operations were successfully on-line, it would be his turn to squeeze again.

IX

It was in the context of carrying out a bitterly contested land reform, then, that the attack on Anaconda was launched a year and a half later.

This attack came, as Chapter 5 described, as the expan-

[82] This account is drawn from interviews with some of the leaders of the *Sociedad de Fomento Fabril* in 1966. After the speech was reprinted in *Industria*, the magazine, which had been published as the official organ of the manufacturers' association since 1889, was discontinued. There were no discussions of reviving it until four years later, in late 1970, under new SFF leadership.

sion programs were being completed and Chile's own decision to take over international pricing policy was producing such spectacular results. Clearly the balance of power
had shifted to Chile at precisely the time when the foreigners' presence was most discounted and the benefit from
ending foreign control was highest.

During Frei's secret negotiations with Anaconda, feelings
of national competence were mixed with a thirst for re-
venge on the part of many as every political party in Chile
talked of nationalization.

On May 17, 1969 the National Party (a fusion of the Conservative and Liberal Parties) made its pronouncement:[83]
the Partido Nacional, said its president Sergio Onofre
Jarpa, was not in favor of *estatismo* in principle, but the
party would nevertheless support some kind of take-over
of Anaconda.

If Anaconda were in fact nationalized, Onofre was asked,
how could Chile carry it out?

His answer was succinct: "The United States told us to
have an Agrarian Reform with 30-year terms of payment of
compensation. I think that we ought to apply the same system to the *Gran Minería*, and I am sure that the United
States won't object. In any case, we won't support Anaconda. . . . If this plan [to nationalize Anaconda] is serious,
we will support it."

Anaconda searched in vain for local support among business, banking, and commercial groups.[84] They had been

[83] Statement of Sergio Onofre Jarpa, president of the *Partido Na-
cional*, in *Tercer de la Hora*, May 17, 1969. On the same day, *El
Diario Ilustrado* reported an "almost unanimous tendency in the
[Partido Nacional] for nationalization".

[84] This account is based on interviews with the top Anaconda officials in Santiago and New York and with Congressional Deputies of
various political parties in Santiago (January–February 1970). The
latter suggested that constituent pressures from landholders, including
middle-class urban landholders who felt that their interests were
threatened, prevented the more conservative members of the Radical
and Christian Democratic Parties, as well as of the National (Liberal

spending a pre-tax budget in Chile of over $180 million— much of it going to Chilean companies and contractors in relation to the new expansion program—and they hoped to swing some weight with that. The result was negative. Not a single important Chilean business group, legal group, or banking group spoke out in their favor. Several prominent conservatives who had been personal friends with the Anaconda hierarchy in New York left Chile and would not return to the country (or answer their phones in Paris) until the movement toward nationalization had been completed.

As Chapter 5 indicated, the Frei administration actually only pressed for 51% control with compensation—that is, for the fulfillment of Chileanization. But President Frei privately informed Anaconda that domestic pressures were so strong that if he could not win a spectacular "deal" from the company, he would be forced to introduce his own nationalization proposal into the Congress.

By now, however, the Anaconda management realized what Kennecott had accepted as a working principle for nearly a decade—that there was little or no dependable domestic support left for them in Chile. Consequently the promise of a new commitment on their part would just see

---

and Conservative) Party from speaking out in defense of the US companies.

As for the position of the United States government, Ambassador Edward Korry in Santiago did what he could to see that Anaconda got the most advantageous settlement possible. But there was little he could do. UPI dispatches in Santiago reported that Ambassador Korry had warned Frei to "be careful" in the Anaconda negotiations or else the United States government would "see with satisfaction the triumph of the Right in next year's elections" (reported May 18, 1969).

At that time, however, the *Partido Nacional* was pushing its own plan for nationalization.

In Washington, when the actual "nationalization by agreement" was announced, UPI quoted Robert J. McClosky of the State Department as saying that "the gradual expropriation of the interests of Anaconda constituted an agreement between a private company and a government". Therefore, the United States government was not a party to any "dispute".

the balance of power swing against them once again at a short time in the future. Anaconda refused to be Chileanized, and they feared that they would be expropriated if they balked at any change whatsoever. So they asked to be nationalized.[85]

In the campaign of 1970, both Salvador Allende, the candidate of the *Unidad Popular* coalition (Socialists, Communists, Radicals, and MAPU), and Radomiro Tomic, the candidate of the Christian Democrats, promised that they would nationalize all the foreign copper companies immediately if elected. Even the Conservative candidate, former

---

[85] The agreement called for the Chilean government to take over 51% of Anaconda's two major operations at Chuquicamata and Potrerillos almost immediately, paid for at book value. The remaining 49% would be bought in subsequent years at a price determined by the earnings of the companies and the speed of nationalization.

Outraged at being upstaged by Frei's nationalization and critical that anything at all was being paid to Anaconda in compensation, the Socialist and Communist Parties called the *nacionalización pactada* a fraud and threatened to call a general strike to protest it.

Frei was apparently angered enough at the reaction of the left (posters of "FRAUD" all over Santiago) and threatened enough by the possibility of a general strike for him to take extraordinary international steps to counter the Socialist–Communist coalition. According to the newspapers *La Segunda* and *El Clarín* (July 3, 1969), Frei demanded to know from the Soviet Union whether the views of the Chilean Communist Party were independent, or came from Moscow; he threatened to withdraw his ambassador from Moscow if the views came from there; he spoke of reversing the trend toward liberalizing relations with the USSR that had taken place during his administration; he even hinted at breaking diplomatic relations.

Immediately afterward, two visiting union leaders from the Soviet Union spoke out suddenly in favor of Frei's nationalization of Anaconda (*La Segunda*, July 4, 1969). On the sixth of July, *El Mercurio* editorialized that the Chilean Communist Party was changing its tone about the nationalization of Anaconda. On the twelfth of July, the Italian Communist Party and the Ecuadorian Communist Party took note of Frei's nationalization of Anaconda and applauded it (*La Nación*, July 12, 1969).

El Siglo, the newspaper of the Chilean Communist Party, kept referring to Frei's nationalization as a swindle (*estafa*), but there was no more threat of a national strike.

President Jorge Alessandri, affirmed that he felt obliged to uphold the nationalization of Anaconda, although he offered the prospect of a long management contract and generous compensation for the company.[86]

Once in office, Dr. Salvador Allende pressed for rapid nationalization of Kennecott and Cerro as well as Anaconda. In a Congress dominated by the opposition and requiring two-thirds approval for the copper legislation, President Allende's nationalization program was passed unanimously on July 11, 1971.

On September 28 President Allende formalized the nationalization of Anaconda, Kennecott, and Cerro. The setting of compensation had been left by Congress to the discretion of the President, and a calculation of back taxes on "excess profits" since the beginning of the *Nuevo Trato* (plus charges for other damages) far exceeded the book value of the companies. The efforts of the United States government to influence the process of providing compensation only strengthened Chilean intransigence.

There was extreme domestic discord about many aspects of Allende's administration. But national support for the act of taking over the foreign copper companies was overwhelming. The opposition parties of the center and right, like the *Unidad Popular* coalition, defended the nationalization in terms of restoring sovereign control over national development and welfare. Even the head of Chile's Roman Catholic bishops, Raúl Cardinal Silva Henríquez, felt moved to declare that the nationalization of the large US copper companies was right and just.[87]

[86] The promises of Allende and Tomic to nationalize the US mining companies were repeated in almost every campaign speech as well as in their electoral platforms. For Alessandri's position on copper, see his statement in *El Mercurio*, February 7, 1970.

[87] Cardinal Silva said: "The process of nationalization has been constitutionally impeccable. With the respect for the law that is traditional in Chile, the principle consecrated by the United Nations that every country has the right to reclaim its basic resources has been put into practice." (*New York Times*, October 24, 1971.) In addition, the

X

The first part of this chapter developed a model of the relations between foreign investors and host governments based on the evolution of their bargaining strengths. Short-run swings in the balance of power between foreign investors and host governments are a product of sharp reversals in the perception of uncertainty. A cumulative shift in the balance of power is the result of a national learning process, the result of an increase in domestic skills and confidence.

The chapter then attempted to build on top of the formal bargaining model an analysis of what made domestic groups in the Chilean context produce a policy outcome that took advantage of, or did not take advantage of, the relative balance of power.

From the Chilean case, then, it is possible to extract the beginnings of a general theory of host country–foreign investor relations. By combining the dynamic bargaining model developed here with the analysis of disaggregated domestic group interests, one can try to generalize about what must be examined across many cases in order to test the extent to which the course of host country–foreign investor relations can be predicted.

The Chilean experience with copper suggests a general theory of host country–foreign investor relations in which conflict or cooperation is a function of variables along three dimensions:

(1) one dimension specifying the *target* of domestic concern—that is, a dimension in which it is necessary to try to measure the "prominence" or "sensitivity" of the foreign-controlled industry in the national economy, national prestige, or national political tradition.

(2) a second dimension specifying the *setting* for any

Chilean bishops asked the Synod of Bishops then meeting in Rome to study the "morality" of nationalization without compensation of foreign interests in developing countries.

negotiation—that is, a dimension in which it is necessary to measure host-country perceptions of the advantages that the foreign investor contributes to the conduct of the industry, and to measure host-country perceptions of the cost of replacing or doing without those advantages. This dimension would have to incorporate an analysis of at what point in the swings in the balance of power the host country and foreign investor find themselves.

(3) a third dimension specifying how *policy formation* takes place—that is, a dimension in which it is necessary to measure the value (in social, political, or economic terms) to various domestic groups of maintaining or expelling the foreign presence, and to weigh their relative abilities to influence public policy in line with their interests.

The presence or absence, strength or weakness of measurements in these three dimensions will predict the presence or absence, strength or weakness of conflict or cooperation in the relations between any host country and any foreign investor in any industry.[88]

These three dimensions constitute the theoretical structure within which all attempts to analyze economic nationalism, joint maximization, foreign domination, and international exploitation should be made in order to be complete. They offer a richer perspective than the conventional paradigms of "reactionary alliances", "neo-imperialism", and the "consolidation of underdevelopment"—which may describe relations between host countries and foreign investors at

---

[88] Manufacturing investments in industries where there are continuous changes in technology or marketing would not have the abrupt swings in the balance of power between foreign investors and host countries that accompany the large lump-sum investments in natural resources. Therefore, although they might be extremely "sensitive" in the first dimension, the perception of the cost of doing without the foreigner in the second dimension would suggest greater stability for them in the host countries. On the other hand, manufacturing investments at the low end of the product cycle—where technology is stable and production standardized—might generate a very low perception of the contribution of the foreigner.

217

particular points in time, but which have no way of explaining the movement from one state to another. Similarly, they offer possibilities for more dynamic prediction than the popular paradigms of "harmony of interests" and "mutual advantage"—which mistake the suppression of tension for its absence.

To be sure, this constitutes only the beginnings of a general theory of foreign investor–host country relations, because the three dimensions will be clearly interrelated in some ways and independent in other ways that can scarcely be determined without many more case studies of different industries and different countries in different stages of development.[89]

Nevertheless, in the remainder of the chapter, I shall suggest how I think the three dimensions are related in large natural-resource investments in developing countries.

The historical experience of almost all countries compels them to define as "sensitive" or "vital" certain areas in which dependence on the performance of a foreigner constitutes a potential threat to national sovereignty, welfare, or security.[90] This is as true for developed as for underdeveloped

[89] At the same time, chance events such as the introduction of the Alliance for Progress land reform would have to be factored out of a general theory.

[90] This analysis draws on the history of economic nationalism in developed countries (such as Canada, Australia, and Western Europe) as well as in diverse developing countries.

On Canada, see Albert Breton, "The Economics of Nationalism", *Journal of Political Economy*, Vol. LXXII, No. 4 (August 1964); Harry Johnson, "An Economic Theory of Protectionism: Tariff Bargaining, and the Formation of Customs Unions", *Journal of Political Economy*, Vol. LXXII (June 1965); Kari Levitt, *Silent Surrender: The Multinational Corporation in Canada* (New York: St. Martin's Press, 1970); A. E. Safarian, *Foreign Ownership of Canadian Industry* (Toronto: McGraw-Hill Co. of Canada, 1966).

On Australia, see T. H. Moran, "Australian Nationalism: Economic and Political Considerations", paper presented to the Georgetown University study of economic nationalism in Australia, November 1972; Donald T. Brash, *American Investment in Australian Industry* (Cam-

countries. The French may seek autonomy in the defense sector; the Canadians in the communications sector; the Japanese in the export sector. In developing countries where a single foreign-controlled industry determines the pace of domestic economic activity and the availability of foreign exchange for growth, the foreign companies cannot avoid being exposed to reactions against the condition of "dependence".

Albert Hirschman has used the term "privileged problems" to describe areas of concern that are easily brought to the attention of governments by groups within the society, or areas of conflict about which feelings can be easily aroused within the populace by governments or elite groups.[91] The concerns about economic growth, employment, social welfare were "privileged problems" in Chile, as in other developing countries, after the Second World War. Through intimate linkage to these public concerns, the foreign-controlled copper export industry could not help becoming just such a "privileged problem", too. Even political and economic groups whose ideological stance

---

bridge, Mass.: Harvard University Press, 1966); Edith T. Penrose, "Foreign Investment and the Growth of the Firm", *Economic Journal*, June 1956; B. L. Johns, "Private Overseas Investment in Australia: Profitability and Motivation," *Economic Record*, June 1967.

For general overviews, see Vernon, *Sovereignty at Bay*; Charles P. Kindleberger, *American Business Abroad* (New Haven: Yale University Press, 1969), *The International Corporation: A Symposium* (Cambridge, Mass.: MIT Press, 1970), and *Power and Money* (New York: Basic Books, 1970); Jean-Jacques Servan-Schreiber, *The American Challenge* (New York: Atheneum, 1968); Jack N. Behrman, *National Interests and Multinational Enterprise* (Englewood Cliffs, N.J.: Prentice-Hall, 1970); Michael Kidron, *Foreign Investments in India* (New York: Oxford University Press, 1965); Mikesell, ed., *Foreign Investment in the Petroleum and Mineral Industries: Case Studies in Investor–Host Country Relations*; Wionczek, *El nacionalismo mexicano y la inversión extranjera*; and Harry Johnson, ed., *Economic Nationalism in Old and New States* (Chicago: University of Chicago Press, 1967).

[91] Albert O. Hirschman, *Journeys Toward Progress* (New York: Doubleday, 1965), Part II.

might lead them to welcome the foreign presence were drawn into a process of monitoring and criticizing the behavior of the companies ever more closely.

There is a "mobilization" effect in foreign investor–host country relations in a poor country that springs from the process of development itself, similar to what Karl Deutsch has described in the area of populace–government relations.[92] In the Deutsch model of "mobilization", many of the stresses and strains and instabilities of developing countries are caused by the promises of development itself. As old patterns of social and economic stability are broken, new expectations are aroused, new groups are brought the consciousness of benefiting from change, and new demands are made on the governing elites. If expectations rise faster than they can be fulfilled and if demands increase at a rate greater than the capacity of the system to deal with them, then tension, conflict, and instability result.

When this mobilization model is transposed to the area of foreign investor–host country relations, one might predict the same results. In a developing economy that depends to a predominant extent on a single foreign-dominated industry for taxes and hard currency revenues, one would expect growing pressure on the foreign companies to the extent that needs are increasing faster than tax revenues and exchange earnings are being supplied. As more groups perceive that they are in fact "dependent" on the behavior of the foreigners, the foreign companies will be blamed and criticized when their contribution to the national economy is weak, when they "transmit" bad condi-

---

[92] On social mobilization, see Karl W. Deutsch, "Social Mobilization and Political Development," *American Political Science Review*, Vol. 55 (September 1961); Samuel P. Huntington, *Political Order in Changing Societies* (New Haven: Yale University Press, 1968); also Mancur Olson, Jr., "Rapid Growth as a Destabilizing Force," *Journal of Economic History*, Vol. 23 (December 1963); and Raymond Tanter and Manus Midlarsky, "A Theory of Revolution", *Journal of Conflict Resolution*, Vol. 11 (September 1967).

tions into the host country. And, rather than being praised when their contribution to the national economy is strong, they may be told merely that current behavior proves that prior criticism was justified.

In a poor and stagnant country where the foreign exporters actually formed an isolated enclave, investors would in all likelihood feel little tension from the traditional upper classes. The host country demands for dollar revenues to supply luxury imports to a small domestic oligarchy could probably be easily accommodated. Here the conventional model of "reactionary alliances" would apply—only the ideological left ("class-conscious" workers, students, and intellectuals) would call for increasing pressure on the foreign companies. The domestic right would ally with the foreigners to defend the status quo that served them both.

But once the traditional pattern is broken and there are rising demands for growth, development, and welfare, the prominent foreign companies, like the national government in the mobilization model, will find more and more eyes, including conservative eyes, watching and measuring corporate performance against national needs. There may, indeed, be clear and costly instances of "exploitation" and "complicity" in which elite groups arrange political or economic payoffs to foreign companies to serve their own particular domestic interests at the public expense. But the value of supporting the international investors will be restricted more and more exclusively to those periods when the balance of power is on the side of the foreigners, under conditions where they can be enticed to bring new corporate resources to the service of the host country—that is, only when the perception of the cost of replacing or doing without the foreigners is very high.

Unless the fiscal contributions of the foreign companies are far beyond the real or imagined needs of the country, one can predict rising demands for more dynamic performance on the part of the foreign corporations. When foreigners in a particular sector occupy such a sensitive position in public attention that political groups can win support by constantly maneuvering to force more out of them, then it will be a rational decision to invest time and energy in a systematic drive to chip away at the bases of foreign invulnerability. Economic nationalism, as Albert Breton and Harry Johnson suggest, can then be thought of as a kind of "social good" in which there is a consensus to invest scarce national talents.[93]

As abrupt changes in the perception of uncertainty swing the balance of power back and forth between foreign investors and the host country, domestic concern about the performance of those investors leads to a systematic drive to take over functions, gain expertise, acquire knowledge that were previously the monopoly of the foreign corporations. Thus, for the "prominent", "sensitive" foreign companies, national *concern* inevitably shifts toward the potential for national *control*, no matter what the ideological proclivities of the host government or of the critical elites.

As the host country works itself up a learning curve, the accumulated domestic skills result in a decline in the perception of the relative value of the contribution of the foreign investors. Just as the foreign investors were welcomed into the country because they had some quasi-monopoly advantage to offer,[94] so the burden falls on them, if they oc-

[93] Breton, "The Economics of Nationalism", *Journal of Political Economy*; Johnson, "An Economic Theory of Protectionism: Tariff Bargaining, and the Formation of Customs Unions", *ibid.*

There is no attempt here, however, to estimate the economic or political opportunity costs of nationalism.

[94] This model has been developed as a general theory of foreign investment by Stephen Hymer, "The International Operations of National Firms: A Study of Direct Foreign Investment," unpublished Ph.D. dissertation, MIT, 1960; Raymond Vernon, "International Investment and International Trade in the Product Cycle", *Quarterly Journal of Economics*, Vol. 80 (May 1966), and *Sovereignty at Bay*; Kindleberger, *American Business Abroad*; Louis T. Wells, Jr., "Test of a Product Cycle Model of International Trade", *Quarterly Journal of*

cupy a politically or economically sensitive position, to demonstrate that their presence continues to offer clear advantages that would be very costly to replace or do without. As domestic capacities increase, they must be willing to bring more and more corporate resources to the national arena each time the balance of power shifts against them, just to get back to the same relative position.

Doubtless there are some corporations whose expertise is so valuable and so tightly held that they can occupy unassailable positions in various host countries for long periods of time. And doubtless there are some corporations that are willing to respond to the challenge of nationalism by bringing more and more resources to the service of the country for a considerable period of time. But a final point will probably come inevitably[95] for any foreign investor whose presence is a challenge to national sovereignty or whose behavior is considered rarely dynamic enough for the multiplying needs of national welfare. That point will come when beleaguered corporate boards of directors decide that making greater and greater commitments in a deteriorating situation is simply throwing good money after bad, or when ambitious politicians decide that the benefits of nationalization that accrue to themselves and to the country are greater than the costs of doing without the foreigner.

When the precariously exposed foreign investors no longer have advantages to offer greater than the national preference for domestic control, or when they decide that they will stand and be pushed no farther along a course moving constantly to their disadvantage, they will be taken over.

Economics, Vol. 83 (February 1969), and *International Trade: The Product Cycle Approach* (New York: Basic Books, 1973); and Richard Caves, "International Corporations: The Industrial Economics of Foreign Investment", *Economica*, February 1971.

[95] Hypotheses that host-country tensions about "foreign control" could diminish under certain conditions in many underdeveloped countries are discussed in Chapter 8.

Given the dynamics of economic nationalism, such foreign corporations in the long run, to paraphrase Keynes, are all dead.

The trick for the nationalist is to take as full advantage of the foreign corporations as he can while they are within his range, and not to push them out until he is as close as possible to being able to duplicate or surpass their feats on the international as well as the national scene.

CHAPTER 7

Chile and the Future of *Dependencia*

Chapter 2 traced the evolution of strategy in the international copper industry as a series of efforts to preserve and protect the ability of producers to exact an economic rent from final industrial consumers. Chapters 3 through 6 outlined the conflict between Chile's drive for sovereign control over a dynamic national development and the private decision-making processes that were determining strategy for the multinational copper companies. The process of closing in on and ultimately nationalizing Anaconda and Kennecott (and Cerro) sprang from the collective desire in Chile to take control of the domestic copper industry and use its full strength to serve the needs of domestic development.

The idea of *dependencia* described the power of the foreign companies as something that had to be seized. It described the moderation in the use of power on the part of the foreign companies as something that had to be overcome. The idea of *dependencia* inspired the country to learn how to pull, push, and shove the foreign companies to bring more of their corporate resources to the service of Chilean development. It inspired the country to learn how to duplicate the feats of the foreign companies in managing domestic production.

Unfortunately, however, the idea of *dependencia* did not help the country to learn how best to use the power it struggled for as an "independent" producer in the international market.

With the nationalization of the copper companies, *dependencia* was replaced in Chile by a hard-won *independencia*, a longed-for *autonomía*, with regard to pricing, production, and marketing. The country had "recovered" control of its own natural resources, "restored" sovereignty

225

over the course of its own national destiny. The new independence or autonomy or sovereignty would not easily again suffer anything that could be construed as surrender to the dictates of foreigners.

Herein lies the subtle problem that faces all the new nationalistic producers: how to make successive governments and their opponents recognize that the cautious manipulation of interdependence (with other producers, including the private corporate producers, as well as with fabricators and consumers) leads to greater strength than the raw exercise of autonomous power. The cautious manipulation of interdependence requires self-restraint and dependability in the use of market power. Further, it requires the ability to make a credible promise that the self-restraint and dependability will continue into the future. For this, the heritage of economic nationalism does not provide a good preparation.

This chapter will analyze how the international copper industry (both producers and fabricators or consumers) has reacted to the rise of economic nationalism in the major copper-exporting countries, and what alternative courses of evolution are likely for the industry in the future. The chapter will then examine the position of an independent national producer like Chile vis-à-vis such projected evolutions of the international industry, and suggest the margins within which the country can exercise its independence and autonomy to best serve the needs of national development and welfare.

I

The mid-1960's marked a peak—perhaps the last peak for some time—in the flow of equity venture capital to develop or expand copper-mining facilities in "insecure" countries of the underdeveloped world. Chile was just beginning its mammoth expansion program through negotiations with Kennecott, Anaconda, and the Cerro Corporation. Peru was on the verge of opening the rich Cuajone, Cerro Verde, and

Quellaveco properties in the south, and the Michiquillay properties in the north, with the capital of Anaconda, Cerro, and American Smelting and Refining. In Zambia, President Kenneth Kaunda seemed to be providing independence with stability for the British and American interests, and the Japanese were talking of moving in, too. The one uncertain major copper-producing area was the Congo, with all its bloody upheaval, where the Union Minière was in the process of being nationalized.

By the beginning of the 1970's, however, economic nationalism seemed to be the rule rather than the exception. General Velasco had taken over the government in Peru, and, after the nationalization of the International Petroleum Corporation, had imposed stiff new controls over the copper industry as well. The nationalization in the Congo had been completed. To the south, in Zambia, President Kaunda had taken over 51% of the operations of Roan Selection Trust and the Anglo-American Corporation—thereby damaging, at the same time, the interests of American Metal Climax and the Rio Tinto Zinc Corporation. Kaunda had threatened to demand the remaining 49%, and had placed himself in personal charge of all the country's international copper operations. Finally, of course, Eduardo Frei in Chile had nationalized Anaconda, and Salvador Allende had followed with rapid take-overs of Kennecott and Cerro as well.

The immediate reaction to the challenge of economic nationalism by the traditional giants in the international copper industry—both those directly affected by nationalizations and those not directly affected—has been simple and predictable:[1] (1) they have shifted their investment plans and their exploration efforts to "secure" areas; (2)

---

[1] The reactions of the major international copper companies and projections of future behavior have been estimated on the basis of data published in the *American Metal Market, Metals Week, Metal Bulletin*, and *Engineering and Mining Journal*, as well as on the basis of interviews with officials of the leading companies.

they have tried to keep their former market share by "replacing" threatened or lost output; (3) they have been trying to preserve their network of ties to customers, to maintain the selling patterns that they built up with such effort, expense, and patience in the past.

The search for alternative sources of production has been directed toward the United States and Canada, Australia, and the South Pacific. Increased exploration in these geographical areas has been combined with concentration on the technology and techniques necessary to exploit large-scale, low-grade ore-bodies. In the South Pacific, for example, Rio Tinto Zinc has brought a mine of 200,000 tons per year capacity on-line in 1973 in Bougainville (the Papua-New Guinea protectorate of Australia) that works ore of only 0.49% copper content—that is, a mine equal in size to (pre-1967) El Teniente in Chile with ore of one-half the richness.[2] With terms arranged so that the large fixed capital costs can be recovered quickly, this property, like other low-grade operations in Canada and the United States, is expected to have operating costs that make it competitive with mines of much higher grade ore elsewhere.

Since copper producers, like other natural resource oligopolists, traditionally keep claims on many more reserves than they need to meet current commitments in their share of the market, it is particularly difficult to evaluate to what extent truly "new" discoveries have been required in the attempts of threatened producers to regain their shares.

Anaconda, under completely new management after the Chilean nationalization, has at least thirteen major undeveloped ore deposits in non-Spanish speaking countries (plus one in Mexico) under consideration for bringing on-line in

[2] Cf. "Bougainville Copper", Harvard Business School Case No. 9-372-146, prepared by Michael Dubin, 1971; "Bougainville: The New Face in Copper Mining", *Engineering and Mining Journal*, February 1973; and "Facing the Change in Copper Technology", *Engineering and Mining Journal*, April 1973.

the course of the 1970's.[3] Nine are in the United States, and others are in Canada, Australia, and Iran.

Kennecott has new properties and new explorations under way in the United States, Puerto Rico, and Southeast Asia–Oceania.

American Smelting and Refining, forced to give up mining concessions in Peru, has been engaged in bringing new production to the market from Canada, Australia, and Mexico, and has the option of increasing output in the United States.

The Roan Selection Trust group, nationalized in Zambia, was negotiating in competition with Anaconda for major new copper mines in Iran for the mid-1970's, has begun to work new ore-bodies in Botswana, and has bid for concessions in Indonesia and Australia.

The Anglo-American Corporation of South Africa, also nationalized in Zambia, and the Union Minière, nationalized in the Congo, have both been expanding their ore bases in Canada and Australia.

The threat of economic nationalism has hurt all of these corporations not only through the loss of revenues from the mines that were taken over but also through the threat to their places as major oligopoly members in the semi-integrated world industry. To maintain scale economies of size, managerial expertise, and international marketing position, then, they have been investing to replace output and keep their global structures intact even in periods when the short-term outlook for demand has been weak and prices have been falling.

II

The challenge of economic nationalism has already contributed to the dilution of the international producers' oligopoly through adding four new actors—the state agencies of Chile, Peru, Zambia, and Zaire (the Congo). More im-

[3] Cf. *Wall Street Journal*, June 21, 1971, p. 22.

portantly, the behavior of these four state agencies is likely to spur the further dilution of oligopoly concentration and oligopoly strength. In the jargon of the industry, they have not devoted enough attention to "customer relations"; in the jargon of economics, they have not been willing, in a situation of bilateral oligopoly with customers, to share the burden of fluctuations in supply and demand. They have not given fabricators and consumers a "secure" source of supply.

In 1966 Chile began, as we have seen, to raise its price above the US producers' price in response to the stiff demand resulting from escalation in Vietnam. Together with other nationalistic governments, Chile agreed to peg its quotation for copper to the high level then reflected on the thin London Metals Exchange. Disregarding all cautions to the contrary, these countries decided to go for all the market would bear under conditions of wartime shortage. During the course of the Vietnam War, the prices borne by the customers of these four countries rose from about 35¢ per pound to levels frequently above 80¢, while the US producers' price stayed from 20¢ to 30¢ per pound lower.

Not only did these producing countries try to use full market power during periods of strong demand by leaving the low US producers' price and switching to the higher open market price, but they also sought to cut back production when demand sagged in order to maintain prices at the high level. In 1967 Chile met in Lusaka with representatives of Zambia, Peru, and Zaire and formed a producers' organization, the Intergovernmental Council of Copper Exporting Countries (CIPEC), modeled after the Organization of Petroleum Exporting countries, to coordinate price and production policy. At least three times since the Lusaka Conference, the CIPEC countries have tried to obtain agreement for cutbacks in production when prices dropped to force them back up. Each time the divergent interests of the member countries have prevented effective harmonization of plans for production quotas during periods of slack demand. But the intent of the independent national producers was clear—the new state agencies would try to take advantage of short-run inelasticities of supply and demand at each stage of the business cycle to gain the most revenues possible to fund their needs for national welfare and development. The strategy of the CIPEC countries—to confront customers with full market power at every stage of supply and demand—was precisely what the processors and consumers wanted to avoid most.

Such a strategy would work only if consumers had no feasible alternatives. Unfortunately for CIPEC, many major consumers (and their governments) are beginning to calculate the costs of one alternative—namely, integrating backward to their own "secure" supplies—and finding that the results may be worth the effort. The initial CIPEC strategy of capitalizing on the position of strength under conditions of extreme copper shortage (1966–1969) provided the stimulus for industrial fabricators and consumers, and their governments, to take unprecedented steps to develop new sources of copper. Such steps have now been continued even through periods of weak demand.

For the first time, the West German government has been following the pattern of the Japanese in financing new mining operations on the basis of repayment in ore. The Kreditanstalt für Wiederaufbau, the German state reconstruction bank, has lent substantial amounts of development capital to American companies in Southeast Asia–Oceania and to British and American companies in some parts of Africa (not Zambia) in return for long-term contracts for a share of the output. West Germany's largest smelter-refinery (Norddeutsche Affinerie of Hamburg) and largest fabricator group (Metallgesellschaft A.G.)—neither of which had ever been formally integrated backward to the production stage before—have been participating in both of these regions with official backing.

West German, Swedish, Belgian, and French capital have flowed to Canada to finance or take equity participation in new mines. The Pechiney–Tréfimétaux group in France, formerly interested primarily in aluminum and nickel, are becoming copper producers in Australia. The Australian government has advanced loans to British and Australian companies to bring new copper sources into production.

The Japanese Ministry of International Trade and Investment, coordinating the efforts of governmental agencies, private trading groups, banks, and mining and fabricating companies, has continued that country's voracious search for copper in Canada, the South Pacific, Southeast Asia, and some parts of Africa. Providing development capital in return for long-term contracts for ore has continued to be the favored Japanese method of securing new sources of capital, but there have also been an increasing number of direct equity participations taken by groups of Japanese companies.

In the United States under President Nixon, a special subcommittee of the Council of Economic Advisors, headed by Dr. Hendrik Houthakker, asked why new production was sluggish and asked how increases might be stimulated in the United States.[4] A new "Paley Report" recommended increasing government support and financial backing for domestic mine production to offset any threat of producer cartels.[5]

Most of the US reserves consist of large, low-grade deposits in Arizona, Utah, and Montana. Newly discovered Canadian reserves are of the same type. These are not nearly so rich as ore-bodies in some other countries, but once

[4] Hendrik H. Houthakker, *Report of the Subcommittee on Copper to the Cabinet Committee on Economic Policy* (Washington, D.C.: The White House, May 1970), "Copper: The Anatomy of a Malfunctioning Market", "The Copper Industry in a Changing World"; and the press conference of Dr. Houthakker, Washington, May 22, 1970.

[5] National Commission on Materials Policy, *Final Report: Material Needs and the Environment Today and Tomorrow*, (Washington: GPO 1973). Cf. C. Fred Bergsten, "The Threat from the Third World", *Foreign Policy*, No. 11 (summer 1973); and Bension Varon and Kenji Takeuchi, "Developing Countries and Non-Fuel Minerals", *Foreign Affairs*, Vol. 52, No. 3 (April, 1974).

the huge initial capital investments are sunk and the mines brought on-line, the marginal costs of production appear to be competitive with much higher grade deposits elsewhere. Thus, a well-constructed system of depreciation or depletion allowances to permit the rapid return of fixed investment could stimulate the outlays necessary to expand the North American production base by a substantial factor.

In summary, the entry of new competition at the production stage that was traced since the end of the Second World War in Chapter 2 has been continuing—indeed, accelerating—since the beginning of the Vietnam War. Consumers and fabricators of copper in the major industrial countries have been integrating backwards to develop their own secure sources. Their governments have been encouraging them to move upstream and have also been supporting the formation of other mining companies that can be depended upon to be regular suppliers of copper. CIPEC use of untempered "monopoly power" in the past, inspired by Chile, has stimulated this movement to weaken the producers' oligopoly. CIPEC policy for the untempered use of "monopoly power" in the future, led by Chile, will insure that the weakening process continues.

III

There is a danger posed by the pricing and marketing strategy of the CIPEC producers, however, that is more immediate than the long-term dilution of the international copper oligopoly. It consists in the potential development of a dual market system in which the CIPEC countries gradually become suppliers of last resort, outside the main network of semi-integrated ties between corporate producers and consumers, onto whom will be shifted the major costs of uncertainty about supply and demand for the entire industry.

The reason for the evolution of a new dual structure lies in the persistence of a preference among consumers for ties

233

of informal integration to the mining stage—ties that the new independent state producers have been unwilling or unable to maintain.

To understand the likelihood of such an evolution, it is helpful to re-explore the rationale for vertical integration.

The impetus for vertical integration can come from two directions—from producers who want "secure" outlets, and from processors or consumers who want "secure" sources of supply. "Security" is a judgment about the relative risk that the producer, processor, or consumer runs of meeting sudden market power being wielded against him—especially market power wielded *unevenly* against himself and not against his competitors—at some stage that he does not control. If there is a high risk, he measures the cost of the threat to his operations against the costs of neutralizing or minimizing the threat. Calculations of this sort are never exact. They are impressionistic and subjective. But they are the basis for any strategy of constructing ties of vertical integration.

The formal and informal bonds of vertical integration in the copper industry were built up because inelasticities of supply and demand in the short run have tended to shift market power abruptly back and forth from producer to fabricator or consumer. In a situation of bilateral oligopoly such as this, where there is a large exposure to risk, both sides may be willing to pay a premium to reduce that exposure.

From the point of view of the consumer in the international copper industry, the risk of large blocs of copper being removed unpredictably from the market, creating sudden and severe shortage, remains high. Transportation difficulties for Zambian copper moving through Rhodesia or Tanzania create periodic uncertainty about delivery, as do port strikes in the United States or Europe. A cave-in at Mufulira in Africa in 1970 took 150,000 tons, or 20% of Zambian production, from the market in one blow; a mudslide in West Irian or Bougainville in the monsoon season of the South Pacific could do the same thing. New production simply cannot be brought on-line in the short run in time to prevent a sharp rise in price with an absolute shortfall for many users—and a temporary switch to aluminum, plastics, or specialized steels is not easily accomplished at the margin by fabricators, nor, once accomplished, easily reversible.

These risks have been compounded by labor difficulties. Twice in the 1960's there were prolonged strikes among copper workers in the United States, cutting off almost all American production; in 1971 there was a short strike, after the threat of a long one. Unfortunately, as the CIPEC countries move toward complete national control of production, their labor problems appear to be becoming more serious, too. In the past, despite frequent short strikes with political or economic motivation, the aggregate production record of Chile, Zambia, Peru, and Zaire has been quite good. Allende's efforts to keep miners' salaries within the limits of his stabilization program, however, provoked a 75-day strike in 1973 and the stoppage of all exports for almost three months. It may prove to be more difficult for governments with direct control to minimize strikes, keep production costs competitive, and insure a steady flow of output than was accomplished through the intermediation of the private foreign companies.

An additional uncertainty for consumers has been introduced by the debates in various CIPEC countries, especially Chile, about selling copper to communist countries. After the election of Dr. Allende, Chilean copper administrators suggested on repeated occasions that they wanted to withdraw substantial amounts from the country's former trading partners (sometimes as much as 10% on a single occasion) to sell to China, but later, after the old customers scrambled to react, it was not clear if the sales would live up to the pronouncements. Unfortunately, the military coup in Chile in 1973 and the domestic reaction to it will insure that international marketing policy remains a political issue.

The major problem in this for consumers is uncertainty in the face of inelastic supply—not ideology. If some or all of the CIPEC countries were to establish regular trading patterns that allocated, for example, 10% of their annual output to Eastern Europe and 5% to China, the uncertainty would be removed.[6] But there is no predictability about supply when trade policy changes, or threatens to change, with each new President or each new Congress or each new state administrator.

To hedge against the threat of undependable supply, against the threat of market power being wielded unevenly against them, the major copper consumers have been continuing to show a strong preference for establishing ties of formal or informal vertical integration.[7] The private corporate producers are responding sympathetically to that preference, as they have for decades. The new national producers are not.

The private mining companies have been continuing to act on their belief that aggregate demand for copper would be maximized over the long term if consumers could be somewhat insured against the risk of meeting sudden scarcity. They have continued to feel that their oligopolist position would be best preserved by a willingness to absorb short-run demand shocks through inventory variation or excess capacity. This would be backed by faithful allocation of production on the basis of historical trading patterns and (for American mining companies) producers' prices.[8] Dur-

[6] The Soviet Union is a net exporter of copper, with plans to become a large net exporter, and is thus unlikely to provide a strong market for CIPEC countries.

[7] With the penetration of US sellers of copper products into the Common Market countries (and Japan), one would predict a drive on the part of domestic fabricators and consumers to integrate backward to sources as "secure" as those supplying the Americans. This is supported by the evidence thus far available (discussed in this chapter on pages 231–232).

[8] Such a strategy is not inconsistent with econometric findings about price-elasticity of demand for copper and cross-elasticity of demand

ing the copper shortages of 1968–1969, George Munroe, the president of Phelps Dodge, said that he would eventually like to see world productive capacity at an *average* level at least 10% above projected consumption—to provide consumers with a margin of safety against interruptions in production or surges in demand.[9] Other producers felt that secure supplies would temper the drive of fabricators and consumers to integrate backward to the mining stage. Some mining companies even looked forward to a period of abundant supplies that might reverse the process of substitution, especially among electrical utilities, that had been so pronounced after CIPEC adopted its LME pricing strategy in 1966.[10] These companies wanted their customers to be insured against getting pushed to the wall by sudden monopoly power. And they were willing, often with the help of their governments, to pay the insurance premium.

But the danger for the new independent national producers is that they may end up paying the insurance premium for the entire international industry. The major private corporations and their governments may well not in fact have to bear most of the costs of maintaining excess capacity, or maintaining inventories, or providing consumers with insurance against meeting unavoidable monopoly power at the production stage.

Rather, the danger for the national producers like Chile is that their policies may unwittingly lead them to be forced to accept those costs for the entire industry.

---

with aluminum. Cf. Charles River Associates, Inc., *Economic Analysis of the Copper Industry* (Cambridge, Mass.: March 1970); and Franklin M. Fisher and Paul H. Cootner, in association with Martin Neal Baily, "An Econometric Model of the World Copper Industry, I + II", *Bell Journal*, Vol. 2, No. 2 (Autumn 1972)—both of which are discussed in Chapter 3, pp. 81–83.

[9] George Munroe, president of Phelps Dodge, *Engineering and Mining Journal*, February 1969.

[10] Cf. James Boyd, president of Copper Range, *Engineering and Mining Journal*, March 1971. See also "Annual Review and Survey: Copper", *Engineering and Mining Journal*, March 1973.

It is quite possible that planners in the governments of Chile, Peru, Zambia, and Zaire have too easily accepted the conventional marxist argument that large industrial societies need the raw materials of the Third World and will collapse without them. This has led the nationalists to assume that by controlling the sources of raw materials, they would be in a position of consummate strength. More properly, the argument should be put that the large industrial countries need secure sources of raw materials so badly that they will be willing to pay the price of neutralizing economic nationalists who threaten to upset the old and dependable system. There is nothing in history or logic to suggest that corporate boards of directors (or the governments they and their customers influence) will simply sit and let the price and terms of supply be dictated to them by outsiders, if they have other options available to them. Without the necessity of alleging either malice or conspiracy, it is now evident that fabricators and consumers and their governments are willing to act to the extent of their powers to protect themselves.

It is also possible that the CIPEC countries have seen their position as being more similar to the OPEC (Organization of Petroleum Exporting Countries) countries than the evidence warrants.[11] The cost of alternative sources of energy are much higher for the industrial countries than are the costs of alternative sources of copper (or substitutes for it). And the OPEC countries control a much larger share of the world market in petroleum than the CIPEC countries control in copper. Thus, the range of alternatives

[11] On the Organization of Petroleum Exporting Countries, see M. A. Adelman, *The World Petroleum Market* (Baltimore: Resources for the Future, Johns Hopkins Press, 1972); Edith Penrose, *The Large International Firm in Developing Countries* (London: Allen & Unwin, 1969); Zuhayr Mikdashi, *The Community of Oil Exporting Countries* (Baltimore: Resources for the Future, Johns Hopkins Press, 1973); and T. H. Moran, "New Deal or Raw Deal in Raw Materials", *Foreign Policy*, No. 5 (Winter 1970-1971), and "The Politics of Oil: Coups and Costs", *Foreign Policy*, No. 8 (Fall 1972).

open to industrial consumers and their governments is much smaller and more costly for fuel than it is for non-ferrous metals.

By adopting the strategy of using the full extent of their market power at every point of the business cycle, the independent national producers offer no incentive for a fabricator or consumer to maintain ties with them rather than seek alternative sources or integrate backwards to develop supplies of its own. They make themselves into suppliers of last resort. Their share of world production is still in the early 1970's sufficiently large (35%–40%) that there cannot and will not be a massive defection from them as suppliers. But there has been a trend for major consumers to try to cover the bulk of their needs from the semi-integrated system of corporate producers as fast as the companies can expand output, while treating the CIPEC production more and more like a spill-over market.

With current expansion plans, it is reasonable to estimate that by the mid- or late 1970's, about 70% of projected world demand can be met from the copper supplies of the traditional companies in "secure" areas. That is, 70% of the "Free World" market—and an increasing amount of the socialist-bloc market—will consist of sales between regular buyers and sellers in the historical semi-integrated pattern.

If one assumes that investment in new production by private corporations, backed by their governments, will continue at a higher rate than investment by the state agencies of the capital- and credit-starved economic nationalists, then by the end of the decade the CIPEC share could be less than 30% of world production.

The new "independents" will have a difficult job of maintaining their sales positions in the face of this persistent semi-integrated market. Paradoxically, the stronger a cartel CIPEC can create in the 1970's, the weaker its position will become. The stronger the CIPEC cartel, the more rapid will be the evolution of the industry in the direction of dual markets and isolation for the independents.

The greatest danger for the national producers is that onto the CIPEC market, for which Chile will be either the first or the second largest supplier, will be shifted the major burden of fluctuations in demand. If consumers cover the bulk of their needs from sources in the integrated industry during both the expansion and the contraction phases of the business cycle, a 10% variation in aggregate demand that is passed onto the CIPEC market would require a 30% change in production (or inventories) for them, and a much greater change in net revenues.

Those proud and independent nationalists like Chile who have taken over production, breaking the corporate organic ties to the industrial consumers, and who have been unable or have disdained to build their own strong vertical ties into the major industrial markets, will find their small (and probably competitive) market getting only the notoriously unstable edge of demand. Industrial consumers will provide for the majority of their orders through scrupulously regular positions on the sales books of the major private producers, reserving for the independents only the variable margin of their needs. If the CIPEC countries make themselves into a spill-over market as suppliers of last resort through the full use of their individual or collective market power, they will operate at full capacity only in the boom phase of the industrial business cycle, and hold inventories for the entire industry (or clear their production in price competition with each other at discounts that may fall below average cost) the rest of the time.[12]

Their position may come to be equally appalling, over time, in relation to the Soviet bloc and to China. As a rule, socialist or communist state trading agencies have outdone their capitalist corporate counterparts in desiring to avoid risk, in desiring to insure the dependability of suppliers for

[12] The inability of their economies to do without foreign exchange earnings for long would push them toward price competition rather than holding inventories.

all basic needs. And, as the centrally controlled economies are increasingly penetrated by the major capitalist corporations, the latter may be recognized as more dependable suppliers of copper or copper-intensive products than the CIPEC countries. In any but the shortest run and for any but the materials least important to an industrial economy (sugar, cotton), socialist governments, like capitalist governments, will try to avoid buying from producers that exploit the extent of their monopoly power at every moment of time.

The economic nationalists who have talked so much of their new-found "independence" will find themselves more unhappily "dependent" than ever. They may have to finance their own national development out of highly fluctuating, highly unpredictable, and perhaps even declining real earnings. They may come to inhabit the worst of all possible worlds: a fast weakening international copper oligopoly, with themselves relegated to the position of a spill-over market onto which has been shifted the burden of market uncertainty and instability for the entire industry.

IV

The future need not be so dismal.

There seem to be two clear courses of possible evolution for the relations between the new independent national producers and the larger world industry:

First, there is the course that has been followed thus far, in which the independents continue systematically to break ties, pursuing something called *independencia* or *autonomía*, and scorning close dependable relations with final customers in the large industrial countries.

Second, there is an alternative course, in which the independents seek reintegration with the world industry, reestablishing informal vertical ties of their own and conducting themselves like the other producers, recognizing and emphasizing and taking advantage of interdependence.

241

The second course for Chile will require a turn away from the rhetorical dichotomy of *dependencia/independencia,* now that the production stage has been nationalized.

To occupy a strong position within an industry that values backward integration to secure sources at the mining stage, a national producer like Chile must offer its buyers the same inducements as a private corporate producer. This will require maintaining production volume and servicing sales contracts as dependably as the private companies do. It requires building up and scrupulously maintaining regular marketing relations with major customers equal to the concern of traditional companies for semi-integrated ties. It requires a pricing system, based either on open-market quotations or on a producers' price (or on a combination of the two) that does not represent major disadvantages in comparison to the pricing policy of the corporate producers.[13] It requires a moderation in coordinating production that is not aimed at exploiting inelasticity of demand to the fullest extent possible in both boom and slack markets.

It requires, in effect, joining the oligopoly and playing according to its rules.

If Chile, as a leader of the CIPEC countries, can turn away from fashioning a strategy that is systematically directed at taking fullest advantage of the short-run needs and weaknesses of industrial consumers, then the country may come to occupy a strong position within the semi-integrated structure of the world industry. Fabricators and consumers want to minimize their risk by diversifying sources of supply. They want to buy from an array of dependable suppliers offering similar terms. Chile and other

[13] Since the formation of CIPEC, there has been an active debate within the North American copper industry about the fate of the producers' price system. Some of the major companies quote a producers' price but sell according to a formula that reflects the CIPEC quotation as well. The CIPEC producers could match this practice.

CIPEC countries could even come to be considered the pre-ferred suppliers.

This point was stressed in 1970 by the chairman of American Metal Climax, Ian MacGregor:[14]

> If you go back over a period of time . . . you'll find that the Congo, Zambia, Peru and Chile have a star perform-ance in terms of reliability of production. They have achieved an average of about 93% to 95% performance against capacity in the last 10 years. The one that really gives the trouble in terms of uncertainty is the U.S. supply.
> Why?
> Because of our labor problem we've had recurring long serious stoppages. The market takes into account the imagined political problems. But the main difficulties stem from real U.S. labor problems, which in the last dec-ade have exhausted the domestic flow of copper on two occasions.

On balance the production performance of the CIPEC countries under corporate management was good. During the 1960's the Congo went through a civil war, Zambia had transportation problems in shipping its copper to the coast after independence, and Chile and Peru experienced agita-tion in the strong copper-mining unions. But they achieved an average output above 90% of capacity. This is an impres-sive record, far superior to the strike-prone industry in the United States. The task for Chile and the other CIPEC countries now is to duplicate their record under national management in the 1970's. This will not be easy, as Allende's serious labor difficulties in 1973 showed, but it should be possible.

If so, there is no reason why, with proper stress on per-formance and reliability, the economic nationalists cannot

[14] In *Barron's*, "The Experts' Corner: Copper's Future", March 9, 1970.

occupy a position within the international industry as strong or stronger than any private multinational copper corporation. Unless the CIPEC countries deliberately fashion a price and marketing strategy to make themselves into suppliers of last resort, the large corporate consumers may come one day to consider them suppliers of first resort—since domestic pressures for foreign exchange could limit the probability of long interruptions in production. In the United States, Western Electric and General Electric, General Motors and Westinghouse will be happy to import a regular portion of their needs from Chile if the country will insure them of dependable supplies in the event of a domestic strike. In Europe and Japan, British Insulated Callender's Cables, Norddeutsche Affinerie, Volkswagen, or Mitsubishi will continue to be content to get most of their copper from Chile, Zambia, Peru, and Zaire, even with the increasing penetration of their economies by vertically integrated foreigners, if they are not put at a competitive disadvantage to their rivals from the United States. What the CIPEC producers must devise is a pricing and marketing strategy calculated to moderate the pressure felt by fabricators or consumers to integrate backwards themselves, and to eliminate the pressure felt by the fabricators or consumers to seek closer and more durable ties with alternative producers.

In short, the new national producers must carefully learn to exploit the consumers in the industrial countries exactly the way the multinational corporations do.

V

The possibility of playing the delicate oligopolists' game, however, is particularly difficult for a country such as Chile, where copper policy is so prominent in public consciousness and national politics. As we have seen in the Chilean case, a government in office, whatever its ideological beliefs, would have trouble explaining why it frequently accepted prices lower than the full use of its powers could

exact, why it did not use every bit of leverage to exact higher revenues whenever it had the chance. Nor can a strongly
nationalistic government, without access to adequate domestic capital, adequate foreign credit, or the latest technology, easily adopt a strategy of increasing earnings by
taking a smaller margin while expanding production, rather
than by taking a larger margin through higher prices on a
given production. In addition, "aggressive" marketing
makes it easier to hide, rather than restrain, swelling labor
costs. Furthermore, even if a government in office could devise a proper strategy to strengthen its position within the
international oligopoly, then parties out of power, or economic groups eager for more foreign exchange and added
revenues, would find it easy to exploit the issue of restraint
in national politics.

In such a situation, the government of a nationalistic producing country that has taken direct control of natural resource production has a double problem: it must not only
control domestic disputes over ways to exact more revenues, but must also credibly persuade buyers that it will be
able to maintain such control into the future.

The politics of economic nationalism as determined by
the interplay of groups pursuing their own interests and
their own visions of the national interest—the politics of
economic nationalism that we have been following in Chile
for a quarter of a century—does not stop on call.

The dynamics of economic nationalism seem to have set
Chile on a course that served the country for a while, but
now has ceased to. It will be difficult to change those dynamics or the direction of that course. But if such a change
is achieved, then the ideas of *dependencia*, which served to
release creative energies in the past, will not become fetters
on the forces of production in Chile in the future.

If Chile is successful in fashioning a strategy to build
close integrated relations to processors and consumers in
the major industrial markets of the globe, both capitalist
and socialist, then there are some years ahead of using care-

ful oligopoly power to gain a greater share from exploiting the industrial consumer with nationalized production than the country has been getting for years under the system of corporate integration.

In a curious sense, some would argue, this would represent progress.

CHAPTER 8

Economic Nationalism and the Future

A national interest in building the economy, providing for the welfare of the society, and controlling national sovereignty propelled successive Chilean administrations and their opponents to push against the foreign copper companies. Despite ebbs and flows of confidence as elites from across the domestic spectrum tested their strengths and abilities against the uncertainties of having to duplicate complicated foreign corporate skills, the broad thrust of policy tended toward tighter regulation, closer supervision, more control.

In the process of moving up a learning curve of experience and expertise, the Chilean perception of the costs of economic nationalism declined—on the part of those both in and out of government—and the perception of the benefits of domestic control rose. Solemn bargains were struck but always revised. Although there were certain clear cases of "complicity" and "exploitation" at crucial periods of negotiation and renegotiation, the conventional model of "neo-colonialism" must be replaced with the model of economic nationalism developed here. The Chilean experience suggests that foreign investors in prominent natural-resource industries in developing countries have few permanent domestic allies. In the course of history their lives become increasingly solitary, poor, nasty, brutish, and short.

The broad consensus to nationalize the foreign copper sector despite readily apparent economic costs reflected the culmination of a process that was probably irreversible and whose outcome was probably inevitable. The land reform of the Alliance for Progress may have speeded the disaffection of the right, just as the narrow election of Dr. Allende speeded the arrival of the left. But it seems impossible to conceive, in any case, of the survival of the copper companies in Chile for more than one presidential term after the Frei administration, even if Allende had never taken office. The military junta of 1973, just like the proposed treachery of ITT in 1970, will have scant possibility of re-establishing foreign ownership under Anaconda or Kennecott (or Cerro) on a permanent basis with legitimacy sufficient to maintain operations.

It is quite likely that the Chilean dictatorship may hire foreign management consultants to tighten efficiency of production at Chuquicamata, El Teniente, and El Salvador. It is even more likely that the dictatorship will award long-term compensation to the former owners in return for US aid. But no military dictatorship, no matter how suppressive of democratic politics, can reverse the movement toward Chilean control of basic natural resources for long. A Chile that is free to express the least part of its popular will can never settle back into a stable system of foreign corporate domination from mine to consumer.

But as Chile now tries to recover from the bloody challenge to its democratic institutions, it will be extraordinarily difficult to put the struggle against *dependencia* into a perspective that will serve the country's interests. The struggle against *dependencia* was in fact a struggle of pure sovereignty—to replace foreign control with domestic control—and a struggle of pure self-interest—to gain all the rents (surplus) from the existing copper industry for itself. It was not, as the rhetoric of *dependencia* drew the picture, a struggle against a malign system of corporate integration whose dynamics worked to deprive the producing country of the proceeds from the industry. To serve its self-interest now, Chile must discard the rhetoric of *dependencia* with regard to the international industry and study the business of becoming a conservative and secure member of the global oligopoly. The military repression, combined with foreign glee at the demise of Allende, will make this shift toward the dispassionate calculation of self-interest all the more difficult.

I

Chilean achievements in maintaining production after nationalization have been substantial. The problems that the country has encountered, although severe, have not been insurmountable. Chile, under Frei and then Allende, took over the domestic mining industry at an advantageous moment—a moment of power and confidence just after remarkable investments by the foreign companies in new productive capacity. Few analysts expected that the country would be able alone to manage the large mining properties as well as Anaconda or Kennecott or Cerro right from the moment of nationalization. Rather, like the new administrators of any operation after a take-over, Chile had to suffer a period of settling-down expenses. Total Chilean mine production in 1971 and 1972 was firmly above 700,000 metric tons, of which 593,000 metric tons (1972) came from the mines formerly owned by Anaconda, Kennecott, and Cerro. This was much lower than the estimate of 880,000 metric tons targeted for the US companies under their own management,[1] and of 210,000 metric tons targeted for the small mining companies in Chile if copper prices had remained high, conditions stable, and machinery available for import. Nevertheless, during the first two years of nationalization, Chile did maintain the highest production in its history— 13% more output than the private companies' peak year (1969) and 20% more than the average production in the 1960's before the beginning of the Chileanization expansion program. Despite a simultaneous nationalization and social revolution, despite the exodus of technicians, despite an economic blockade of replacement equipment from the United States, even *Barron's* (which had predicted and hoped for disaster in Chile) had to admit by 1973 that Chilean production was "holding up reasonably well".[2]

---

[1] Several independent mining engineers from the United States felt that the company estimates of increased capacity were exaggerated.

[2] January 1, 1973; for prior positions reflected in *Barron's* editorial

Unless there are negotiated phase-outs of foreign owner-ship in natural resource industries according to timetables agreed upon in advance, it is unlikely that final take-overs in such industries will come at the optimal moment when the host countries are perfectly able to duplicate the skills and services of the foreign corporations. Rather there will be clear costs of transition, in which the country establishes its own equilibrium production-level and production-costs before it moves on up the learning curve as an independent producer.

While Allende was in office, there were three major fac-tors that augmented the transition costs of nationalization in Chile.[3]

First, there was featherbedding and a clear decline of labor discipline after nationalization. President Allende warned the workers of Chuquicamata in 1971, for example, that wildcat stoppages for petty grievances, combined with extra time spent at lunches, dinners, and tea breaks (and at the beginning or end of each work shift) had caused sharply rising unit costs of production and a loss of $36 mil-lion in output in 1970.[4] At El Teniente, where the Kennecott

---

commentary, see "Point of No Return", April 19, 1971, and "Kenne-cott's Private War", October 23, 1972.

On the exodus of technicians, the best estimates suggest that in 1971 400–500 Chilean supervisers and skilled personnel left the *Gran Minería*, plus about 150 North Americans or other expatriates in managerial or technical positions.

Anaconda and Kennecott contributed to the exodus by helping their most skilled employees find mining jobs outside of Chile.

[3] A good portrait of some of the post-nationalization mining prob-lems in Chile can be found in "Copper Is the Wage of Chile", by Norman Gall, American Universities Field Staff *Fieldstaff Reports*, Vol. xix, No. 3 (August 1972). In addition I have relied on inter-views with pro- and anti-Allende Chileans who are knowledgeable about the accomplishments and the problems in the copper industry, and with officials of US companies who have had dealings with Codelco.

[4] Reprinted in *Cobre*, the newspaper of the Copper Workers Con-federation, Santiago, October–November 1971, p. 22. For other views,

expansion program had called for a work force of 6,800, employment during the Allende administration rose above 13,000. In 1973, Dr. Allende complained that the miners "lack the revolutionary spirit. . . . They are acting like true monopolistic bankers, asking for more money for their pockets without considering the situation of the country."[5] At the same time, carelessness took its toll in machinery— for example, a new locomotive was destroyed by a rail left out of place; a giant converter was ruined when left filled with molten copper and tilted on its side. Some, but by no means all, of the incidents causing lost production were blamed on sabotage by the right or by the companies. In addition, several North American mining engineers have suggested that there were serious defects in the Anaconda and Kennecott expansion projects. Whatever the cause, such errors and accidents and difficulties became exaggerated in impact because of the scarcity of skilled personnel remaining at the mines to perform repair or maintenance work. And the Allende administration was unable simply to call in engineering experts from the United States, as the companies had done, when something went wrong.

Second, there were sectarian struggles in the supervision of the mining sector. To satisfy the complex requirements of maintaining checks and balances among the constituent members of the *Unidad Popular*, the Allende government developed elaborate procedures for political overlap in the management of all the major state enterprises. This meant that not only in the Codelco offices in Santiago but also in the on-site supervision of mining operations there were representatives of the major coalition parties watching and challenging each other with a high propensity to foul up

---

see "Ineficiencia, Despilfarro y Sectarismo en Chuquicamata" by Senator Ramón Silva Ulloa of the Union Socialist Party, *El Mercurio*, May 29, 1972; and "Chuquicamata por Dentro" by Carlos A. Correa Iglesias (a former Chilean official of Chuquicamata), *El Mercurio*, December 23, 1971.

[5] Reported in the *Wall Street Journal*, February 26, 1973.

decision-making. At El Teniente, for example, which was experiencing severe difficulties with its smelter, the Communists and the Socialists agreed to share control. Their respective managers, a lawyer and an administrator from the State Technical University (who had obtained a master's degree in mine technology at Berkeley on a Kennecott scholarship), had never worked at a mine before.[6] To the political rivalries were added struggles between the traditional union leaders in the Copper Workers Confederation and the new political appointees from Santiago, who were given important management posts without having to work up through the ranks. Such administrative disputes were placed on top of the celebrated tradition of bureaucratic proliferation and bureaucratic *trámites* (red-tape) in Chile. The results magnified the effect of having few experienced personnel who could make authoritative decisions, magnified the difficulty of enforcing labor discipline.

Third, there was more effective international retaliation on the part of the expropriated companies than many Chileans had anticipated. This retaliation, combined with the intransigence of various political figures in both Chile and the United States against permitting any kind of compromise on compensation, hindered the procurement of spare parts.[7] The writs of attachment against the US assets of Codelco and Corfo (discussed in Chapter 5) forced the Allende administration into the complicated business of ordering inexact replacements for US machinery and parts from outside of the United States. As maintenance and re-

---

[6] Norman Gall, "Copper Is the Wage of Chile", p. 16.

[7] In October 1971 Chilean Foreign Minister Clodomiro Almeyda, Ambassador to the US, Orlando Letelier, and Henry Kissinger appeared to negotiate a face-saving agreement on compensation that would have given the US companies some payment over a long period of time in return for easing the US economic blockade against Chile. It came to naught, however, owing to pressure from hard-liners (John Connally, Carlos Altamirano) in both countries.

In addition to interviews with some of the principals, I have relied on the *New York Times*, October 8 and 10, 1971.

pair problems became more severe at the mines, the improvisation of logistical support for operations that had used US equipment intensively became a very costly business. In less than a year after nationalization Codelco hired and fired three managers of procurement in Santiago. Delays and errors in trying to manage some $200 million per year in procurement via new suppliers in Europe, Japan, and the Soviet bloc contributed to the loss of production.

II

What is the future of economic nationalism and natural resource development in the Third World? Will other underdeveloped countries and other multinational corporations have to repeat the experience of Chile up to and including the acrimonious nationalization—will they have to suffer all the costs to get the benefits? Is there no permanent place for the large international natural-resource companies within the Third World?

There are two appealing approaches to predicting the future. The first is to argue that what has been taking place in the past will exactly repeat itself over and over again—that other countries in Asia, Africa, and Latin America will recapitulate the course that history took in Chile as long as there are foreign investors rash enough to commit their funds. The second is to declare an end to history—to declare that lessons will be learned once and for all and that old patterns of interaction will be transcended.

Between these extremes, however, one can advance three hypotheses about how to produce a dampening effect on the tense sequence of pulling, pushing, and shoving in the relations between foreign investors and host countries in the Third World that may enable both sides to gain benefits from natural resource development while minimizing the costs.[8] All of the hypotheses, however, are built upon the

[8] These arguments have been developed and expanded in my paper and testimony presented to the Senate Foreign Relations subcommittee on multinational corporations ("The Evolution of Concession Agree-

conviction that multinational corporations and consuming countries cannot turn the clock back to a world of impotent, quiescent host countries. Any recommendations, then, have to be measured against a world in which mining companies have few alternatives except to adapt to tougher bargaining, or not invest at all (and see their rivals move in instead).

(1) The first hypothesis suggests that a greater symmetry of power between the investors and the host from the very beginning of their relationship might reduce the accumulation of tension. If the governments of underdeveloped countries had more equal access to international expertise from the initiation of a concession (through training programs set up for this purpose and/or through hiring consultants to aid their side of the negotiations), it would be less likely that an entire political tradition in the host country would be built upon frustration and suspicion. More open negotiations, clearer expectations about costs and benefits, surer understanding of occult business practices might result in more confident acceptance of the foreign investors' presence. In all likelihood, the cycle of negotiation and renegotiation in accordance with shifting bargaining power would continue, but the premiums and discounts might become standard and more palatable— without the long accumulation of host-country resentment.

The petroleum exporting countries have been leaders in developing international programs to train nationals in negotiation, taxation, accounting, production, and exploration, and in hiring the best international economists, lawyers, accountants to consult with their governments. From time to time, the United Nations and the World Bank have suggested programs to do the same in copper, bauxite, iron ore, and agricultural commodities. The movement in this direction could be substantially accelerated.

---

ments in Underdeveloped Countries and the U.S. National Interest", June 5, 1973).

(2) The second hypothesis concerns introducing the option of systematic divestment into broader usage in natural resource investments.[9] Some countries (and some companies) may continue to think that direct investment via equity ownership is the only feasible means of setting up a large-scale development project—even though both sides realize that this places the foreigner in a politically and economically sensitive position. In these cases, it would be wise to introduce an anticipation of swings in the pendulum of power—including a possible final swing in the host country's favor when the domestic benefits of nationalization finally appear to outweigh the costs of doing without the foreigner—into the expectations of both sides. It may be valuable to the foreign corporation as well as to the host country to think seriously about establishing an option of systematic divestment with the margins of compensation agreed to in advance in the initial negotiations. To protect such an agreement, perhaps a certain sum from taxes and/ or from depletion/depreciation allowances could be put aside in escrow in the hands of an independent third party. This would spread the risk of nationalization between host country and foreign investor, while insuring that successor governments would bear identical costs if they chose nationalization (namely, the loss of the services of the foreigner plus the loss of the amount agreed to as compensation). In many cases (perhaps most cases), of course, the option to nationalize would never be exercised. But the mere existence of such a clear option agreed upon in advance might itself serve to reduce tensions associated with "foreign ownership".[10]

[9] Cf. Albert Hirschman, "How to Divest in Latin America and Why", in *A Bias for Hope: Essays on Development and Latin America* (New Haven: Yale University Press, 1971). For a critical view, see Jack N. Behrman, "International Divestment: Panacea or Pitfall?", *Comments on Argentine Trade*, Vol. 50, No. 10 (May 1971).

[10] Even in those cases where the option was exercised, the time period of divestment would still reflect the host-country valuation of the foreigner's services and evaluation of its own expertise—that is, the

(3) The third hypothesis suggests that experiments with new forms of mineral development may increase the benefits and reduce some of the unnecessary costs associated with direct foreign ownership. Host countries and foreign companies should be encouraged to find formulas for sharing scarce corporate talents in such a way that many of the tensions of "foreign control", "subsoil rights", and "threats to sovereignty" do not arise. Straight equity investment may have to give way to management contracts, service contracts, exploration contracts, and producer sharing agreements, in order to avoid the political reactions that accompany foreign ownership.

Such repackaging of the relations between foreign companies and host country would not necessarily eliminate periodic readjustments to reflect changing bargaining strengths, but might keep such adjustments within limits more tolerable to the expectations of both sides. The for-

---

time period of divestment would depend upon the learning curve of the host country. Companies whose time horizon was thus reduced from the infinitude of traditional concessions to 10–12 years of actual operation would be reflecting accurately the discounted present value of returns accruing 99 years in the future (that is, a value approaching zero).

Mining companies seldom have the complicated centralized strategies that make systematic divestment in manufacturing so unappealing. Natural resource producers may object that by agreeing to "phase out" at some point they are creating their own potential competition. But if they do not agree to the demand for the option of systematic divestment, they may be replaced by Japanese or European or Canadian or American contractors who do. Then their choice is between potential competition 15 years in the future or real competition in the present.

The phase-out option could only work to the benefit of the host country in those natural-resource industries where the greatest barriers to entry are found at the production stage—such as copper, petroleum, natural gas, nickel. For the dangers that follow a national take-over where the point of oligopoly control is farther downstream than the mining stage—such as in bauxite and perhaps iron ore—see T. H. Moran, "New Deal or Raw Deal in Raw Materials?" *Foreign Policy*, No. 5 (Winter 1970–1971).

eign company would be paid directly for services rendered (with incentives for successful performance) rather than be invited to create an operation on its own, from whose ownership it then would expect to collect a stream of rents in perpetuity.

The capital necessary for natural resource development in the Third World could increasingly be raised through debt rather than through equity. To a large extent, this shift has already been taking place. In the past decade, since the first experiments of Kennecott in 1964, more and more capital for mineral and petroleum projects has been raised in advance from processors and consumers and/or from financial institutions through various kinds of factoring (that is, selling collection rights on long-term contracts to a financial intermediary at a discount).[11] There are currently many US companies in South Asia, Africa, and Latin America that went into business only after processors or customers in Japan or Western Europe advanced them money for contracts for output stretching to the end of the life of the mine or the well. In relation to traditional practices, they have high debt-to-equity ratios in which as little as 15% of the risk capital has been raised in the name of the US parent.

Yet a shift toward high debt-equity ratios merely so that the producing company can avoid the risk of broader direct exposure does little to eliminate the fundamental causes of that risk. Under current conditions, the equity is still owned by the US parent. The US company is the actual or potential target of nationalistic attack. And the US government is the "imperialistic power" liable to become drawn into a diplomatic dispute (directly, or via multilateral lending agencies) with the host country. The Japanese or West European consortia for whom the US mining or drilling companies are working (with some of the attributes, al-

---

[11] For evidence from the copper, petroleum, natural gas, and nickel industries, see T. H. Moran, "Transnational Strategies of Protection and Defense by Multinational Corporations: Spreading the Risk and Raising the Cost for Nationalization in Natural Resources", *International Organization*, Vol. 27, No. 2 (Spring 1973).

ready, at a service contract) are viewed, meanwhile, as providing kindly access to final markets.

It might be much more sensible for mining companies to move out of equity altogether and supply their scarce talents and services on a direct contract basis. If given the proper encouragement, it seems reasonable to predict that the more agile corporate managements could be highly imaginative in working out new arrangements that would avoid the tensions of direct ownership.[12]

It should be emphasized that repackaging company–country relations to avoid direct ownership, or introducing the option of systematic divestment, will not necessarily be less costly to host countries, in purely financial terms, than the traditional arrangements are now. (Indeed, by having to bear new costs, host countries may come to appreciate just exactly what have been the benefits of the old system.)

---

[12] See Peter P. Gabriel, "Importing Corporate Capabilities without Exporting Ownership and Control: Alternatives to Foreign Direct Investment", paper prepared for the Conference on Latin American–United States Economic Interactions, University of Texas at Austin, March 18–21, 1973, and *The International Transfer of Corporate Skills: Management Contracts in Less Developed Countries* (Boston, Mass.: Harvard University, Division of Research, Graduate School of Business Administration, 1967). See also the National Commission on Materials Policy, *Final Report: Material Needs and the Environment Today and Tomorrow* (Washington, D.C.: GPO, June 1973), ch. 9.

For evidence of successful foreign participation via service and management contracts in a setting of nationalism, see Louis Kraar, "Oil and Nationalism Mix Beautifully in Indonesia", *Fortune*, July 1973. Similar results have been obtained in the petroleum industry in post-IPC Peru, and in the copper industry in Iran.

In my paper for the Senate Foreign Relations Committee subcommittee on multinational corporations I argued that the US guarantee program for equity investment works as a large disincentive to experimentation with such new arrangements. It is implausible to expect the management of a US corporation to waste valuable time and effort trying out methods of avoiding potential disputes far in the future, if the US government stands ready to assume the burden of risk and become a party to any dispute when called upon by the company.

Host countries may have to supply more of the venture capital for new projects themselves, or, if they try to raise it by selling long-term contracts, they will find that the expense is quite high. To make their agreements on compensation credible, they may have to forgo some tax revenue or to post a lump-sum bond. They may have to bear more of the burden of risk of failure for new projects themselves and not be able to share such risk with, or push it off onto, the foreign companies. They may find that operating at arm's length with foreign companies on service or management contracts is more (rather than less) costly than the system of direct foreign investment. They may discover, as the evidence indicates,[13] that jointly managed ventures (especially where the host government or host country nationals are the controlling partner) are charged a higher proportion of common overhead expenses by the foreign partner's parent than wholly owned subsidiaries are.

The benefits will come through avoiding the major breakdowns and major losses that occur through acrimonious nationalizations, sudden expropriations, destructive waves of economic nationalism. A realistic approach to accommodating the demands of economic nationalism can reduce the uncertainty, and hence the costs, borne by all sides in the international production of natural resources. It may produce gains that show up through fewer unproductive disputes about whether a course of foreign investor–host country relations that is empirically inevitable is morally just. It may, perhaps, free national energies and national resources that can be more creatively engaged attacking other domestic problems.

[13] Cf. John Stopford and Louis T. Wells, Jr., *Managing the Multinational Enterprise: Organization of the Firm and Ownership of the Subsidiaries* (New York: Basic Books, 1972); Lawrence G. Franko, "Strategy Choice and Multinational Corporate Tolerance for Joint Ventures with Foreign Partners" (D.B.A. dissertation, Graduate School of Business Administration, Harvard University, 1969); and Raymond Vernon, *Sovereignty at Bay: The Multinational Spread of U.S. Enterprises* (New York: Basic Books, 1971).

If concession agreements moved away from equity ownership, or included the option of systematic divestment, and if procedures were adopted for regular renegotiation of terms, both sides could begin to operate within some arrangement that anticipates the kind of course their relations will follow anyway. Given the dialectical relations between foreign investors and host countries, there would be political as well as economic profit in making a virtue of necessity, instead of spending bitter years arguing futilely about the necessity of virtue.

Statistical Appendix

1. Copper Production

Year	Free World	Chilean Production	Chilean Percentage of Free World Market
1945	2,024	446	22%
1946	1,694	365	21%
1947	2,053	415	20%
1948	2,129	444	20%
1949	2,050	367	17%
1950	2,286	361	15%
1951	2,382	378	15%
1952	2,443	407	16%
1953	2,459	360	14%
1954	2,485	355	14%
1955	2,731	433	15%
1956	3,031	488	16%
1957	3,094	482	15%
1958	2,958	463	15%
1959	3,153	549	17%
1960	3,614	536	14%
1961	3,715	551	14%
1962	3,812	591	15%
1963	3,871	604	15%
1964	4,009	633	15%
1965	4,150	585	14%
1966	4,337	637	14%
1967	4,066	660	16%
1968	4,412	658	14%
1969	4,842	688	14%
1970	5,148	692	13%
1971	4,145	708	17%
1972			

2. Profits of the Gran Minería del Cobre en Chile

	(thousand dollars)			
	Andes (Anaconda)	*Braden* (Kennecott)	*Chilex* (Anaconda)	*Total*
1945	407	5,174	13,268	10,050
1946	1,449	3,821	16,335	21,645
1947	1,699	10,888	22,404	34,991
1948	4,975	19,261	24,605	48,842
1949	1,487	9,620	15,372	26,479
1950	2,363	10,815	17,039	30,217
1951	1,356	17,036	20,652	39,223
1952	2,107	18,556	14,731	36,394
1953	522	4,476	4,715	9,713
1954	412	4,825	13,896	19,134
1955	1,147	20,950	31,738	54,835
1956	2,523	23,964	49,284	75,771
1957	(35)	19,013	18,957	37,935
1958	(44)	15,370	11,957	27,203
1959	62	20,932	34,905	55,900
1960	2,693	23,752	21,357	47,802
1961	602	9,285	25,533	35,420
1962	2,130	10,089	31,237	43,456
1963	3,628	6,410	29,259	39,296
1964	906	12,879	34,311	48,096
1965	3,276	8,525	32,084	43,885
1966	(1,881)	22,149	61,622	81,890
1967	19,209	5,199	72,897	174,541
	El Teniente*	77,235		
1968	25,007	78,299	73,796	177,103
1969	17,087		61,613	

*Of the profits from the El Teniente joint venture, 51% were remitted to the Corporación del Cobre and 49% to Braden/Kennecott. On this 40%, Braden was charged a withholding tax of 30%.

3. Book Value Recorded by the Major Copper-mining
Companies in Chile

		(thousand dollars)		
	Andes (Anaconda)	*Braden* (Kennecott)	*Chilex* (Anaconda)	*Chilex* * (Anaconda)
1945	87,018	36,197	44,274	138,258
1946	83,185	36,535	44,274	138,159
1947	84,165	30,895	43,858	144,625
1948	82,181	34,368	50,636	151,254
1949	83,646	37,741	57,267	157,576
1950	83,276	37,032	63,591	167,630
1951	83,038	40,802	73,646	176,800
1952	82,703	48,891	82,724	183,977
1953	63,377	49,472	89,993	184,429
1954	63,503	50,209	86,627	200,272
1955	60,193	48,381	99,932	219,585
1956	63,011	52,453	139,050	256,914
1957	63,860	53,920	137,027	259,331
1958	84,188	53,217	138,424	264,889
1959	84,244	58,007	162,810	292,865
1960	86,944	71,695	162,435	296,771
1961	87,557	59,016	200,066	294,051
1962	89,805	59,217	206,158	300,142
1963	93,197	69,307	213,060	307,044
1964	91,752	64,614	213,313	307,297
1965	90,955	60,115	200,650	294,434
1966	83,161	67,360	222,011	315,995
1967	87,780	73,056	273,015	366,999
	El Teniente 215,654**			
1968	97,651	285,789	288,435	
1969	NA		279,404	

*Anaconda claims that the Chile Copper Company, which is 100% owner of Chilex, paid $93,984,065 for rights and properties that were transferred to Chilex in 1913, but the value was never transferred to the books of Chilex "for internal and tax reasons". Thus, Anaconda claims that the "real" book value of Chilex is about $94 million more than the Corporación del Cobre shows on the books of Chilex.
**The difference is due to the revaluation of assets for Braden before those assets were sold to the new joint company.

4. Profit Rate (net profits/book value) of the Major Copper-mining Companies in Chile

	Andes (Anaconda)	*Braden* (Kennecott)	*Chilex* (Anaconda)	*Chilex* * (Anaconda)
1945	0.5%	14.3%	30.0%	9.6%
1946	1.8%	10.5%	38.3%	11.8%
1947	2.0%	35.2%	51.1%	15.5%
1948	6.1%	56.0%	48.6%	16.3%
1949	1.8%	25.5%	26.8%	9.8%
1950	2.8%	29.2%	26.8%	10.2%
1951	1.6%	41.8%	28.0%	11.7%
1952	2.5%	38.0%	17.8%	8.0%
1953	0.8%	9.0%	5.2%	4.6%
1954	0.6%	9.6%	16.0%	11.1%
1955	1.9%	43.3%	31.8%	17.9%
1956	4.0%	45.7%	35.4%	20.8%
1957	—	35.3%	13.8%	9.0%
1958	—	28.9%	8.6%	6.1%
1959	0.7%	36.1%	21.4%	13.1%
1960	3.1%	33.1%	13.1%	8.6%
1961	0.7%	15.7%	12.8%	8.7%
1962	2.4%	17.0%	15.2%	10.4%
1963	3.9%	9.2%	13.7%	9.5%
1964	1.0%	19.9%	16.1%	11.2%
1965	3.6%	14.2%	16.0%	10.9%
1966	—	32.9%	27.8%	19.5%
1967	23.1%		26.7%	19.9%
1968	25.5%		25.6%	19.3%
1969			22.2%	16.6%

*This series corresponds to Anaconda's claim to have a $94 million carry-over from 1913 that was never recorded as part of the book value of Chilex. See p. 22-23.

5. Direct Taxes Paid by the Major Copper-mining Companies
to the Chilean Government

	Andes (Anaconda)	*Braden* (Kennecott)	*Chilex* (Anaconda)	*Total*
	(thousand dollars)			
1945	1,525	5,418	11,155	18,097
1946	1,897	3,364	12,262	17,523
1947	1,965	11,887	23,529	37,381
1948	4,856	19,476	24,377	48,709
1949	1,295	9,412	15,362	26,070
1950	3,855	16,397	21,998	42,250
1951	2,221	20,932	23,954	47,107
1952	1,829	22,789	18,363	42,982
1953	724	11,318	5,427	17,469
1954	921	7,622	22,158	30,701
1955	6,871	51,214	62,910	120,995
1956	6,596	56,239	67,787	130,622
1957	2,672	42,927	31,298	76,897
1958	390	32,429	20,391	53,210
1959	2,012	42,584	40,940	85,536
1960	74	53,669	34,418	88,161
1961	—	39,155	33,715	72,870
1962	—	36,895	52,452	89,347
1963	1,287	38,316	46,785	86,387
1964	2,871	47,766	54,475	105,112
1965	3,549	52,902	69,887	126,338
1966	10,559	89,498	96,625	196,683
1967	17,993	28,290	102,030	157,937
	El Teniente*	9,624		
1968	23,606	45,617	98,543	209,789
1969	31,065	34,774	149,885	215,724

*The taxes for El Teniente include levies against the profits of the joint
venture and also the 30% tax on Braden dividends.

6. Implicit Taxes Through Exchange-rate Discrimination on the Major Copper-mining Companies in Chile, 1948–1954

	Andes (Anaconda)	*Braden* (Kennecott)	*Chilex* (Anaconda)	*Total*
(million dollars)				
1948	5.5	12.9	13.8	32.2
1949	NA	NA	NA	NA
1950	4.3	21.7	13.6	29.7
1951	5.9	23.7	16.5	46.2
1952	6.4	27.5	19.1	53.0
1953	1.2	4.8	3.9	9.8
1954	3.8	11.3	11.0	26.5

Note: This covers only the period when the artificial exchange rate for the copper companies of 19.36 pesos per dollar became most burdensome. Prior to 1948 there was an implicit tax of lesser magnitude owing to the exchange rate, and after 1954 there were complaints that the "official" exchange rate was perpetually overvalued. Thus, a strong case can be made that there were smaller implicit taxes both before and after the period 1948–1954.

These figures have been calculated according to the following formulas: the "real" cost of production in dollars times the "real" (official) exchange rate equals the "legal cost" of production times the artificial exchange rate.

The indirect tax equals the "legal cost" minus the "real" cost. Figures used for the "real" (official) exchange rate and the "legal cost" of production come from Markos Mamalakis, "The American Copper Companies and the Chilean Government, 1920–1967: Profile of an Export Sector."

For a spot check on these calculations, Braden reported in 1952 (*Boletin Minero*, February 1953) that the company calculated it was paying an implicit tax of $30 million owing to the artificial exchange rate.

7. Effective Tax Rate of the Major Copper-mining Companies in Chile*

	Andes (Anaconda)	*Braden* (Kennecott)	*Chilex* (Anaconda)
1945	78.9%	51.2%	45.7%
1946	56.0%	46.8%	42.9%
1947	53.6%	52.2%	51.2%
1948	68.0%*	62.9%*	60.8%*
1949	46.5%	49.5%	50.0%
1950	76.6%*	77.9%*	67.7%*
1951	85.3%*	72.3%*	66.3%*
1952	79.6%*	73.1%*	71.8%*
1953	79.2%*	78.2%*	65.0%*
1954	92.2%*	79.7%*	70.6%*
1955	85.7%	71.0%	66.5%
1956	72.3%	70.1%	57.9%
1957	—	69.3%	62.3%
1958	—	67.8%	63.0%
1959	97.0%	67.0%	54.0%
1960	2.7%	69.3%	61.7%
1961	—	80.8%	56.9%
1962	—	78.5%	62.7%
1963	8.6%	85.7%	61.6%
1964	76.0%	78.8%	61.4%
1965	52.0%	86.1%	68.5%
1966	—	80.3%	61.0%
1967	60.4%	44.0%**	58.3%
1968	48.6%	44.0%**	57.2%

*The years 1948 and 1950–1954 include the indirect tax burden through artificial exchange rates. A certain amount of indirect taxation had been building up in the years prior to 1948 and an argument can be made that exchange rates were generally overvalued after 1955, too. (For purposes of calculating consistent percentages, the estimate of taxable income and gross tax includes the amount of the implicit tax for the years 1948 and 1950–1954. For other years, it does not.)

**Estimated purely on the basis of company statements.

8. Investments Made by the Major Copper-mining Companies in Chile

	Andes (Anaconda)	Braden (Kennecott)	Chilex (Anaconda)	Total
		(thousand dollars)		
1945	2	415	886	1,304
1946	—	635	907	1,542
1947	—	827	1,166	1,994
1948	12	1,054	5,588	6,654
1949	203	1,520	20,641	22,364
1950	—	2,311	22,446	24,757
1951	28	1,048	37,716	38,792
1952	4	2,397	28,521	30,921
1953	36	2,560	17,584	20,179
1954	49	275	—	323
1955	—	1,091	1,218	2,309
1956	11,359	3,398	11,933	26,691
1957	28,707	3,548	14,078	46,333
1958	41,717	2,189	10,275	54,182
1959	22,400	2,609	14,087	39,095
1960	3,099	2,940	10,080	16,120
1961	1,727	9,906	5,571	17,204
1962	1,333	4,790	8,461	14,584
1963	4,441	4,438	9,807	18,686
1964	3,388	5,283	7,207	15,878
1965	5,181	5,556	9,000	19,737
1966	13,293	2,611	22,593	38,497
1967	6,918	854	43,611	70,165
	El Teniente 18,781			
1968	10,164	98,494	62,324	170,982

9. Depreciation Claimed by the Major Copper-mining Companies in Chile

	Andes (Anaconda)	(thousand dollars) Braden (Kennecott)	Chilex (Anaconda)	Total
1945	2,493	898	2,619	6,000
1946	2,455	875	2,319	5,649
1947	2,298	877	2,436	5,611
1948	2,639	824	2,293	5,756
1949	1,908	859	1,930	4,697
1950	1,822	927	1,723	4,473
1951	1,629	893	1,802	4,324
1952	1,350	944	2,495	5,288
1953	1,575	1,109	5,621	8,304
1954	1,526	1,217	6,675	9,418
1955	1,653	830	7,503	9,986
1956	1,571	778	6,003	8,352
1957	1,575	1,015	9,937	12,527
1958	1,309	2,046	9,370	12,725
1959	5,432	2,231	12,875	20,538
1960	11,649	2,550	11,734	25,933
1961	5,488	1,936	7,209	14,633
1962	10,172	2,917	8,476	21,565
1963	15,518	2,669	9,172	27,359
1964	13,432	3,017	10,264	26,715
1965	14,396	4,503	14,265	33,165
1966	13,875	4,783	15,801	34,459
1967	3,148	1,058	11,075	19,881
	El Teniente 4,600			
1968	3,430	3,930	10,985	18,345

Bibliography

I. *Books and Manuscripts*

Adelman, M. A., *The World Petroleum Market* (Baltimore: The Johns Hopkins Press, 1972).

Aharoni, Yair, *The Foreign Investment Process* (Boston: Division of Research, Graduate School of Business Administration, Harvard University, 1966).

Alexander, Robert J., *Communism in Latin America* (New Brunswick, N.J.: Rutgers University Press, 1957).

Allison, Graham, *Essence of Decision* (New York: Little, Brown, 1971).

Bain, Joe S., *Barriers to New Competition* (Cambridge, Mass.: Harvard University Press, 1956).

Baran, Paul A., *The Political Economy of Growth* (New York: Monthly Review Press, 1957).

Behrman, Jack N., *National Interests and Multinational Enterprise* (Englewood Cliffs, N.J.: Prentice-Hall, 1970).

Beraschina Gonzáles, Mario, *Constitución política y leyes complementárias* (Santiago: Editorial Jurídica de Chile, 2nd ed., 1958).

Bernstein Marvin D., *The Mexican Mining Industry, 1890–1950* (Albany, N.Y.: SUNY Albany, 1965).

Bowers, Claude G., *Chile Through Embassy Windows: 1939–1953* (New York: Simon and Schuster, 1958).

Brash, Donald T., *American Investment in Australian Industry* (Cambridge, Mass.: Harvard University Press, 1966).

Brown, Martin S., and Butler, John, *The Production, Marketing, and Consumption of Copper and Aluminum* (New York: Praeger, 1967).

Brubaker, Sterling, *Trends in the World Aluminum Industry* (Baltimore: Resources for the Future, Johns Hopkins Press, 1967).

Cabezas Pares, Rubén, *Pensamiento económico de los partidos políticos históricos chilenos* (Santiago: Editorial Universitaria, 1964).

Cockcroft, James D., Frank, André Gunder, and Johnson, Dale L., eds., *Dependence and Underdevelopment: Latin America's Political Economy* (Grove City, N.Y.: Doubleday, 1972).

271

Dos Santos, Theotonio, *Dependencia y cambio social* (Santiago: Centro de Estudios Socio-Economicos, Universidad de Chile, 1970).

Einhorn, Jessica, "Effect of Bureaucratic Politics on the Expropriation Policy of the Nixon Administration: Two Case Studies, 1969–1972" (unpublished Ph.D. dissertation, Department of Politics, Princeton University, 1973).

Elliott, William Y., *et al.*, *International Control in the Non-Ferrous Metals* (New York: Macmillan, 1937).

Ellsworth, P. T., *Chile: An Economy in Transition* (New York: Macmillan, 1945).

Encina, Francisco A., *Nuestra inferioridad económica, sus causas y sus consequencias* (Santiago: Imprenta Universitaria, 1912).

Frank, André Gunder, *Capitalism and Underdevelopment in Latin America: Historical Studies of Chile and Brazil* (New York: Monthly Review Press, 1967).

———, *Latin America: Underdevelopment or Revolution* (New York: Monthly Review Press, 1969).

Franko, Lawrence G., "Strategy Choice and Multinational Corporate Tolerance for Joint Ventures with Foreign Partners" (unpublished D.B.A. dissertation, Graduate School of Business Administration, Harvard University, 1969).

Gabriel, Peter P., *The International Transfer of Corporate Skills: Management Contracts in Less Developed Countries* (Boston: Harvard University, Division of Research, Graduate School of Business Administration, 1967).

Gil, Federico, *The Political System of Chile* (Boston: Houghton Mifflin, 1966).

Griffin, Keith, *Underdevelopment in Spanish America: An Interpretation* (Cambridge, Mass.: MIT Press, 1969).

Halperin, Morton, *Bureaucratic Politics and National Security Policy* (Washington, D.C.: Brookings Institution, 1974).

Herfindahl, Orris C., *Copper Costs and Prices: 1870–1957* (Baltimore: Resources for Freedom, Johns Hopkins Press, 1960).

Hirschman, Albert O., *Journeys Toward Progress* (New York: Doubleday, 1965).

———, "How to Divest in Latin America and Why", in *A Bias*

for Hope: Essays on Development and Latin America (New Haven: Yale University Press, 1971).

Huntington, Samuel P., *Political Order in Changing Societies* (New Haven: Yale University Press, 1968).

Hymer, Stephen, "The International Operations of National Firms: A Study of Direct Foreign Investment" (unpublished Ph.D. dissertation, MIT, 1960).

Jobet, Julio César, *Ensayo crítico del desarrollo económico-social de Chile* (Santiago: Editorial Universitaria, 1955).

Johnson, Harry, ed., *Economic Nationalism in Old and New States* (Chicago: University of Chicago Press, 1967).

Kaufman, Robert, "Chilean Political Institutions and Agrarian Reform: The Politics of Adjustment" (unpublished Ph.D. dissertation, Government Department, Harvard University, 1967).

————, *The Politics of Land Reform in Chile* (Cambridge, Mass.: Harvard University Press, 1972).

Kaulen, Julio, *Las empresas mineras extranjeras en Chile y la economía nacional* (Santiago: 1916).

Kidron, Michael, *Foreign Investments in India* (New York: Oxford University Press, 1965).

Kindleberger, Charles, *Economic Development* (New York: McGraw-Hill, 1965).

————, *American Business Abroad* (New Haven: Yale University Press, 1969).

————, *The International Corporation: A Symposium* (Cambridge, Mass.: MIT Press, 1970).

————, *Power and Money* (New York: Basic Books, 1970).

Lagos, E. Ricardo, *La concentración del poder económico* (Santiago: Editorial del Pacífico, 1965).

Levitt, Kari, *Silent Surrender: The Multinational Corporation in Canada* (New York: St. Martin's Press, 1970).

Lieuwen, Edwin, *Petroleum in Venezuela: A History* (Berkeley: University of California Press, 1954).

————, *Venezuela* (London: Oxford University Press, 1965).

Mamalakis, Markos, and Reynolds, Clark, *Essays on the Chilean Economy* (Homewood, Ill.: Richard D. Irwin, 1965).

Marcosson, Isaac F., *Anaconda* (New York: Dodd, Mead, 1957).

Bibliography

McMahon, A. D., *Copper: A Materials Survey* (Washington, D.C.: U.S. Department of the Interior, Bureau of Mines, 1964).

Mikdashi, Zuhayr, *The Community of Oil Exporting Countries* (Baltimore: Resources for the Future, Johns Hopkins Press, 1973).

————, *Business and Government in the Extractive Industries* (forthcoming, 1974).

Mikesell, Raymond, ed., *Foreign Investment in the Petroleum and Mineral Industries: Case Studies in Investor–Host Country Relations* (Baltimore: Johns Hopkins Press, 1971).

Muñoz G., Oscar, *Crecimiento industrial de Chile, 1914–1965* (Santiago: Instituto de Economía y Planificación, Universidad de Chile, 1968).

Novoa Monreal, Eduardo, *La batalla por el cobre* (Santiago: Quimantu, 1972).

O'Connor, Harvey, *The Empire of Oil* (New York: Monthly Review Press, 1955).

————, *World Crisis in Oil* (New York: Monthly Review Press, 1962).

Olavarría Bravo, Arturo, *Chile bajo la democracia cristiana* (Santiago: Editorial Nacimiento, 1966).

Peck, Merton J., *Competition in the Aluminum Industry, 1945–1958* (Cambridge, Mass.: Harvard University Press, 1961).

Penrose, Edith, *The Large International Firm in Developing Countries* (London: Allen & Unwin, 1969).

————, *New Orientations: Essays in International Relations* (New York: Humanities Press, 1970).

Pinto Santa Cruz, Aníbal, *Hacia nuestra independencia económica* (Santiago: Editorial del Pacífico, 1953).

————, *Chile: Un caso de desarrollo frustrado* (Santiago: Editorial Universitaria, 1959).

Prebisch, Raúl, *The Economic Development of Latin America and Its Principal Problems*, Economic Commission for Latin America (Lake Success, N.Y.: United Nations, Department of Economic Affairs, 1950).

Ramírez Necochea, Hernán, *Balmaceda y la contrarevolución de 1891* (Santiago: Editorial Universitaria, 1958).

274

Bibliography

————, *Historia del imperialismo en Chile* (Santiago: Austral, 1960).

Rhodes, Robert I., ed., *Imperialism and Underdevelopment: A Reader* (New York: Monthly Review Press, 1970).

Ruiz, Félix, *Tributación directa e indirecta a las grandes empresas de cobre* (Santiago: Sección Estadística del Banco Central, August 1953).

Sáez, Raúl, *Chile y el cobre* (Santiago: Departmento del Cobre, January 1965).

Safarian, A. E., *Foreign Ownership of Canadian Industry* (Toronto: McGraw-Hill Co. of Canada, 1966).

Schelling, Thomas, *The Strategy of Conflict* (London: Oxford University Press, 1963).

Servan-Schreiber, Jean-Jacques, *The American Challenge* (New York: Atheneum, 1968).

Smith, Peter H., *Politics & Beef in Argentina: Patterns of Conflict and Change* (New York: Columbia University Press, 1969).

Stigler, George, *The Theory of Price* (New York: Macmillan, 1961).

Stopford, John, and Wells, Louis T., Jr., *Managing the Multinational Enterprise: Organization of the Firm and Ownership of the Subsidiaries* (New York: Basic Books, 1972).

Tanzer, Michael, *The Political Economy of International Oil* (Boston: Beacon Press, 1969).

Tilton, John E., "The Choice of Trading Partners: An Analysis of International Trade in Aluminum, Bauxite, Copper, Lead, Manganese, Tin, and Zinc (unpublished Ph.D. dissertation, Department of Economics, Yale University, 1966).

Varas, Machiavello, *El problema de la industria del cobre* (Santiago: 1923).

Vera Valenzuela, Mario, *La política económica del cobre en Chile* (Santiago: Universidad de Chile, 1961).

————, *Una política definitiva para nuestras riquezas básicas* (Santiago: Prensa Latinoamericano, 1964).

Vernon, Raymond, *Sovereignty at Bay: The Multinational Spread of U.S. Enterprises* (New York: Basic Books, 1971).

Wionczek, Miguel, *El nacionalismo mexicano y la inversión estranjera* (Mexico City: Siglo veintiuno editores, 1967).

Zeitlin, Maurice, and Ratcliff, Richard Earl, *Landlords and Capitalists* (New York: Harper and Row, forthcoming).

II. *Reports and Reference Works*

American Bureau of Metal Statistics, *Yearbook* (New York, annual).

Beerman's Financial Yearbook of Europe (New York: International Publishers Service, 1970).

Charles River Associates, Inc., *Economic Analysis of the Copper Industry* (Cambridge, Mass.: March 1970).

Expropriation of the El Teniente Copper Mine by the Chilean Government (New York: Kennecott Public Relations Department, 1971–1973), 6 sections.

Federal Trade Commission, *Report of the Federal Trade Commission on the Copper Industry* (Washington, D.C.: U.S. Government Printing Office, 1947).

Foreign Relations of the United States, 1946 (Washington, D.C.: U.S. Government Printing Office, 1969), Vol. xi.

Historia de la ley 11.828 (Chilean Congressional hearings on the *Nuevo Trato*), Vols. 1–3, 1954–1955.

Historia de la ley 16.425 (Chilean Congressional hearings on "Chileanization"), Vols. 1–3, 1964–1966.

Houthakker, Hendrik, *Report of the Subcommittee on Copper to the Cabinet Committee on Economic Policy* (Washington, D.C.: The White House, May 13, 1970, mimeo).

Metal Statistics (Frankfurt am Main: Metallgesellschaft A.G., annual).

National Commission on Materials Policy, *Final Report: Material Needs & the Environment Today and Tomorrow* (Washington, D.C.: U.S. Government Printing Office, June 1973).

Non-Ferrous Metal Works of the World (London: Metal Bulletin Books, Ltd., 1967).

President's Materials Policy Commission, *Resources for Freedom* (Washington, D.C.: U.S. Government Printing Office, 1952), 5 vols.

Subcommittee on Antitrust and Monopoly of the Committee on the Judiciary, *Concentration Ratios in Manufacturing Industry, 1958* and *Concentration Ratios in Manufacturing Industry, 1963*, Reports prepared by the Bureau of the Census for the Subcommittee on Antitrust and Monopoly of the Committee on the Judiciary, U.S. Senate, 87th Congress,

2nd Session (Washington, D.C.: U.S. Government Printing Office, 1962) and 89th Congress, 2nd Session, 1963 (Washington, D.C.: U.S. Government Printing Office, 1966).

III. *Articles*

Baer, Werner, "The Economics of Prebisch and ECLA", *Economic Development and Cultural Change*, Vol. 10, No. 2, Part II (January 1962).

Baklanoff, E. N., "Taxation of United States-Owned Copper Companies in Chile: Economic Myopia vs. Long-Run Self Interest", *National Tax Journal*, Vol. 14, No. 1 (March 1961).

Behrman, Jack N., "International Divestment: Panacea or Pitfall?" *Comments on Argentine Trade*, Vol. 50, No. 10 (May 1971).

Breton, Albert, "The Economics of Nationalism", *Journal of Political Economy*, Vol. LXXII, No. 4 (August 1964).

Caves, Richard, "International Corporations: The Industrial Economics of Foreign Investment", *Economica*, February 1971.

Deutsch, Karl W., "Social Mobilization and Political Development," *American Political Science Review*, Vol. 55 (September 1961).

Ellsworth, Paul T., "The Terms of Trade between Primary Producing and Industrial Countries", *Inter-American Economic Affairs*, Vol. 9 (Summer 1956).

Fisher, Franklin M., and Cootner, Paul H., in association with Martin Neal Baily, "An Econometric Model of the World Copper Industry, I + II", *Bell Journal*, Vol. II, No. 2 (Autumn 1972).

Flanders, M. June, "Prebisch on Protectionism: An Evaluation", *Economic Journal*, Vol. LXXIV, No. 294 (June 1964).

Gabriel, Peter P., "Importing Corporate Capabilities without Exporting Ownership and Control: Alternatives to Foreign Direct Investment", paper prepared for the Conference on Latin American–United States Economic Interactions, University of Texas at Austin, March 18–21, 1973.

Gall, Norman, "Copper Is the Wage of Chile", American Universities Field Staff *Fieldstaff Reports*, Vol. XIX, No. 3 (August 1972).

Bibliography

Gann, L. H., "The Northern Rhodesian Copper Industry and the World of Copper: 1923–1952", Human Problems in British Central Africa XVIII, *Rhodes-Livingstone Journal*, No. 18, 1955.

Haberler, Gottfried, "Terms of Trade and Economic Development", in *Economic Development for Latin America*, Howard S. Ellis, ed. (London: Macmillan, 1961).

Johns, B. L., "Private Overseas Investment in Australia: Profitability and Motivation", *Economic Record*, June 1967.

Johnson, Harry, "An Economic Theory of Protectionism: Tariff Bargaining, and the Formation of Customs Unions", *Journal of Political Economy*, Vol. LXXIII, No. 3 (June 1965).

Kraar, Louis, "Oil and Nationalism Mix Beautifully in Indonesia", *Fortune*, July 1973.

Krasner, Stephen, "Are Bureaucracies Important?" *Foreign Policy*, No. 7 (Summer 1972).

Loving, Rush, Jr., "How Kennecott Got Hooked with Catch–22", *Fortune*, September 1971.

Lutgen, George P., "Open-pit Guide: Sierrita Makes It with Big Equipment", *Engineering and Mining Journal* (August, 1970), pp. 70–73.

Mamalakis, Markos, "The American Copper Companies and the Chilean Government, 1920–1967: Profile of an Export Sector", Economic Growth Center, Yale University, Discussion paper No. 37, September 22, 1967.

———, "An Analysis of the Financial and Investment Activities of the Chilean Development Corporation: 1939–1964", *Journal of Development Studies*, Vol. 5, No. 2 (January 1969).

Mann, H. Michael, "Seller Concentration, Barriers to Entry, and Rates of Return in Thirty Industries, 1950–1960", *Review of Economics and Statistics*, Vol. 48 (August 1966).

McCarthy, James L., "The American Copper Industry, 1947–1955", *Yale Economic Essays*, Vol. IV (Spring 1964).

McDonald, John, "The World of Kennecott", *Fortune*, November 1951.

Moran, Theodore H., "New Deal or Raw Deal in Raw Materials", *Foreign Policy*, No. 5 (Winter 1970–1971).

———, "The Politics of Oil: Coups and Costs", *Foreign Policy*, No. 8 (Fall 1972).

Bibliography

——, "Transnational Strategies of Protection and Defense by Multinational Corporations: Spreading the Risk and Raising the Cost for Nationalization in Natural Resources", *International Organization*, Vol. 27, No. 2 (Spring 1973).

——, "The Evolution of Concession Agreements in Underdeveloped Countries and the U.S. National Interest", U.S. Senate Foreign Relations subcommittee on multinational corporations (testimony and report), Washington, D.C., July 1973.

——, "A Model of National Interest, Balance of Power, and International Exploitation in Large Natural Resource Investments", in James Kurth and Stephen Rosen, eds., *Testing the Theory of Economic Imperialism* (New York: Heath, 1974).

O'Hanlon, Thomas, "The Perilous Prosperity of Anaconda", *Fortune*, May 1966.

Olson, Mancur, Jr., "Rapid Growth as a Destabilizing Force", *Journal of Economic History*, Vol. 23 (December 1963).

Penrose, Edith, "Foreign Investment and the Growth of the Firm", *Economic Journal*, June 1956.

——, "Profit Sharing Between Producing Countries and Oil Companies in the Middle East", *Economic Journal*, June 1958.

Petras, James and LaPorte, Robert, "Can We Do Business with Radical Nationalists?—Chile: No," *Foreign Policy*, No. 7 (Summer 1972).

——, "An Exchange on Chile", *Foreign Policy*, No. 8 (Fall 1972).

Prebisch, Raúl, "Commercial Policy in the Underdeveloped Countries", *American Economic Review*, Vol. xlix, No. 2 (May 1959).

Singer, H. W., "The Distribution of Gains between Investing and Borrowing Countries", *American Economic Review, Papers and Proceedings*, Vol. xl, No. 2 (May 1950).

Stewardson, B. R., "The Nature of Competition in the World Market for Refined Copper", *Economic Record*, June 1970.

Stobaugh, Robert, "Systematic Bias and the Terms of Trade", *Review of Economics and Statistics*, Vol. xlix (November 1967).

Tanter, Raymond, and Midlarsky, Manus, "A Theory of Revolution", *Journal of Conflict Resolution*, Vol. 11 (September 1967).

Tilton, John E., "The Choice of Trading Partners: An Analysis of International Trade in Aluminum, Bauxite, Copper, Lead, Manganese, Tin, and Zinc", *Yale Economic Essays*, Vol. VI (Fall 1966).

Vernon, Raymond, "International Investment and International Trade in the Product Cycle", *Quarterly Journal of Economics*, Vol. 80 (May 1966).

———, "Long-Run Trends in Congression Contracts", *Proceedings of the American Society for International Law*, April 1967.

Wells, L. T., "Test of a Product Cycle Model of International Trade", *Quarterly Journal of Economics*, Vol. LXXXIII (February 1969).

———, "The Evolution of Concession Agreements in Developing Countries", Harvard Development Advisory Service, March 29, 1971.

Index

Chana, Julio, 202
Chilex (Chile Exploration Company—subsidiary of Anaconda working Chuquicamata mine), 104n, 107n
China, 235–36, 240
Christian Democratic Party, 69, 72, 119–46, 183, 186, 199, 203, 205–10, 212, 214
Chuquicamata (copper mine of Anaconda), 22–23, 64, 100n, 214, 248, 250
CIPEC (Intergovernmental Council of Copper Exporting Countries), 142–43, 230–44
Codegua Project, 131–32, 202–203
CODELCO (Corporación del Cobre de Chile), 22–23, 107n, 124–25, 141, 150, 251–53. *See also* Copper Department
COMEX (New York Commodities Exchange), 53, 78
Communist Party, 27, 41, 64–65, 77n, 146, 173, 175, 177–78, 180, 182, 204–206, 214, 252
compensation, 75, 147–52, 212, 216n
competition: perfect, 45–96, 98–99; imperfect, 4, 16, 55. *See also* oligopoly
conflict (between foreign investor and host country), 6, 55, 114, 152
Congo, 30, 37, 142, 227, 229, 243–44. *See also* Zaire
Connally, John, 252
Conservative Party, 62, 74n, 132, 146, 172, 176–77, 179, 185–86, 188, 192–96, 199–207, 212–13
"consolidation of underdevelopment", 14–15, 154, 170, 187, 217

construction industry (uses of copper in), 20, 38, 42, 82
consultants, 9, 166, 254
Copper Department, 97, 123–24, 140. *See also* CODELCO
Correa Letelier, Hector, 201–202
Corvalán, Luís, 41
costs in the copper industry: fixed costs, 49; variable costs, 39–40, 49; average costs, 39–40, 49, 76, 250
Cuba, 198–99
Cuevas Mackenna, Francisco, 124n, 193n

de Dios Reyes, (Senator) Juan, 202n
Defense Production Act (of 1950), 33–34
dependencia: origins, 3, 54, 56, 61, 66, 76, 86–87, 90, 99, 106, 118–19, 153, 182, 186–87, 189; meaning, 4–5, 7–8, 11–14, 19, 57–61, 121, 144, 147, 152, 248; future, 241, 245, 248
diversification (out of copper industry), 35–36, 48–49, 109, 111, 114–15
divestment, 250, 255–56, 258
Dungan, Ralph, 206
Durán, Julio, 64, 72–73, 123, 183

ECLA (United Nations Economic Commission for Latin America), 59–60, 66–71, 79–83, 181
economic nationalism, 12–15, 34, 57, 89, 106, 153, 155–58, 167–69, 172, 184, 186, 217–24, 226–29, 238–45, 247–48, 253, 257, 259
elasticities (in copper industry), 50, 79–83, 234, 236

Related Books Written Under the Auspices of the
Center for International Affairs, Harvard University

United States Manufacturing Investment in Brazil, by Lincoln
Gordon Engelbert L. Grommers. Harvard Business School,
1962.

The Dilemma of Mexico's Development, by Raymond Vernon.
Harvard University Press, 1963.

Export Instability and Economic Development, by Alasdair I.
MacBean. Harvard University Press, 1966.

Elites in Latin America, edited by Seymour M. Lipset and Aldo
Solari. Oxford University Press, 1967.

Pakistan's Development: Social Goals and Private Incentives, by
Gustav F. Papanek. Harvard University Press, 1967.

Aid, Influence, and Foreign Policy, by Joan M. Nelson. The
Macmillan Company, 1968.

Political Development in Latin America, by Martin Needler.
Random House, 1968.

The Brazilian Capital Goods Industry, 1929-1964 (sponsored
jointly with the Center for Studies in Education and Development), by Nathaniel H. Leff. Harvard University Press, 1968.

Economic Policy-Making and Development in Brazil, 1947-1964,
by Nathaniel H. Leff. John Wiley & Sons, 1968.

*Agricultural Development in India's Districts: The Intensive
Agricultural Districts Programme*, by Dorris D. Brown. Harvard University Press, 1970.

Taxation and Development: Lessons from Colombian Experience,
by Richard M. Bird. Harvard University Press, 1970.

*Lord and Peasant in Peru: A Paradigm of Political and Social
Change*, by F. LaMond Tullis. Harvard University Press, 1970.

Korean Development: The Interplay of Politics and Economics,
by David C. Cole and Princeton N. Lyman. Harvard University Press, 1971.

Development Policy II—The Pakistan Experience, edited by
Walter P. Falcon and Gustav F. Papanek. Harvard University
Press, 1971.

Studies in Development Planning, edited by Hollis B. Chenery.
Harvard University Press, 1971.

Political Mobilization of the Venezuelan Peasant, by John D. Powell. Harvard University Press, 1971.

Sovereignty at Bay: The Multinational Spread of U.S. Enterprise, by Raymond Vernon. Basic Books, 1971.

Transnational Relations and World Politics, edited by Robert O. Keohane and Joseph S. Nye, Jr., Harvard University Press, 1972.

Latin American University Students: A Six Nation Study, by Arthur Liebman, Kenneth N. Walker, and Myron Glazer. Harvard University Press, 1972.

The Politics of Land Reform in Chile, 1950-1970: Public Policy, Political Institutions, and Social Change, by Robert R. Kaufman. Harvard University Press, 1972.

The Andean Group: A Case Study in Economic Integration among Developing Countries, by David Morawetz. M.I.T. Press, 1974.

LIBRARY OF CONGRESS CATALOGING IN PUBLICATION DATA

Moran, Theodore H   1943-
    Multinational corporations and the politics of dependence.

    Bibliography: p.
    1. International business enterprises—Case studies. 2. Copper industry and trade—Chile. I. Title.
HD69.I7M59   1975   338.8′8   74-2973
ISBN 0-691-04204-7